THE CHANGING FACE OF MARITIME POWER

The Changing Face of Maritime Power

Edited by

Andrew Dorman

Senior Lecturer
Defence Studies Department
Joint Services Command and Staff College
Bracknell

Mike Lawrence Smith

Lecturer
Department of War Studies
King's College
London

and

Matthew R. H. Uttley

Senior Lecturer
Defence Studies Department
Joint Services Command and Staff College
Bracknell

First published in Great Britain 1999 by
MACMILLAN PRESS LTD
Houndmills, Basingstoke, Hampshire RG21 6XS and London
Companies and representatives throughout the world

A catalogue record for this book is available from the British Library.

ISBN 0–333–73407–6

 First published in the United States of America 1999 by
ST. MARTIN'S PRESS, INC.,
Scholarly and Reference Division,
175 Fifth Avenue, New York, N.Y. 10010

ISBN 0–312–22037–5

Library of Congress Cataloging-in-Publication Data
The changing face of maritime power / edited by Andrew Dorman, Mike
Lawrence Smith, Matthew R. H. Uttley.
p.   cm.
Includes bibliographical references and index.
ISBN 0–312–22037–5
1. Sea-power.   2. Security, International.   3. Naval strategy.
I. Dorman, Andrew M., 1966–   . II. Uttley, Matthew.   III. Smith,
M. L. R. (Michael Lawrence Rowan), 1963–   .
V25.C43   1999
359—dc21

98–31156
CIP

This book is printed on paper suitable for recycling and made from fully managed and
sustained forest sources.

10   9   8   7   6   5   4   3   2   1
08   07   06   05   04   03   02   01   00   99

Printed and bound in Great Britain by
Antony Rowe Ltd, Chippenham, Wiltshire

Contents

Notes on the Contributors

George Baer is the Alfred Thayer Mahan Professor of Maritime Strategy and Chairman of the Strategy and Policy Department at the US Naval War College, Newport, Rhode Island. A graduate of Stanford (AB), Oxford (BA, MA) and Harvard (PhD) universities, he previously held posts at Dartmouth College and the University of California. His distinguished array of books includes: *The Coming of the Italian–Ethiopian War* (1967); *Test Case: Italy, Ethiopia, and the League of Nations* (1976); *International Organizations, 1919–1945*, comp. and ed. (1981; revised edition 1991) and *A Question of Trust – the Origins of U.S.–Soviet Diplomatic Relations. The Memoirs of Loy W. Henderson*, ed. with Introduction (1986). Professor Baer's highly acclaimed *One Hundred Years of Sea Power: The U.S. Navy 1890–1990* (1994) was the winner of the 1994 Theodore and Franklin D. Roosevelt Naval History Prize, the 1995 Bonnot Award for Naval and Maritime History and the 1996 Distinguished Book Award of the Society for Military History.

Tim Benbow is a DPhil student at St Antony's College, Oxford. His thesis is on the Royal Navy and the impact of air power since 1945. During 1996–97 he was Research Associate on the MacArthur Programme on 'Regional Security in the Global Context' at the Department of War Studies, King's College, London, working on naval power after the Cold War.

Michael Clarke is Professor of Defence Studies and Executive Director of the Centre for Defence Studies, King's College, London. Previously he has held posts and fellowships at the University of Manchester, the University of Newcastle, the Royal Institute of International Affairs and the Brookings Institution, Washington, DC. Professor Clarke's books include: *British External Policy-making in the 1990s* (1992); *The Alternative Defence Debate: Non-Nuclear Defence Policies for Europe* (1985) and *Simulation in the Study of International Relations* (1978). In addition, he has edited numerous volumes including *New Perspectives on Security* (1992), *British Defence Choices for the 21st Century* (1993), *European Defence Cooperation: America, Britain and NATO* (1990) and *Brassey's Defence Yearbook* between 1993 and 1996. In addition to a range of consultancies that have included Membership of the High Level Group of Experts on CFSP matters advising Commissioner Hans van den Broek and Special Adviser to the House of Commons Foreign Affairs Committee and the Defence Committee, Professor Clarke makes regular television appearances commenting on defence and security-related issues.

Andrew M. Dorman is a Senior Lecturer in the Defence Studies Department, Joint Services Command and Staff College, and a Research Assistant at the Security Studies Research Programme, University of Birmingham. He was formerly Senior Lecturer in the Department of History and International Affairs at the Royal Naval College, Greenwich, and Lecturer in the Department of Political Science and International Studies at the University of Birmingham. He completed an undergraduate degree at Sunderland Polytechnic in 1987, a masters degree at Birmingham in 1992 and has recently submitted his doctorate. In between time he trained and qualified as a chartered accountant with KPMG Peat Marwick. Mr Dorman is a specialist in British defence policy, European security and the use of force. His publications include a co-authored book *European Security: An Introduction to Security Issues in Post-Cold War Europe* (1995) and the co-edited *Military Intervention: From Gunboat Diplomacy to Humanitarian Intervention*, (1995). He is currently working on a co-authored book entitled *British Defence Policy since 1945*.

Christina Goulter is a Senior Lecturer in Defence Studies at the Joint Services Command and Staff College. Between 1994 and 1997, she was Associate Professor of Strategy at the US Naval War College, Rhode Island. Her last book, entitled *A Forgotten Offensive: Royal Air Force Coastal Command's Anti-Shipping Campaign, 1940–1945*, was published in 1995. Her other publications include articles and co-authored works on strategic bombing, economic warfare and British intelligence during the Second World War, including a recent study of the Special Operations Executive in occupied Greece in *Knowing Your Friends: Intelligence Inside Alliances and Coalitions from 1914 to the Cold War* (1998). She is currently writing a book on the Ministry of Economic Warfare and British air strategy between 1939 and 1945.

Eric Grove is Senior Lecturer in Politics and Deputy Director of the Centre for Security Studies at the University of Hull. He was Deputy Head of Strategic Studies at the Britannia Royal Naval College, Dartmouth, and has held visiting posts at the United States Naval Academy, Annapolis, Cambridge University, the Royal Naval College, Greenwich, and the University of Wollongong. His many books include: *Vanguard to Trident, British Naval Policy since 1945* (1987) and *The Future of Sea Power* (1990), and co-authorship of the most recent history of the Britannia Royal Naval College, Dartmouth. He has edited Sir Julian Corbett's *Some Principles of Maritime Strategy* and is an international authority on maritime strategy and modern naval history. Dr Grove has served as consultant to both the Ministry of Defence and the Royal Navy. He was a co-author of BR1806, *The Fundamentals of British Maritime Doctrine*.

Andrew Lambert is a Senior Lecturer in the Department of War Studies, King's College, London. He is also Secretary of the Navy Records Society, Chairman of the Publications Committee of the Society for Nautical Research, Vice President of the British Commission for Maritime History and Fellow of the Royal Historical Society. His books include *The Crimean War: British Grand Strategy against Russia 1853–1856* (1990) and *The Last Sailing Battlefleet: Maintaining Naval Mastery 1815–1850* (1991). Recent articles include: 'The Naval War', in John Pimlott and Stephen Badsey (eds), *The Gulf War Assessed* (1992); 'Seapower 1939–40: Churchill and the Strategic Origins of the Battle of the Atlantic', *Journal of Strategic Studies*, 1994; 'The Royal Navy 1856–1914: Deterrence and the Strategy of World Power', in K. Neilson and J. Errington (eds), *Navies and Global Defence: Theories and Strategies* (1995); and 'Seizing the Initiative: the Arctic Convoys 1944–45', in N. A. M. Rodger (ed.), *Naval Power in the Twentieth Century* (1966). At present he is completing a biography of Professor Sir John Knox Laughton entitled *The Foundations of Naval History: John Knox Laughton, the Royal Navy and the Historical Progression*.

Colin McInnes is a Reader in the Department of International Politics, University of Wales, Aberystwyth. He was formerly a lecturer in the Department of War Studies, the Royal Military Academy Sandhurst, and Visiting Research Fellow at the Centre for Defence Studies, King's College, London. He has published widely on the British independent deterrent, NATO strategy, conventional war-fighting doctrine and the British army. His most recent book is *Hot War, Cold War: the British Army's Way in Warfare, 1945–95*.

Malcolm H. Murfett is an Associate Professor in the Department of History at the National University of Singapore. He is the author of *Fool-Proof Relations: the Search for Anglo-American Naval Cooperation during the Chamberlain Years, 1937–1940* (1984), *Hostage on the Yangtze: Britain, China and the Amethyst Crisis of 1949* (1991), *In Jeopardy: the Royal Navy and British Far Eastern Defence Policy, 1945–1951* (1995) and the editor of *The Limitations of Military Power* (1990) and *The First Sea Lords: from Fisher to Mountbatten* (1995). Dr Murfett is also a Fellow of the Royal Historical Society.

Norman Polmar is an analyst, historian and author specializing in naval and strategic issues. He has served as a consultant to three Secretaries of the Navy, three members of the US Senate, one member of the House of Representatives and the Director of the Los Alamos National Laboratory as well as to the Deputy Counsellor of President Reagan. He also served from 1982 to 1986 as a member of the Secretary of the Navy's Research Advisory Committee (NRAC). Mr Polmar has written or co-authored more than thirty books. These include co-authoring with Thomas B. Allen the best-selling biography, *Rickover: Controversy and Genius* (1982) and the controversial *Codename Downfall: the Secret Plan to Invade Japan and Why Truman Used the Bomb* (1995). He is also co-author of two Random House encyclopaedias, the author of the Naval Institute reference books *The Ships and Aircraft of the U.S. Fleet* and *Guide to the Soviet Navy*, a regular columnist for the Naval Institute *Proceedings*, and a former editor of the US and several other sections of the annual *Jane's Fighting Ships*. He is currently writing a history of submarine design during the Cold War era with Academician I. D. Spassky, Head of the RUBIN submarine design bureau.

Michael Pugh is Reader in International Relations, Department of Politics, University of Plymouth. He is the Director of the new International Studies Centre at the University of Plymouth and is also directing a research project on peacebuilding in Bosnia and Croatia. He is the editor of the quarterly journal *International Peacekeeping*. He has written many articles on maritime security issues and is the editor of the book *Maritime Security and Peacekeeping* (1994).

Mike Lawrence Smith is Lecturer in the Department of War Studies, King's College, London. Formerly he was Senior Lecturer in the Department of History and International Affairs at the Royal Naval College, Greenwich. Between 1992 and 1995 he was Lecturer in the Department of History at the National University of Singapore.

Geoffrey Till is the Dean of Academic Studies at the Joint Services Command and Staff College, Bracknell, and is the Head of the Defence Studies Department. He is also Visiting Professor in Maritime Studies in the Department of War Studies at King's College, London, and before that was in the Department of Management and Systems at the City University. In addition to many articles and chapters on various aspects of defence, he is the author of a number of books including *Air Power and the Royal Navy* (1979); *Maritime Strategy and the Nuclear Age*, 2nd edn (1984); *Modern Sea Power* (1987); and, with Bryan Ranft, *The Sea in Soviet Strategy*, 2nd edn (1989). More recently he has edited *Coastal Forces* (1994) and *Sea-Power: Theory and Practice* (1994). Professor Till's work has been translated into eight languages and he lectures regularly at defence and academic institutions around the world.

Matthew Uttley is Senior Lecturer in the Defence Studies Department, Joint Services Command and Staff College (JSCSC), and Director of the JSCSC Defence Technology Research Group. He was formerly Senior Lecturer in the Department of History and International Affairs at the Royal Naval College, Greenwich, and has been a Research Fellow at the Centre for Defence Economics at the University of York and the Centre for Defence and International Security Studies, Lancaster University. During 1987 he was the Ford Foundation Scholar in Science, Technology and International Affairs at Lancaster University, and was elected Fellow of the Royal Society of Arts in 1994. Dr Uttley has published widely on defence procurement, technology transfer and West European defence integration. In addition, he is co-editor with Richard Coopey and Graham Spinardi of *Defence Science and Technology: Adjusting to Change* (1993).

1 Tradition and Innovation in Maritime Thinking

Mike Lawrence Smith and
Matthew R. H. Uttley[1]

FROM COLD WAR TO POST-COLD WAR

During the Cold War, the security environment on which Western naval planning was premised had a number of characteristics. The bipolar structure of the international system meant that East–West security relations were organized around two strong and opposing alliances – NATO and the Warsaw Pact. Against this strategic backdrop, the main tenet of Western defence strategy was deterring the threat posed by the Soviet Union. By the latter stages of the Cold War, planning assumptions were relatively stable because the 'active deterrent role played by the military was well-defined and clearly understood',[2] and NATO force levels were based on threat-based calculations and configured primarily for high-intensity war-fighting roles. Collective security was based primarily on the NATO alliance; bipolarity meant that other multilateral organizations, including the United Nations (UN), the West European Union (WEU) and the European Union (EU), played only a marginal role in East–West security affairs.

In the maritime sphere, the major Western powers' assumptions about bipolarity were reflected in naval force dispositions which were organized primarily for deterrence, achieving sea control and battle-space dominance.[3] In light of the increase in Soviet blue-water naval capabilities during the 1970s,[4] the NATO alliance prepared for the struggle for control of the sea and the containment of the Soviet Navy, reflected in forces capable of anti-surface, anti-air and deep-water anti-submarine warfare, as well as the ability to protect sea lines of communication for extended periods. The apogee of Cold War naval planning was the United States Navy's 1986 document *Maritime Strategy*, which 'will probably be remembered as the highwater mark of "blue water" naval thinking in the post-war era'.[5] The emphasis of the *Maritime Strategy* was

> on offensive sea control and horizontal escalation using the USN's command of the sea (for example, attacking the Soviet Far East if the

1

Soviet Union had attacked Europe). The primary task was war at sea through sea control. Indeed, throughout the Cold War period, the focus of Western maritime strategy was the containment of Soviet power at sea by Western sea control.[6]

NATO maritime forces were thus designed for high-intensity conflict and structured to contain, defend in depth and maintain the initiative against a specific blue-water adversary.

Since 1989, the end of the Cold War has had two major implications for the milieu confronting Western maritime strategy and naval planning. The first has been the dramatic decline in the blue-water threat presented by the former Soviet Navy:

> Lack of funds; ships in deteriorating condition; loss of ports, ship-building and repair facilities and industrial suppliers; loss of manpower; under recruitment; loss of training establishments; the high cost of the nuclear disposal programme and enforced, continued retrenchment in overseas deployments: all of these circumstances have already reduced the Russian navy to a shadow of its former Soviet self. The prospect of regeneration in the near future is excluded by government defence and foreign policies which place overriding priority on the "near abroad" and therefore by implication on forces other than the navy, thus reaffirming the traditional emphasis on a continental rather than maritime strategy.[7]

Even when residual capabilities are taken into account, the fact that the Russian Navy is so much smaller and less well equipped than the former Soviet Fleet has significantly reduced 'the capabilities and skills needed to counter it, when compared to the levels obtained in the Cold War years'.[8] The second implication is that security issues previously suppressed by bipolar stability, or at least largely neglected by strategists, during the Cold War have intensified. These include an increase in the relative salience of territorial disputes and regional confrontation following the drawdown of superpower presence in Asia,[9] the growth in intra-state hostilities and confrontation clearly evident following the fragmentation of the former Soviet Union and Yugoslavia,[10] the rise in nationalism and evidence of the proliferation of conventional defence equipment and weapons capable of mass destruction.[11] Cold War 'certainties' in Western naval planning have been replaced by perceptions of a more diffuse set of risks on a global scale. As Till points out:

> We are now witnessing quite radical change in the global security system ... Even the continued dominance of the nation state can no

longer be taken for granted, with its power apparently leaking away to supranational, transnational and sectional organisations and interests... [T]he assumptions of national statesmen are shifting too: old enemies are new friends; bipolarity has been replaced by multi-polarity; order by disorder; the familiar alliance systems of the past are shifting beneath our feet.[12]

These developments have affected Western maritime planning assumptions. With the demise of the former Soviet naval capability, the fundamental shift in Western concerns has been 'away from having to deal with a global maritime threat and towards projecting power and influence across the seas in response to regional challenges'.[13] Confronted with post-Cold War instability, planning emphasis has moved away from sea control and sea denial towards 'littoral operations to contain crises or support land forces in "small" wars as the primary task for navies in the foreseeable future'.[14]

INNOVATION AND TRADITION IN MARITIME STRATEGY

Against this shift in the geostrategic backdrop, the major focus of this volume is continuity and change in maritime power. The emphasis is on identifying and analysing the central tenets of contemporary maritime strategy, doctrine, roles and organization in light of the changed international environment since the end of the Cold War. The post-Cold War era is now sufficiently advanced in years for it to be something of a cliché for analysts to proclaim how portentous the 'new' strategic environment is in terms of the new power relationships forged and the new areas of conflict. However, precisely because the post-Cold War era is sufficiently advanced, this experience does allow an assessment of continuity and change in the maritime sphere.

The volume is based on papers originally presented at 'The Changing Nature of Maritime Power' Conference which took place at the Royal Naval College, Greenwich, between 28 and 29 April 1997.[15] There are two caveats concerning the scope of the book. First, the primary focus is the British dimension of maritime thinking, a reflection of the Greenwich Conference and the various speakers who were mainly British-based. However, attention is also focused on evolving naval thinking in the United States as the dominant sea power in the world today. This volume therefore contains an explicitly Anglo-American perspective on maritime power which will inevitably reflect certain value assumptions about the utility of naval forces based on historical, cultural and geographical traditions and predispositions. That is to say, most of the commentary accepts that the functions of navies are likely to encompass significant world roles, including peacekeeping and peace-support operations, projection of power ashore and the retention of traditional roles such as protection of sea lines of communication. This is not to suggest that the number of larger naval powers is irrevocably fixed, as the significant expansion in naval forces in the Asia-Pacific region, most notably the ongoing development of the Chinese navy, testifies.[16] However, clearly the outlook is going to be of less relevance for those smaller naval powers with coastal navies, the major concerns of which are likely to be limited to roles such as, *inter alia*, defence of the littoral,[17] fishery protection and territorial policing.[18]

Second, debates about the extent and nature of continuity and change in the maritime sphere since the end of the Cold War are inherently open to dispute because it depends to a degree on the level of analysis adopted to address the issues. For example, it is possible to argue that at the highest strategic level – the use of maritime forces for the attainment of political objectives – little or nothing has changed fundamentally. Conversely, at the level of doctrine it could plausibly be argued that the transition has ushered in a new era of planning and operating assumptions. Consequently, any volume can only hope to provide a partial rather than a comprehensive evaluation. With these caveats in mind, there has been a deliberate attempt in this volume to focus on some of the key trends and issues affecting contemporary maritime power.

THE APPLICATION OF MARITIME THEORY AND DOCTRINE TODAY

Michael Handel has commented that 'the development of the study and theory of war is (and probably will always remain) in a pre-Newtonian, pre-scientific, or non-formal stage'[19] because the conduct of war is based less on formal developed theories and more on intuition, experience and an understanding of the rules or 'laws' of action. To a greater degree this understanding holds true for maritime strategy. In the sphere of maritime strategy, two of the most influential thinkers of the twentieth century have been Alfred Thayer Mahan and Sir Julian Corbett. The first section of the volume examines the relevance of each strategist to post-Cold War debates about maritime power.

During the Cold War, commentators on Mahan focused on specific aspects of his writings: those that emphasized the achievement of security through command of the sea based on a strategy of offensive annihilation of a blue-water threat with a battle fleet. This is not surprising given the immediate relevance of Mahan's ideas at a time when the focus of Western planning was on open-ocean sea control against an adversary possessing a great-power fleet. George Baer examines the relevance of Mahan's thinking for the US Navy in the post-Cold War scenario where open-ocean sea control now exists, there is no blue-water security threat, no competing great-power fleet, and in which the US Navy operates in a joint, littoral and peacetime environment. George Baer addresses two important questions: How, with command of the sea, do Mahan's ideas justify naval forces today? And, what is today's US Navy for?

Geoffrey Till demonstrates the salience of Sir Julian Corbett's writings for contemporary maritime policy. Corbett emphasized that strategy needs to be consciously related to foreign policy, and naval strategy to land strategy. Over the last few years Corbett has benefited from a renaissance in popularity because the post-Cold War shifts in planning towards littoral warfare and the projection of power from the sea appear to vindicate much of what he said. Geoffrey Till's approach is to demonstrate Corbett's importance as a maritime thinker by formulating what Corbett might well have made his 'Ten Commandments' for those contemplating the use of sea power in the post-Cold War world.

Maritime doctrine forms a bridge between the principles derived from the 'lessons of history'[20] encapsulated in the writings of Mahan, Corbett and others, and the practices and procedures governing the employment of maritime forces. Doctrine provides

> a framework of principles, practices and procedures, understanding of which provides a basis for action. Maritime Doctrine fulfils this function for the use of military power at sea to achieve policy objectives.[21]

The subsequent two chapters analyse the emergence and characteristics of naval and maritime doctrine in the United Kingdom. Andrew Lambert charts the role in doctrinal development played by the Royal Naval College, Greenwich, from the nineteenth century through to the 1995 launch of the Royal Navy's BR1806 *The Fundamentals of Maritime Doctrine*. Eric Grove develops the themes introduced by Andrew Lambert when he considers the factors and considerations leading to the production of BR1806, and outlines the major tenets of contemporary UK maritime doctrine.

MARITIME ROLES

In the 1980s Western Cold War maritime planning emphasized deterrence, achieving sea control and battle-space dominance. On a day-to-day basis, however, navies were utilized primarily for lower-intensity roles and missions that included, *inter alia*, diplomacy and international maritime assistance. In this regard, despite the post-Cold War shift in planning away from achieving sea control towards littoral operations:

> As part of the wider concept of the utility of maritime power, navies have other military, diplomatic and policing roles to fulfil and, despite recent changes on the global security scene, navies continue to fulfil these roles – only the emphasis between the roles, and within each, may have changed.[22]

This post-Cold War shift in 'emphasis' can be illustrated by a simple matrix (Figure 1.1). Naval roles fall on a spectrum, ranging from high-intensity war-fighting against major opposition, coercive diplomacy and alliance building through to the relatively low-intensity role of maintaining good order at sea (protection of sea-based resources including oil, gas and fish, hydrographic surveys, anti-piracy operations, etc.). The major effects of the decline in the former Soviet naval threat and the increased salience of security issues previously suppressed by bipolar stability have been a reduction in the likelihood (frequency) of blue-water naval operations at the high-intensity end of the spectrum but an increase in the probability of naval operations at the low-intensity end. In light of this shift, the subsequent three chapters investigate continuity and changes relating to three naval roles.

On the one hand, the contemporary desire and ability to project power for policing, crisis management and conflict prevention and to obtain influence in the world order reflects a strategic environment freed from the imperatives of the Cold War. On the other, the freedom to project maritime power is now paradoxically constrained, *inter alia*, by the structure of international interdependence that finally finished off the Cold War. Developing these themes, Professor Michael Clarke analyses the opportunities and constraints confronting maritime power projection using the United Kingdom as a case study.

In the post-Cold War world, doctrinal and planning assumptions that emphasize littoral warfare and the projection of naval power from the sea have been accentuated at the expense of operational plans that were premised on large-scale naval confrontation with powerful adversaries.

One consequence has been the recrudescence of what may be loosely described as 'gunboat'-type operations that typified naval activities in the nineteenth century.[23] Malcolm Murfett evaluates the contemporary use of navies for gunboat, or coercive, diplomacy. Through an examination of why gunboat diplomacy continues to be a major naval function in the changed strategic environment of the post-Cold War era, the chapter demonstrates just what relevance this political application of naval power in peacetime has as Western states approach the twenty-first century.

		INTENSITY HIGH	FREQUENCY LOW
War-fighting	Against relatively major opposition		
	Against relatively minor opposition		
Naval diplomacy	Coercive		
	Alliance building		
	International maritime assistance		
Good order at sea			
		LOW	HIGH

Figure 1.1   The spectrum of naval tasks
Source: Till, G., 'Maritime strategy and the twenty-first century', *Journal of Strategic Studies*, vol. 17, no. 1, March 1994, p. 180.

The end of the Cold War has had two important consequences in terms of the military roles and activities of the UN. First, the decline in bipolar stability has been reflected in the emergence or re-emergence of a range of inter- and intra-state conflicts.[24] Second, the Cold War characteristics of the international system that militated against East–West cooperation through the UN has been replaced by a spirit of cooperation.[25] In the period since the demise of the former Soviet Union, the use of the maritime environment has been discovered, or more accurately rediscovered, by UN member states. Michael Pugh analyses this post-Cold War growth of naval involvement in international peace support operations. The chapter reviews the contemporary politics and strategic value of peace support operations, outlines why the UN rediscovered this role after 1989, considers the 'credibility crisis' precipitated by the problems that have enveloped recent UN-authorized operations, and assesses the institutional interests invested in peace support operations.

A major question that has emerged about the utility of naval forces since the end of the Cold War is: what role can navies efficiently fulfil when there is no major opposing navy that they may have to defeat? Tim Benbow investigates this issue by examining the two major regional conflicts in which Western powers have been involved since the end of the Cold War – the 1990–91 Gulf War and the conflict in the former Yugoslavia. The chapter outlines the role of maritime forces in each of the conflicts and considers whether there were vital functions performed by navies for which other armed forces could not have been substituted.

THE TECHNOLOGICAL DIRECTION OF THE US

The changed international setting since the early 1990s, in particular the disappearance of a single all-consuming threat and the rise to prominence of regional instability and conflict, has prompted a re-evaluation and change of emphasis by the world's remaining superpower – the United States. In the words of the Department of the Navy's seminal document *Forward...From the Sea*, 'a landmark shift in operational focus and a reordering of co-ordinated priorities of the Naval Service'[26] was promulgated in September 1992. A consequence has been that the concept of power projection is now an explicit and firmly entrenched aspect of post-Cold War US strategic thinking,[27] and it is this change in emphasis that has produced shifts in maritime planning at the technological level.

Contemporary US debates concerning the future direction of naval technology can be categorized under a range of headings. First, attention is centring on the potential implications of the concept of the 'Revolution in Military Affairs' (RMA) for naval operations, or the 'strategic consequences of the marriage of systems that collect, process and communicate information with those that apply military force'.[28] On the basis of trends in US technological innovation, advocates of this revolution believe that 'if this marriage can be consummated then it will reinforce established tendencies towards the creation of an American military capability far superior to that of any country or groups of countries.'[29] A second strand of debates revolves around the optimum mix of maritime platforms and their desired characteristics to meet emerging and potential naval missions.[30]

A third element in the technology equation includes active consideration of how national naval strengths can be measured and quantified in light of the proliferation of advanced weapons among Third World countries, the acute reduction of the Soviet-Russian fleet, the 'downsizing' of the US Navy, and the reshaping of US defence policy. Norman Polmar's chapter addresses these issues through an analysis of the factors that affect predictions about the measurement of naval strength in the twenty-first century. Using the contemporary Russian Navy as a case study, Norman Polmar introduces a new criteria for evaluating naval strength and effectiveness which generates generic factors that can be applied to the analysis of other states.

THE DIRECTION OF THE UK: NAVAL POWER, 'JOINTERY' AND THE OTHER SERVICES

The transition since the Cold War has had important implications for debates about the level and nature of cooperation between navies and the other armed services within individual NATO states. During the Cold War 'a distinction between the institutional and operational arrangements for the armed forces made some sense'[31] because of the functional roles of each service within NATO's overall force posture. That is not to say inter-service cooperation was absent: in the United States, for example, the Air Force and the Army jointly developed the 'AirLand Battle Concept' to counter the Warsaw Pact conventional threat to Western Europe.[32] However, the primary focus of the Alliance's maritime assets was anti-submarine warfare in the North Atlantic while land assets and supporting air elements were concentrated on the Central Front in West Germany. The consequence was that operational integration was primarily combined between the maritime, land and air forces of the different Alliance members rather than with the other armed services of a particular state.

Since the Cold War, however, the requirement to project military power has created an imperative for a more systematic integration of national forces and doctrines, or as the current terminology has it, 'jointery': planning for 'military operations in which elements of more than one service participate'.[33] The primary drivers for jointery, or 'jointness',[34] are the requirement for the projection of power from littoral areas of the sea by naval forces[35] and the deployment of expeditionary forces[36] which are supported by air elements, as a means to meet contingencies on a global scale. In this regard, the fundamental shift away from

Cold War planning assumptions is that jointery 'signifies a reverse order of [Cold War] priorities; it connotes the fusion of effort in place of *ad hoc* arrangements and, most important, it subordinates all... operations directly to events on land'.[37]

The contemporary orthodoxy from the naval perspective is that

> it is impossible nowadays to talk about the fleet in isolation. Those who believe that military matters can be easily categorised into land, sea and air, in our modern technologically agile world, are making a facile and anachronistic judgement.[38]

The final three chapters evaluate this assumption by focusing on the introduction of 'jointery' in the United Kingdom. Colin McInnes analyses the relationship between land and sea power focusing specifically on the British Army's views on the future of warfare and the role of sea power within its vision of future operations. The chapter charts the changes in the relative importance of the Army and Navy to British defence policy over the course of the past hundred years and outlines the Army's view of the relationship between land and sea power immediately prior to the end of the Cold War. The analysis then suggests the rationale for a change in this relationship with the end of the Cold War, and details the Army's current perspective on jointery.

Like the other two services, the Royal Air Force (RAF) has been compelled to reassess its roles since the end of the Cold War. Maritime aviation played an important role during the Cold War and trends suggest that in the era of expeditionary warfare there is likely to be as much, if not more, of a need for shore-based maritime aviation. Christina Goulter evaluates current RAF doctrine and investigates why the RAF needs to maintain a strong maritime force in the context of new joint service structures.

Andrew Dorman's focus is the Royal Navy's role within the changed internal and external environments brought about by the end of the Cold War. The chapter addresses three key themes: first, how UK government policy towards the use of military power has evolved since the end of the Cold War; second, the extent to which the Royal Navy's planning has adapted to these changes; and third, the compatibility of the UK government and Royal Navy views in terms of the extent to which the Royal Navy's plans are likely to be implemented into the next century.

In the final chapter Mike Lawrence Smith and Matthew Uttley draw together the major themes and issues that emerge. The broad context of the volume is the extent to which the transition from Cold War to post-Cold War has impacted on maritime power. Drawing on the scope and coverage of the individual contributions, the concluding chapter provides a tentative assessment of the extent to which the shift from the bipolar environment since the end of the Cold War has changed the face of maritime power, and in which areas it is taking place.

NOTES

1. The views expressed in this chapter are those of the author and do not necessarily reflect official opinion in any way.
2. Admiral P. D. Miller, 'Both Swords and Plowshares: Military Roles in the 1990s', *RUSI Journal*, April 1993, p. 13.
3. For an authoritative exposition of the Cold War naval posture of the West see Norman Freidman, *The US Maritime Strategy* (London: Jane's, 1988).
4. For more detailed accounts of Soviet naval capabilities, see: Brian Ranft and Geoffrey Till, *The Sea in Soviet Strategy* (London: Macmillan, 1983); R. Fieldhouse and S. Taoka, *Superpowers at Sea: An Assessment of the Naval Arms Race* (Oxford: OUP, 1989); and the collection of articles in P. S. Gillette and W. C. Frank (eds), *The Sources of Soviet Naval Conduct* (Lexington: Lexington Books, 1990), and, J. Skogan and A. Brundtland (eds), *Soviet Sea Power in Northern Waters* (London: Pinter, 1990).
5. J. S. Breemer, 'The End of Naval Strategy: Revolutionary Change and the Future of American Naval Power', *Strategic Review*, Spring 1994, p. 44.
6. S. Bateman, 'Strategic Change and Naval Roles', in S. Bateman and D. Sherwood (eds), *Strategic Change and Naval Roles and Issues for a Medium Naval Power* (Canberra: Australian National University, 1993), p. 38.
7. S. E. Airey, 'Does Russian Seapower Have a Future?', *RUSI Journal*, December 1995, p. 20.
8. Geoffrey Till, 'Maritime Strategy and the Twenty-First Century', *Journal of Strategic Studies*, vol. 17, no. 1, March 1994, p. 182.
9. See, for example, M. J. Valencia, 'China and the South China Sea Disputes', *Adelphi Paper 298* (Oxford: OUP, 1995); and D. T. Stuart and W. T. Tow, 'A US Strategy for the Asia-Pacific', *Adelphi Paper 299* (Oxford: OUP, 1995). Note that other commentators argue that the draw-down in superpower presence has been exaggerated given the large residual US capability deployed in the region: see, for example, M. L. Smith and D. M. Jones, 'ASEAN, Asian Values and the Security of Southeast Asia in the New World Order', *Contemporary Security Policy*, vol. 18, no. 3, Winter 1997, pp. 127–57.
10. See, for example, V. Gray, 'Beyond Bosnia: Ethno-National Diasporas and Security in Europe', *Contemporary Security Policy*, vol. 17, no. 1, April 1996, pp. 146–73.
11. See, for example, J. C. Baker, 'Non-Proliferation Incentives for Russia and Ukraine', *Adelphi Paper 309* (Oxford: OUP, 1997); M. O'Hanlon, V. Farrell and S. Glazerman, 'Controlling Arms Transfers to the Middle

East: The Case for Supplier Limits', *Arms Control Today*, November 1992, pp. 18–24; and, 'Controlling the Flow of Sophisticated Arms to the Third World: A Modern Dilemma', *Asian Defence Journal*, 6/92, pp. 28–36.

12.   Till, op. cit., p. 166.
13.   United States Department of the Navy, *Forward... From the Sea* (Washington, DC: Department of the Navy, October 1994), p. 32.
14.   Breemer, op. cit., p. 44.
15.   The conference was organized by the Defence Studies Department, Royal Naval College, Greenwich, in conjunction with the Head of Defence Studies (Royal Navy).
16.   See 'Solution to China Puzzle Holds Key to Stability', *Defense News*, 11–17 September 1995, and *International Security Review 1997* (London: RUSI, 1997), pp. 271–302.
17.   Derek Boothby, 'Sailing Under New Colors', *United States Naval Institute Proceedings*, No. 118, July 1992, p. 48 cited in Donald C. F. Daniel, *The Evolution of Naval Power to the Year 2010*, Occasional Paper of the Center for Naval Warfare Studies, Strategic Research Department Research Report 6–94, US Naval War College, p. 5.
18.   For a full discussion of the roles and options for smaller navies see Greg Mills (ed.), *Maritime Policy for Developing Nations* (Johannesburg: South African Institute of International Affairs/Centre for Defence and International Security Studies, Lancaster University, 1995). See also Martin Edmonds and Greg Mills, *Uncharted Waters: A Review of South Africa's Naval Options* (Johannesburg: SAIIA/CDISS, 1996), pp. 19–51.
19.   Michael I. Handel, *Masters of War: Classical Strategic Thought* (London: Frank Cass, 1996), p. xiii.
20.   BR1806, *The Fundamentals of British Maritime Doctrine* (London: HMSO, 1995), Foreword.
21.   Ibid., p. 12.
22.   Bateman and Sherwood, op. cit., p. 33.
23.   For a broader discussion see, for example, James Cable, *Gunboat Diplomacy 1919–91*, 3rd edn (London: Macmillan, 1994).
24.   See, for example, Christopher Greenwood, 'Is There a Right of Humanitarian Intervention?', *The World Today*, February 1993, pp. 34–40.
25.   See, for example, Boutros Boutros Ghali, 'UN Peace-Keeping in a New Era: A New Chance for Peace', *The World Today*, April 1993, pp. 66–9; and Marrack Goulding, 'The Evolution of United Nations Peacekeeping', *International Affairs*, vol. 63, no. 3, 1993, pp. 451–64.
26.   United States Department of the Navy, op. cit., p. 1.
27.   *National Military Strategy of the United States of America 1995: A Strategy of Flexible and Selective Engagement* (Washington, DC: US Government Printing Office, 1995), pp. 13–14.
28.   Lawrence Freedman, 'Britain and the Revolution in Military Affairs', *Defense Analysis*, vol. 14, no. 1, April 1998.
29.   Ibid. For a discussion see: William A. Owens, 'JROC: Harnessing the Revolution in Military Affairs', *Joint Forces Quarterly*, no. 5, Summer 1994; Edward N. Luttwak, 'Towards Post Heroic Warfare', *Foreign Affairs*, May/June 1995; and, Edward N. Luttwak, 'A Post Heroic Military Policy', *Foreign Affairs*, July/August 1996.

30. See, for example, the discussion about the potential role of surface war-ships contained in Reuven Leopold, 'The Next Naval Revolution', *Jane's Navy International*, January/February 1996, pp. 13–20.

31. Lieutenant-Commander J. R. Stocker, 'Canadian Joint Operations', *RUSI Journal*, June 1996, p. 36.

32. See, for example: Admiral Paul D. Miller, op. cit., p. 13; Colin McInnes, *NATO's Changing Strategic Agenda: The Defence of Central Europe* (London: Unwin Hyman, 1990); and, Robert A. Gessert, 'The AirLand Battle and NATO's New Doctrinal Debate', *RUSI Journal*, vol. 129, no. 2, June 1984, pp. 52–60.

33. United Kingdom Doctrine for Joint and Combined Operations, *Joint Warfare Publication 0–10*, 3rd Study draft, 1997, p. 11.

34. The term 'jointery' is employed in the United Kingdom, whereas 'jointness' is the term adopted in the United States. Both share the same meaning and they are used interchangeably in this volume. For a detailed discussion of definitional problems associated with the concept of jointery, see Andrew Dorman, Mike Lawrence Smith and Matthew R. H. Uttley, 'Jointery and Combined Operations in an Expeditionary Era: Defining the Issues', *Defense Analysis*, vol. 14, no. 1, April 1998.

35. See, for example, Rear-Admiral R. Cobbold, 'A Joint Maritime-Based Expeditionary Capability', *RUSI Journal*, August 1997, pp. 23–30.

36. See, for example, Lieutenant-General Sir Robert Ross, 'The Role of Amphibious Forces in a Changing World', *RUSI Journal*, April 1996, pp. 21–3.

37. Breemer, op. cit., p. 46.

38. Admiral of the Fleet Sir Jock Slater, 'A Fleet for the 90s', *RUSI Journal*, February 1993, p. 8.

2 Alfred Thayer Mahan and the Utility of US Naval Forces Today[1]

George Baer

This assessment examines both change and continuity in the post-Cold War US naval services. Let us imagine the Mahan of 1890. For Mahan in the late nineteenth century, security was the main issue, achieved by command of the sea through a strategy of offensive annihilation of a blue-water threat with a battle fleet, the Navy acting almost autonomously. The Navy's other operations – those that are today considered its peacetime concerns, those that are directed beyond the sea towards politics and prosperity, presence, influence, intervention, and the rest – were for Mahan lesser ancillary missions, hidden by the security strategy of battle annihilation and command of the open sea. But now: let us imagine Mahan today in a post-Cold War world where there is only one superpower. Here, for a latter-day Mahan, open-ocean sea control now exists, there is no blue-water security threat, no competing great-power fleet, and the US Navy operates in a joint, peacetime, and littoral environment. With command of the sea attained, how does our Mahan today justify naval forces? What is today's US Navy for?

For the US, the answer is: to assure political stability on the economically vibrant rimlands of, *inter alia*, Europe and Pacific Asia, thereby ensuring access to consequent world markets. The naval services, that is the US Navy and the Marine Corps, support a *peacetime* policy of engagement and influence by naval presence, deterrence, and intervention against the land as desired, to assure the continuation of stability, trade, and security. What were different or lesser included missions for Mahan in wartime are now the key to maintaining the peace.

The naval services stated their doctrine in these terms a few years ago after the Persian Gulf War when they belatedly realized how much things had changed: that by victory or default there was no more Soviet navy, that the Cold War was really over, and that there was a new foreign policy agenda. The Gulf War revealed that the navy was slow in adjusting to this new environment, to joint operations, to changes in central command, and to the institutional imperatives of procuring high-technology weaponry and participating in the information control

14

concepts that the Air Force and Army were calling a 'revolution in military affairs.'[2]

In *Desert Storm*, the naval services had been marginalized in the joint command. Naval officers faced doctrines and plans for which they were simply not prepared. The Joint Forces Naval Component Commander lost influence when he decided to stay aboard ship rather than closeted with the other joint commanders in Riyadh. The Joint Forces Air Component Commander paid little attention to naval concerns and capabilities.[3] The Marine Corps found that its role in joint operations was highly contingent. Ocean-manoeuvering warships found themselves cramped in the Persian Gulf, prevented by mines from maneuvering close to shore, thereby diminishing sea control and strategic value. In short, the naval services faced a future of littoral operations, unified commands, and warfare technologies which they had neither foreseen nor for which they had prepared.

Desert Storm was a wake-up call. A new international environment demanded a new foreign policy and a new joint strategy. Moreover, public expectations of low casualties and short operations demanded a more relevant maritime doctrine in order to justify the retention and use of naval forces on these terms.

In the naval services' post-Gulf War/Cold War internal reassessments two tendencies and lines of argument emerged. Each stressed one aspect of a global maritime policy. The first stressed preventing war through naval presence. Naval services, it advocated, with their sustainable sea-based reach, could assert peacetime influence on the rimlands to shape the strategic environment. This stance would be in support of a policy of political engagement and open commerce, projected from the strategically neutral sea whereby the navy was to support an informal empire of free trade. The vision was Cobden's, with the causality reversed: free trade was seen (correctly) as the effect, not the cause, of peace among trading states. The naval services, therefore, were to ensure that peace; the emphasis was *to avoid war*.[4]

The second tendency stressed the *ability to fight*, to respond immediately with Navy firepower and with the Marines' operational maneuver from the sea, to win a war.[5] Sea-based high-techology capabilities would deter any adversary or it would permit US forces to contain a conflict in its early stages. Littoral dominance would enable a larger joint effort to follow on by denying to an enemy the ability to interfere in the seaward and littoral battle-space. The naval services would maintain sea control (on the sea), and assault the land (from the sea). In other words, this represented the recreation of a nineteenth-century maritime trading tradition. As

Palmerston and Gladstone knew, an informal empire of free trade rests on political stability, and requires 'imperial' protection.

In general, it was the first line of argument, the emphasis on peacetime engagement, that prevailed in the new doctrine, as in the new foreign policy, but not to the neglect of combat capability. Influence and intervention are complementary: two parts of a good maritime strategy. Presence and expeditionary operations have always been staples of naval policy, back to the Greeks, before Mahan, during Mahan, and after Mahan. US naval services today are returning to conventional naval functions that were overshadowed for a century by great-power conflicts and the heroic image of a battle fleet, when the Navy was known more for its prestigious platforms than its many and varied functions.[6]

But peacetime operations come at a high price. Maintaining forward presence is very costly. Lengthy and varied deployments stretch a thinning force and lower morale. Support operations call for a sizing of the force considerably different from that for combat. In short, too great an emphasis on peacetime influence may decrease combat readiness.

Conversely, if the Navy justifies its combat functions (and by extension its ability to sustain its deterrence, and influence) in terms of high-technology low-casualty intervention, in terms of the targets it can hit with massed, precision air and missile strikes, how does that serve the many other operations-other-than-war required by peacetime engagement? And what then distinguishes Navy firepower from the fire and steel that the Air Force stand ready to deliver, at, the Air Force claims, very much less cost?

From the command perspective, the answer to whose firepower to use is that it does not matter: services propose; commands dispose. Services are no longer self-referential. Combatant commanders and the National Military Strategy look to function, not to a particular service, and to joint task forces. With joint surveillance assets in place, even the Navy's core competence of sea control is no longer a solely Navy province.

Both schools of thought combine to offer to commanders-in-chief the particular advantages of water-borne access: sea-based combat readiness near the rimlands, and tactical flexibility. And high-technology firepower is not all. For intervention, the Marine Corps' expeditionary force is a sea-based land army. In short, forward naval presence, sustained reach, though costly in money, puts a naval force into operational range of many of the world's capital cities, nearly all the major marketplaces of international trade, and all the routes of sea transport. This access strategy fits the global, but militarily cautious, national military strategy of the United States. It is a strategy of flexible and selective engagement.

That said, the future will require much further thinking about force structures and operational doctrine, both within the naval services and in terms of alternate options offered by the Air Force, the Army, Special Operations Command, and the Coast Guard. For presence there is no way yet to measure influence, to know the effectiveness of new-style gunboat diplomacy, except testing the loyalty of allies and reactions of foes. The danger is mirror-imaging: the thought that what defeats us might defeat another. As a result, for a strategy of influence to be effectively maintained, intelligence and analysis are imperative.

As for intervention, naval forces must be able to act in dense, littoral, and archipelagic theaters. That means assuring movement through unilaterally restricted zones. So access, sea control, or what Callwell called 'maritime preponderance,' remains a live mission after all. Intervention means risking heavy casualties as vulnerable ships close in on an expeditionary operation. That requires a better defense against stand-off missiles, and much improved mine-countermeasures. It means the Marines must be able to fight in cities to support urban warfare. It means that the Navy must be able to insert Marines, and be able to extract them while protecting its ships. It will mean the restructuring both of a doctrine that is now based on current assets, and the force structure itself, as engagement forces are shaped for emergent non-combat missions, amphibious expeditionary forces for penetration into dense combat environments, and combat firepower as organized perhaps through a network of 'distributed' strike platforms.[7]

The point here is that there is no way to establish a priori the relative value of these naval claims to usefulness, nor the competing claims of the Air Force and the Army. Proof of military effectiveness comes only with experience when forces are used, and that depends on the national goals, the political resolve, the plans of the commanders-in-chief, the reaction of opponents, domestic support, and the nature of the war. As no rival service alone can *set* national strategy, none alone can be the final judge of the utility of naval, or of air/space, or of land, forces. Strategy is a pragmatic activity, and the unified commands will make practical decisions. Commanders-in-chief will call for functions and capabilities, not particular services, in the full-force vision of jointness.[8]

But forecasting *is* possible from national policy. It is possible to define the changing utility of the naval services, and it is likewise possible to restate sea power. Generally speaking, US sea power today is not about platforms. It is not a mechanical response to a maritime threat. It is not an annihilation strategy. Neither is it *just* about sea control, presence, or intervention. Sea power is, and Mahan would agree, what Captain

R. C. Rubel called it: 'a broad process supporting the way a maritime
state gains and defends its global interests.'[9] It is about protecting and
promoting an informal empire of free trade and enlarging political liber-
ties. American naval policy, joined, integrated, and under unified command, is – as it always has been – prescriptive. It is 'about influence,
about ambition, about the way a state presents itself to the world, the way
it coordinates its alliances, deters or defeats its foes, assures its prosperity,
and uses its strategically powerful maritime position in the balance of
world power.'[10]

In this manner the naval services in the 1990s identified their utility
with basic national interests, as they did in the 1890s, in the time of Captain Mahan.

NOTES

1. Copyright © George W. Baer. The views expressed here are those of the
   author writing in a personal capacity and do not necessarily reflect US government policy in any way.
2. William A. Owens, *High Seas: The Naval Passage to an Uncharted World*
   (Annapolis, Md.: Naval Institute Press, 1995), p. 4.
3. Peter P. Perla et al., *The Navy and the JFACC: Making Them Work Together*
   (Alexandria, Va.: Center for Naval Analyses, 1993), pp. 2, 25–30.
4. See Wm Roger Louis and Ronald Robinson, 'The Imperialism of Decol-
   onialization', *Journal of Imperial and Commonwealth History*, vol. 22, no.
   3, September 1994, pp. 462–511.
5. The Navy/Marine Corps' operational concept *Forward...from the Sea* was
   published in 1997. The Marine Corps' ongoing experimentation plan is
   called 'Sea Dragon'; its urban warfare component is called 'Urban Warrior'.
6. A reminder of this is found in Frank Uhlig, Jr., 'The Constants of Naval
   Warfare', *Naval War College Review*, vol. 50, no. 2, Spring 1997, pp. 92–105.
7. For the first, see John Keefe et al., *Sizing and Shaping US Military Forces:
   Ideas for the Navy to Use in the Quadrennial Defense Review* (Alexandria,
   Va.: Center for Naval Analyses, 1966), and Linton F. Brooks, *Peacetime
   Influence Through Forward Naval Presence* (Alexandria, Va.: Center for
   Naval Analyses, 1993), who says: 'In the future, the Navy and the nation
   must treat peacetime operations as important in their own right, not simply as a preparation for war or crisis.' For new combat structures, see
   Andrew F. Krepinevich, Jr., *A New Navy for a New Era* (Washington, DC:
   Center for Strategic and Budgetary Assessments, 1993).
8. See Matthew Allen, 'Are Naval Operations Unique?', *Naval Review*, vol.
   84, no. 1, January 1996, pp. 19–23.
9. Captain R. C. Rubel, United States Navy, personal correspondence.
10. Ibid.

3 Sir Julian Corbett and the Twenty-First Century: Ten Maritime Commandments
Geoffrey Till

INTRODUCTION

This analysis will seek to demonstrate the relevance of Corbett to the changing nature and role of maritime power to tomorrow's world of the twenty-first century. The contention here is that, while the theories of Alfred Thayer Mahan are all very well in their way, the work of Sir Julian Corbett provides a much more appropriate foundation for speculation about the future of sea power in the twenty-first century.[1]

SUMMARIZING CORBETT

Corbett came late to maritime affairs and associated with the great men ushering the Royal Navy painfully into the twentieth century. He was very concerned about the poverty of contemporary naval thought, and hoped to improve it in his lectures at the Naval Colleges at Greenwich and Portsmouth in the first decade of the twentieth century. Evidently he did not enjoy the experience, complaining in one letter, 'my strategy lectures are very uphill work. I had no idea when I undertook it how difficult it was to present theory to the unused organs of naval officers.'[2]

His teaching was supported by an impressive list of naval histories, including several on the Tudor and post-Tudor Royal Navy, a masterpiece on the Seven Years War, a hitherto unpublished work on the Russo-Japanese War, *Some Principles of Maritime Strategy* in 1911, and the first three volumes of the *History of the Great War: Naval Operations*.

Paradoxically, Corbett did most of his writing in that particularly interesting period just before the First World War, when Britain was in fact moving away from the kind of strategy that he advocated. As a lawyer, he perhaps had a more judicious sense than Mahan of the limitations of sea power and, quite crucially, of its place in the wider scheme of things.

19

What is special about Corbett is his emphasis on the importance of putting naval operations in that broader context which does so much to explain their form and purpose, and which, in his view, was affected so much by their result.

In this respect, Corbett emphasized that strategy needs to be consciously related to foreign policy, and naval strategy to land strategy:

> Of late years the world has become so deeply impressed with the efficacy of sea power that we are inclined to forget how impotent it is of itself to decide a war against great Continental states, how tedious is the pressure of naval action unless it be nicely co-ordinated with military and diplomatic pressure.[3]

Naval strategy has to be seen not as a separate entity but simply as part of the art of war. Land power and seapower are *not* in opposition, but their relationship with one another will be different for worldwide imperial states where the sea becomes a 'direct and vital factor' than it would be for those for whose geography makes the 'German or Continental School of strategy' more appropriate. Britain of course was pre-eminently just such a maritime state and had derived enormous benefit from developing a set of principles governing the conduct of war '... in which the sea is a substantial factor.'[4]

Of course, Corbett was not confining himself simply to historical analysis. He was advocating a guide for future policy too. The question is whether what he said then has any salience today.

TEN COMMANDMENTS FOR TOMORROW'S WORLD

Corbett and his contemporary Colonel Charles Callwell have both in the past few years benefited from a renaissance in their popularity because so much of what they said, now virtually a century ago, seems almost unerringly apposite to today's world of economic constraint, political uncertainty, small wars and local conflicts. This chapter will seek to establish Corbett's new relevance by identifying what, were he not so modest a man, he might well have made his Ten Commandments for those contemplating maritime strategy and the future of sea power in the twenty-first century. The first five relate to the aims of a maritime policy, the next four to the manner in which it should be carried through. The tenth is a kind of epilogue.

1. Use the Sea to Limit Your Liability for Cost

Corbett thought that maritime power was, at least potentially, uniquely cost-effective when compared to other forms of military power. A maritime policy should seek to exploit that cost-effectiveness to the maximum effect.

He therefore sought to make the most of the particular characteristics of sea power such as flexibility, mobility and controllability that enabled sailors and diplomats to limit their liability if things went wrong, as they will often do. As Sir Francis Bacon famously remarked:

> This much is certain, that he that commands the sea is at great liberty, and may take as much and as little of the war as he will. Whereas those that be strongest by land are many times nevertheless in great straits.[5]

In the past, power at sea provided opportunities for the British to make limited interventions for limited objectives in unlimited wars. Through this capacity to exert influence on the continent of Europe from outside, the British, unlike many of their more land-bound competitors, had been able to develop a uniquely businesslike approach to the otherwise messy and wasteful processes of war. They generally tried to avoid expensive large-scale military commitments to the continent of Europe and its ferocious wars. Instead, the British had done their best to limit their involvement to the financial support of continental allies and to the exertion of maritime pressure through blockade, the threat of amphibious landings, attacks and raids on threatened coastlines and through the seizure of their adversaries' far-flung colonies and bases.

This background provided the source of Corbett's support for the Dardanelles campaign of 1915. Here his basic proposition was that 'the continental method' of striking decisively '…where the enemy's military concentration was highest' (i.e. in France) only made sense where there was 'sufficient preponderance of force to ensure a decision'. In his view, this was not the situation on the Western Front, and it was therefore best to '…postpone offence in the main theatre and devote our combined energies' to improving the strategic balance by striking elsewhere.[6] By making use of the flexibility of sea power, Britain could make the same amount of military force much more effective when deployed in the Dardanelles than it would have been on the Western Front.

Since the future defence postures of most Western states are likely to be more constrained in terms of resources, because Western states are less likely to be acting in defence of vital national interests and as they will be operating in the full glare of publicity and hence acutely sensitive to prospective loss of life, they will surely place even greater emphasis on the cost-effectiveness of their smaller forces. In terms both of force composition and deployment and in terms of an increased determination to limit liability, future force planners will need to pay particular attention to this injunction.

2. Beware the Continental Commitment

Although it may have a certain political and economic resonance at the moment, this commandment is really a strategic one. Corbett focused on conflicts such as the Seven Years War which, since they concentrated on the prospective acquisition of colonies and commercial benefit, were much more popular with the trading classes than potentially costly entanglements in Europe. Smollet put it like this:

> [M]any friends of their country exclaimed against the projected army of observation in Germany, as the commencement of a ruinous continental war, which it was neither the interest of the nation to undertake, nor in their power to maintain, without starving the operations by sea, and in America, founded on British principles.[7]

The British were generally wary about the acceptance of significant military commitments to the continent of Europe. The extent of their commitment was limited by the fact that their aim was merely to act as a balancing power, not as a major protagonist in continental struggles. Wherever possible, they preferred to limit their involvement in European affairs. However, they were particularly sensitive to the prospect of the Low Countries falling into the hands of an expansionist power. When they had to intervene on the continent of Europe, and when they had the option, the Low Countries were their usual theatre of operations.

Significant land forces were provided in the main by their continental allies. The British only intervened ashore when those allies, even when subsidized, were unable to maintain the balance on their own. Even then, the level of intervention was as limited both in scale and time as possible. But when they did intervene, the British required an army, but one, thought Corbett, of an expeditionary sort.

Were he to consider the options facing the British in the closing years of this century, I suspect that Corbett would be advocating that the Army shift its focus from the conduct of armoured warfare and more towards the 'light and portable' aspirations of the French *Force d'Action Rapide*.[8] This would certainly be the recommendation of Charles Callwell whose 1906 book *Small Wars: their Principles and Practice* has, fortuitously,

been reissued in recent years. Callwell analysed the low-intensity conflicts of his time, which were usually quite limited in their aim and scope,
as potentially costly and in which the commanders were often constrained by the absence or limitations of popular support. The geographic
and technical characteristics of these small wars meant the Army needed
to prepare for them specifically. In all these ways, Callwell's most recent
editor is right to claim that '...although Callwell writes about the past,
he also presents...a vision of future combat.'[9]

3. Realize the Limits of Naval Diplomacy

Having digested the writings of Clausewitz, Corbett was well aware of
the fact that war was a political act and that the first function of the fleet
was '...to support or obstruct diplomatic effort'.[10] But, not unnaturally,
given the more adversarial age in which he lived, the focus of most of his
writing was on the operational characteristics of sea power. His preoccu-
pation was with war, not peace – although he was always anxious to demonstrate the connections between the objectives of war and its form. It
was left therefore to analysts of a much later generation to articulate the
characteristics of what has since become known as naval diplomacy.[11]

   This is not the place for a detailed exposition of their analysis of what
naval diplomacy is and how it works; suffice it to say that their conclusion
that the mobility and flexibility of navies makes them uniquely useful
as instruments of foreign policy would have come as no surprise to the
sailors whose activities Corbett studied. Thus, in Nelson's memorable
phrase: 'I hate your pen-and-ink men; a fleet of British ships of war are
the best negotiators in Europe.'

   It is important to note, however, that there were limits to what sea
power could achieve diplomatically, even at the height of Britain's maritime power in the nineteenth century. The point was made, paradoxically
enough, by Palmerston, when commenting on the lessons of a particular
crisis in the Middle East of the time:

> Every country that has towns within cannon shot of deep water will
> remember the operations of the British fleet on the coast of Syria in
> September, October and November 1840, whenever such a country
> has a difference with us.[12]

But there were many countries with towns that were *not* within cannon
shot of the coast and/or which were relatively impervious to pressure from
the sea. British sea power, for example, was not one of Bismarck's chief
preoccupations when building Germany. The British were concerned

about his victory over Denmark in 1864, for example, but could in fact do very little to prevent it. There were other instances too where, despite its command of the sea, Britain was obliged to stand resentfully on the sidelines watching unwanted events unfold.

The limitations of diplomacy based on sea power are illustrated in various ways. First, by the fact that in Europe, by sea power alone, Britain could hope to be no more than a 'balancer': it could not hope to transform the European power system. It was often the case that the British had to use their successes outside Europe in order to compensate for their relative failures inside it, as for example in the 1801 Treaty of Amiens when they had to give up their recent overseas conquests in order to redress French success within Europe.

Second, a poignant passage from Conrad's *Heart of Darkness* usefully reminds us that some situations, perhaps especially outside Europe, are too messy for limited military forces to solve. This may particularly be the case where, as here, those forces are naval. Conrad describes a little French gunboat impotently firing its pop-gun into the heart of the African continent, and the despairing frustration of its crew facing an impossible situation and invisible adversaries:

> The steamer toiled along slowly on the edge of a black and incomprehensible frenzy... We were cut off from the comprehension of our surroundings; we glided past like phantoms, wondering and secretly appalled, as sane men would be before an enthusiastic outbreak in a madhouse.[13]

In such cases, predominance at sea and even the capacity to project military power ashore is not automatically politically useful.

4. Tailor the Aims to Suit the Fleet

Remembering his debt to Clausewitz, Corbett was well aware of the need for modesty in the definition of foreign policy objectives if one of the aims was to avoid excessive expenditure in blood and treasure, and to keep within the bounds of what was militarily sensible or feasible. Throughout the eighteenth and much of the nineteenth century, Britain avoided vainglory and total objectives, especially on the continent of Europe. The British were manipulating, not transforming, the European balance of power. To be effective, sea power had to be exercised with restraint, just because in the words of Eyre Crowe it was 'but natural that the Power of the State supreme at sea should inspire universal jealousy and fear, and be ever exposed to the danger of being overthrown by a general combination of the world.'[14] Only by moderate behaviour could Britain keep such a possibility in check.

Nor were the British averse to hard-headed efforts to reduce the costs of conflict by seeking economically valuable offsets to their expenditure. There was something at once typical and healthily commercial about the appearance in monthly editions of the *Gentleman's Magazine* in the eighteenth century of lists of British merchant ships lost and French or Spanish ones taken, complete with details of their cargoes. Indeed, the notion of an effectively self-financing style of war – whether by the interception of plate convoys or rich foreign merchantmen or indeed anticipations of prize money among Royal Navy personnel – was a constant if not altogether constructive element in the British attitude towards maritime war.

The extent to which British and American military efforts in the 1990 Gulf War were subsidized by their grateful beneficiaries is a useful reminder of the increasing relevance of Corbett's advocacy of a cool and calculating attitude towards the acceptance of foreign policy commitments and the expenditure of effort. It may well be that naval forces have a particular advantage here, as we have seen, in that their ability to withdraw allows diplomats to respond quickly if the sums seem to be going wrong.

5. Be Combined

The fifth commandment should really start with a quotation from another prophet akin to Corbett, Sir Basil Liddell Hart. His definition of strategy as 'the art of distributing and applying military means to achieve the aims of policy'[15] usefully reminds us that although strategists have tended to concentrate on the kind of military activity that is designed to defeat adversaries, there is more to it than that. Military forces can be used to preserve friends and to influence the behaviour of allies in ways which can serve national interest just as well as those advocated in more orthodox and traditional forms of strategy.

Corbett went out of his way to emphasize the point that the fundamental conception of war was political and was clear that the whole success of what later came to be termed as 'The British Way in Warfare'[16] lay in the construction of coalitions with allies with something to offer – bases, ships but very often military power on land. In such cases, British sea power was a kind of currency that allowed the British to win friends and influence people in peace and in war. All this can reasonably be inferred from Corbett's writings, but, to be honest, Corbett says little on the narrower topic of what might be termed the strategy of multinational naval cooperation.

No doubt one of the reasons for this was the commanding naval position enjoyed by the British in Corbett's era. If others wished to advance their national interests by cooperating with the Royal Navy, they did so on British terms. Since the Second World War, however, staying in the first division has been a difficult challenge for the hard-pressed British. They have sought refuge in the company of others, most especially the Americans. The extent to which this absolutely crucial relationship with allies has been guaranteed and cemented by a plethora of naval connections is difficult to exaggerate. After centuries in which the effectiveness of British sea power was chiefly measured by its perceived influence on adversaries, it is interesting to note that a considerable portion of its contemporary value is now to be found in influencing the behaviour of real or prospective allies around the world. The significant *Ocean Wave* deployment to the Asia-Pacific in 1997 exactly illustrates the point.

With this commandment we have partially crossed the line between aim and method, because when it comes to national policy, the creation and preservation of allies can be both. The next four commandments, however, are more to do with method.

6. Maintain the Navy

As a rule, over the last two hundred years the Royal Navy tended to be best favoured in defence expenditure priorities and certainly better favoured than the navies of its adversaries, especially in the eighteenth century.

As one disputant in the great debate of 1743 about whether Britain ought to pay for 16 000 Hannoverians to fight on the continent of Europe put it in the House of Commons:

> We ought to disband a great part of the troops we have now on foot, in order to be able to encrease [*sic*] our naval Force, because it is upon that alone, after the balance of Power upon the Continent is destroyed, that we must depend for the continuance of our future Independency.[17]

To put it briefly and simply, Britain needed, and could generally afford to have, stronger naval forces than its adversaries, but could make do with significantly smaller land forces. Indeed, the weakness of its army was often seen as a justification for a sea-based strategy, rather than a consequence of it. But sometimes, paradoxically enough, this meant spending more on the Army than the Navy, as often happened in the nineteenth century.

But it was simplistic to see this merely as a case for supporting either the Army or the Navy. Instead it should be a constructive balance between the two. In fact, an acceptance of continental commitments was sometimes a way of buttressing naval power, not weakening it. Thus Horace Walpole, harking back in that same 1743 debate to the lessons of a previous war against the French in good Queen Anne's time:

> By land we beat them out of the Sea. We obtained so great and so many Victories at land that they were forced to neglect their Sea Affairs, in order to apply their whole strength both in Money and men to defend their country … at land.[18]

In many parts of the world there has been something of a shift in the balance struck between sea/air forces and land/air forces to the benefit of the former. This is certainly the case around the Pacific Rim, but it applies to much of Europe too. Sometimes, this shift is a reflection of a decline in the seriousness of the Continental threat – most obviously in post-Cold War Europe, but in Asia too – or an increased interest in preparing for more geographically distant operations, or simply an acceptance of the growing commercial importance of the sea. For all such reasons, Corbett would no doubt now be arguing that unfolding events simply confirm the need to maintain a significant Navy as part of a balanced defence package.

7. Tailor the Fleet to Suit Your Aims

As far as Corbett was concerned, and although sailors sometimes forgot it, securing the command of the sea was a means and not an end. In itself this capacity would do little good, for it was only when that command was exploited that the strategic benefits came. Moreover, attaining command of the sea in Corbett's time was seen to require an open-ocean battle fleet which was likely to be costly in itself and not necessarily strategically rewarding even if the enemy was destroyed. The need to assert themselves *at* sea often constrained the British in their capacity to exert power *from* the sea.

Corbett warned that the 'old British creed' of the relentless pursuit of the battle, although generally admirable and effective, could be taken to excess. In some circumstances, it could lead to a distraction from the real aim of the war. He also pointed out that Britain's adversaries, whose naval forces were normally weaker, often sensibly sought to avoid battle with the Royal Navy. This being so, the British needed to be on their guard against the danger of trying too hard in this direction, lest such purist aspirations undermine their practical capacity to use the sea as fully as they often needed to in the meantime.[19]

Corbett's warning against the dangers of concentrating too much on the pursuit of battle was evident in his carefully nuanced account of the Battle of Jutland and led to a significant degree of criticism. Thus an anonymous contributor to the *Naval Review* of 1931 said of Corbett that:

> He had a legal training and mind, which was shown in his preference for getting the better of the enemy in some other way than coming to blows... his teaching did not preach that to destroy or to neutralise the enemy's armed force was the primary military aim leading to a military decision.[20]

Not unnaturally, when the defeat of the enemy's main forces was the overriding aim, preparing the fleet for battle on the open ocean had to be the main priority, and a very demanding one it was too for much of the time. Even if it meant there was less capacity to *exploit* success when it came, the pursuit of battle had to be the main determinant of the size and shape of the fleet.

But in the post-Cold War environment with the disappearance of the Soviet naval threat and before the appearance of other serious contenders we seem to have moved into a different era in which the US and other Western navies' command of the open ocean is largely uncontested; accordingly sea power, because more of it can be devoted to the exploitation of command, is likely to be more effective in influencing events ashore than it has been for many years.

But this may be conditional, at least to some extent and at least for a little while, on fleets being rebalanced and reshaped to reflect this new reality. Technically, such a reshaping might imply less emphasis on deep-water anti-submarine warfare (ASW) and relatively more on, say, land attack systems. Doctrinally, too, there has been a marked shift in many of the world's navies away from contesting command of the open oceans and towards the capacity to exercise it particularly in the littoral. The US Navy's *Forward... From the Sea*[21] is only the most obvious manifestation of that trend. But Corbett would surely have warned against taking this as anything more than a shift in emphasis.

8. Be Joint

Much as he loved the Navy, Corbett was clear that a sensible strategic policy could not be based on the neglect of the Army – or, had it existed when he was writing, the Royal Air Force:

Since men live upon the land and not upon the sea, great issues between nations at war have always been decided – except in the rarest cases – either by what your army can do against your enemy's territory and national life or else by the fear of what the fleet makes it possible for your army to do.[22]

Britain, he thought, had developed a style of maritime war which combined naval and military power in a uniquely beneficial way. It had allowed the British to '…become a controlling force in the European system'[23] and to maintain and extend their interests by manipulating the balance of power in continental Europe. This they had done by the controlled and careful application of maritime power in peace and in war. Because the secret of British success lay in the combination of land and sea power, Corbett used the word 'maritime' when he reviewed the strategy of sea power rather than the much narrower term 'naval' that Mahan tended to use. This difference is significant.

Corbett advocated a synergistic relationship between the Navy and the Army. These two services were seen as complementary; both could serve the interests of the other. The Army could be used to protect the Low Countries, preventing their vital ports from falling into the hands of hostile navies – an imperative ranging from Elizabeth's war against Spain in the sixteenth century to the Passchendaele campaign in the twentieth century. Indeed, as we have seen, interventions on the mainland were occasionally justified on the grounds that this would protect Britain's position at sea by preventing the emergence of a hostile power or coalition strong enough to generate a dangerous *maritime* threat. Accordingly, as Richmond remarked, nothing was '…more misleading or objectionable than the attribution of success to…[sea power or land power]…separately.'[24] Nowadays, of course, when jointery is the creed of all three services, such sentiments have a salience that does much more to counter single-service preoccupations with the distinctiveness of their element and of their dimension of war than it used to.

9. Be Prepared to go Ashore

As far as Corbett was concerned, the reward for being strong at sea was the capacity it conferred to influence events ashore for that was where events were actually decided. This was what sea power was really about. In the First World War, the nearest approach to a Corbettian strategy was the Dardanelles campaign. This was, arguably, '…the one imaginative strategic idea of the war on the Allied side',[25] but its strategic possibilities were thrown away by the truly appalling way in which the operation was conducted.

Among the many reasons for the failure of this campaign was the fact that much of Navy and Army opinion gave it less priority than it needed. Army opinion was split over the Dardanelles operation, with many regarding it as an eccentric and probably futile diversion from the real business of defeating the Germans on the Western Front. The Navy, too, had its reservations. Successive First Sea Lords were in favour of combined operations, but principally in the North West European theatre where they would help achieve naval objectives. At the time of the Dardanelles campaign, Corbett fair-mindedly pointed out that the appearance of the U-boat, the continuing attacks on shipping and the need to support operations in Africa and elsewhere were all putting a strain on the Navy's ability to contain the German fleet. Fisher was willing to dispatch surplus warships to support secondary operations such as the Dardanelles campaign, but resigned when the campaign's increasing demands seemed likely to undermine 'the plans he was elaborating to secure a perfect control of Home Waters and the Baltic.'[26] This was an example of the tension sailors could often find between the demands of securing command of the sea and those of its exploitation.

Although the Dardanelles campaign failed, Corbett drew much comfort by the 'marvellous evacuation' that concluded it, since this showed that all the necessary lessons had been learned. It reinforced his conviction, based on evidence such as the capture of Havana in 1762, Wolfe's Canadian operations in the Seven Years War, Wellington's Peninsula campaign – the quintessential Combined Operation[27] – and the Crimean War, that when amphibious operations were properly conducted they could indeed be the means by which sea powers could really help decide the outcome of wars, through being able to strike at their enemies' weakest points.

The flexibility and mobility conferred by power at sea, Corbett thought, had allowed Britain to project significant power ashore. Accordingly, the maritime strategy that he advocated required the kind of army that could work with the Navy to conquer overseas territories and to outflank land-bound adversaries by amphibious operations:

> ... more or less upon the European seaboard designed, not for permanent conquest, but as a method of disturbing our enemy's plans and strengthening the hands of our allies and our own position.[28]

In present circumstances, he would certainly conclude that the Royal Navy's capacity to project power ashore, whether by a significant amphibious capacity, by sea-based air and sea power or by continued 'presence' operations – or preferably by all three – was likely to prove an increasingly valuable part of the national armoury as we move into the next century.

10. Think About It

Finally, we should remember that Corbett, as a writer and a lecturer, was not just personally interested in the study of maritime strategy. Instead, he wanted his audience, and especially naval officers, to think constructively about such issues as part of their normal professional development. This was partly in response to his perception that too many people, both inside the Navy and outside it, were arriving at conclusions about maritime strategy that were unsustainable. But his push for thought was also motivated by a strong sense that for a whole variety of technological, political and economic reasons, things were changing and there was a strong need for the Navy to identify the fundamentals and to adapt to a changing reality as necessary.

Given current uncertainties, this advice is particularly salient now in the closing decade of the century. The challenge will be to get future naval officers to think as constructively about this vital aspect of their profession as Corbett would have wished.

CONCLUSION

The conclusion to this study is neither complex nor unexpected. It is quite simply that much of what Corbett wrote at the beginning of this century remains apposite as we approach its end.

NOTES

1. The views expressed in this chapter should not be taken necessarily to reflect official opinion in any way.
2. Quoted in Donald M. Schurman, *Julian S. Corbett 1854–1922* (London: Royal Historical Society, 1981), p. 44.
3. J. S. Corbett, *England in the Seven Years War*, vol. 1 (London: Longmans Green, 1907), p. 5.

4. Cited in J. S. Corbett, *Some Principles of Maritime Strategy* (Annapolis, Md.: USNI Press, 1988), p. 15.
5. Ibid., p. 58.
6. J. S. Corbett, *Naval Operations* (London: Longmans Green, 1920), vol. 2, pp. 41–2.
7. T. Smollett, *History of England* (London, 1760), p. 423.
8. Bruce George and Jonathan Mercus, 'Change and Continuity in French Defence Policy', *RUSI Journal*, vol. 129, no. 2, June 1984, pp. 13–19.
9. Douglas Porch in Charles Callwell, *Small Wars: their Principles and Practice* (Toronto: Bison Books, 1996), p. iv.
10. Ibid., p. 16.
11. See James Cable, *Gunboat Diplomacy: Application of Limited Naval Force*, 2nd edn (London: Chatto & Windus, 1981), and Ken Booth, *Law, Force and Diplomacy at Sea* (London: Allen & Unwin, 1985).
12. Cited in A. Lambert, *The Last Sailing Battlefleet* (London: Conway, 1991), p. 38.
13. Joseph Conrad, *Heart of Darkness* (London: Penguin, 1978), p. 51.
14. Eyre Crowe cited in N. Tracy, *Attack on Maritime Trade* (London: Macmillan, 1991), pp. 101–2.
15. B. H. Liddell Hart, *Strategy: The Indirect Approach* (London: Faber, 1967), p. 335.
16. See Sir Basil Liddell Hart, *The British Way in Warfare* (London: Penguin, 1942); and David French, *The British Way in Warfare 1688–2000* (London: Unwin Hyman, 1990).
17. For an interesting summary of this debate see the 'Journal of the Proceedings and Debates in the Political Club', *The London Magazine*, 1743, esp. pp. 23, 58, 62, 134, 211, 218, 221, 228–9, 279, 427, 437, 438, 541.
18. Ibid.
19. Corbett (1988), op. cit., p. 67.
20. See 'Sea Heresies' and 'Some Notes on the Early Days of the Naval War College', *Naval Review*, 1931.
21. United States Department of the Navy, *Forward... From the Sea* (Washington, DC: Department of the Navy, 1993).
22. Corbett (1988), op. cit., pp. 15–16.
23. J. S. Corbett, *Drake and the Tudor Navy*, vol. 1 (London: Longmans Green, 1916), p. 6.
24. Cited in P. M. Kennedy, *Strategy and Diplomacy 1870–1945* (London: Fontana, 1983), pp. 62–3.
25. Arthur J. Marder, *From the Dardanelles to Oran* (London: Oxford University Press, 1974), p. 1.
26. Corbett (1920), op. cit., vol. 2, pp. 105–6.
27. David A. Baugh, 'British Strategy during the First World War in the Context of Four Centuries', in Daniel M. Masterton (ed.), *Naval History: The Sixth Symposium*, (Wilmington, Del.: Scholarly Resources, 1987), p. 100.
28. Corbett (1988), op. cit., p. 66.

4 'History is the Sole Foundation for the Construction of a Sound and Living Common Doctrine':[1] the Royal Naval College, Greenwich, and Doctrine Development down to BR1806

Andrew Lambert

For 125 years the Royal Naval College at Greenwich provided the higher-level education of the Royal Navy. With a large, dedicated teaching staff that included both naval officers and academics it was ideally placed to act as the focus for the creation and ongoing development of a historically aware doctrine. Yet the haphazard contribution actually made at the College reveals the limitations of institutions and the importance of individuals.

In a multipolar world, composed of numerous overlapping fluid alliances and alignments with a number of dangerously unstable and hostile regimes and organizations, there is much profit to be had from standing back from the present and the single-scenario, quantified, perception-driven thinking that characterized the Cold War. Two examples of how the failure to create a living, historically aware doctrine before 1914 affected the Royal Navy will illustrate the danger. In the nineteenth century, no single power or bloc could command the destiny of the world; Britain, a unique global maritime power, maintained her naval strength on the famous 'two-power standard' not to fight the next two largest fleets, but to deter them. So long as this was understood the nation, and the empire, were safe. After 1890 the world was increasingly polarized, and eventually, in 1904 and 1907, Britain was drawn into a temporary relationship first with France and then with Russia in order to deter German hegemonic ambitions. Yet in 1914 Britain went to war with Germany without even trying to use the naval deterrent that had worked so well for the last century, even against Germany in 1905 and 1911, and without anything approaching a two-power standard. The government of the day simply did not apply the experience of the past. Whether deterrence could have worked in 1914 is an open question, but it was not attempted and for that the responsible ministers deserve censure. Having allowed the German Navy to come close to the battle fleet strength of the Royal Navy, by cutting naval programmes that were intended to crush the German Navy in the shipyards, they allowed the German elite to think that they, and not the British, were wielding a naval deterrent. While the ministers acted for perfectly laudable reasons they were wrong, and the cost of this error was infinitely greater than the price of the dozen extra dreadnoughts that might have done the job in 1907, 1908 or 1909.[2]

At the operational level every war Britain fought between 1815 and 1914 involved naval gunfire support. During the Boer War the guns were hundreds of miles from any navigable water. In 1882 British heavy calibre ammunition performed badly against old fashioned forts. In the 1915 it did exactly the same. This failure can be attributed to the doctrine developed between 1890 and 1914, which marginalized non-naval roles like gunfire support and commercial blockade in favour of fleet battles. The Navy even found a good Nelson quote to the effect that only a fool would use a ship to fight a fort. Yet the record shows that Nelson did exactly that, and more than once. In fact the Navy has engaged in far more power projection and bombardment work than naval combat; and ships have regularly overpowered shore defences, when there has been a purpose to the exercise. Fighting forts for the sake of fighting has always been foolish, but there have often been cases where shore defences have to be destroyed or masked to permit naval forces to accomplish an ulterior object. Yet, because such work was ignored at the level of doctrine, no suitable ammunition was prepared. The fleet that engaged the Dardanelles forts went into action with half empty magazines. The ships fired semi-armour piercing shells with very small black powder bursting charges. These were quite useless against large earthworks. The fleet of 1915 could have suppressed the Dardanelles defences, but only if they were properly prepared. The lesson had been learnt by 1944, when gunfire support was critical to success of D-Day and other major assault landings.[3] Subsequent events suggest that the insight was not retained.

The responsible ministers remained ignorant of the deterrent basis of British strategy, and the need for effective coastal warfare equipment and tactics, because almost all of their senior professional advisers were equally ignorant. It is this lack of understanding among senior professionals that brings us back to the role of the Royal Naval College in the development of doctrine.

The Royal Naval College was moved from Portsmouth to Greenwich in 1873 to placate the electors of Greenwich. It was to provide a new source of government employment to replace the hospital and the two dockyards which had been closed in 1869. The urgency of the decision, which was forced through against the opposition of every naval officer on the relevant Committee, is explained by the poor relations then existing between the local electorate and their MP, William Ewart Gladstone, the Prime Minster.[4]

The move was seen as an opportunity to expand naval education, and improve links with the universities. In the 1860s two lecturers and a technical assistant had provided a mathematics-based curriculum for junior officers who were qualifying for the gunnery course aboard HMS *Excellent*. However, while the move witnessed a marked increase of staff to 15 and a broadening of the curriculum, the courses for anyone above the rank of sub-lieutenant remained voluntary, and they were entirely technical in character. The courses of study proposed and largely carried into effect were:

1. Pure mathematics, including geometry and calculus.
2. Applied mathematics, including mechanics, optics and the theories of heat, light, electricity and magnetism.
3. Applied mechanics, theories of structures and machines.
4. Nautical astronomy, surveying, meteorology and chart drawing.
5. Experimental science, physics, chemistry, metallurgy.
6. Marine engineering.
7. Naval architecture.
8. Fortification, military drawing and naval artillery.
9. International law, law of evidence, and naval courts martial.
10. Naval history and tactics, including naval signals and steam evolutions.
11. Modern languages.
12. Drawing.
13. Hygiene, naval and climactic.

The examination syllabus, as set out in 1874, awarded marks for all subjects, to a maximum of 1500. Of these 500 were for algebra, geometry and trigonometry, and 400 for navigation and nautical astronomy.[5] This syllabus, with the exception of naval artillery, law of evidence and courts martial, was being taught by the end of the decade to a large but amorphous body of officers, many of whom were still volunteers. However, the overwhelming importance of mathematics and scientific subjects reflected the mood of the age and the needs of the service, up to a point. The course did nothing to prepare officers to exercise command, develop judgement, tactical acumen, strategic insight or political wisdom. It completed their 'training', but it did not start their education.

Yet even this was too much for the service. By 1880 the number attending the college had dropped from 237 to 180, revealing a fundamental flaw. Because the senior Greenwich course was never made compulsory it was never incorporated into the naval career structure. Doubtless the reason was the same one that has always been advanced against intellectually stimulating studies that require time for reading and reflection, the lack of time in a crowded career.[6] Typically Admiral Sir Geoffrey Hornby, a man of ability and a supporter of the College, complained there would not be enough lieutenants for sea service if they all took a one-year course ashore. The weakness of such arguments, which conflated a fixed intake of cadets with a fluctuating demand for sea service, can hardly be exceeded. Any profession that does not make time to contemplate the higher direction of its core activity is doomed to disappointment at the very least. More seriously the six-month sub-lieutenant's course, which all officers attended, did little to advance understanding, consisting as it did of little more that a repetition of what had been taught at HMS *Britannia*, with some meteorology and hydrography thrown in.[7]

These two courses were the special province of John Knox Laughton, the only lecturer to be transferred from Portsmouth.[8] Laughton (1830–1915) had come ashore in 1866 after 12 years' service as a naval instructor. As a mathematician and scientist he believed that the only way to master any subject was to understand the principles upon which it was based. After applying his methodology to College text books on meteorology and hydrography, Laughton began to work on naval doctrine.

While serving at Portsmouth Laughton recognized that the Navy was losing touch with the past, which he believed was the key to sound doctrine. Faced by a constant and accelerating technical revolution men who had gown up with the centuries old certainties of the wooden sailing ship were convinced that the past had become 'a useless branch of knowledge'. Laughton stressed that a 'scientific' study of history, in contrast to the haphazard, romantic stuff that then passed for naval history, would produce 'lessons of the gravest meaning' for the study of strategy, administration, tactics, discipline and all other aspects of naval service. Indeed, he argued that history was the *only* basis from which a coherent written doctrine could be developed. He did this work in his own time.

Initially Laughton devoted his efforts to tactical doctrine, combining rigorous scientific analysis of the known capabilities of modern ships and weapons with the principles to be derived from the experience of the past. Although the two committees that set up the College had hoped to include history in the core curriculum, this was not done. Instead the first President, Admiral Sir Astley Cooper Key, could only provide time and funds for Laughton to give half a dozen lectures a year. Not only was the provision totally inadequate, but it was only an option on a course that was, itself, optional.

Laughton's work on tactics produced two major texts. The *Essay on Naval Tactics* of 1873 was as close to an officially sanctioned tactical doctrine as the Navy would go.[9] The second, *Letters and Despatches of Horatio, Viscount Nelson*, published in 1886, was developed with Admiral Sir Geoffrey Hornby, the pre-eminent fleet commander and tactician of the age, and President of the College in 1882–83. Although normally, and incorrectly, associated with the development of rigid, formalized squadron handling,[10] Hornby, like Laughton, stressed that no formal system of tactics should be adopted. Both men understood that 'square-bashing' fleet evolutions were only intended to develop the ship-handling skills of the practitioners and were far too complex to be attempted under combat conditions. In his College lectures on fleet tactics, Hornby declared:

> It is often asked, what is to be our fighting formation in future? None has been prescribed: it is to be hoped that none will be prescribed. To prescribe any would be exceedingly foolish and in a high degree presumptuous. Foolish; for all our past history shows us the evil of having a prescribed formation for fighting in; it needed the genius of a Nelson to disentangle us from the mess. Foolish; for, unless perhaps the state of his enemy's bunkers, there are few things an admiral would give more to know beforehand than the formation in which his enemy was going to fight. Presumptuous; because in the present day, we have no business to speak with authority.[11]

Instead naval history would provide the basis for doctrine. When Laughton published the *Nelson* letters in 1886 he dedicated the book to Hornby. In the introduction he demolished the myth that Nelson's tactical ideas could be summed up in Lord Cochrane's phrase 'never mind manoeuvres, always go at them'.[12] He also rebutted the commonly held notion that a modern naval battle would rapidly degenerate into a mêlée.[13] Laughton stressed that Nelson's tactical appreciation was built on personal study, the lessons of the past as transmitted by senior officers like Lord Hood and his own genius. Only the combination of these elements could explain his success. For him the most important part of an officer's education was provided by personal study. Nelson had used his time on the beach to study his profession. Here was a task that Greenwich could take on: the provision of an intellectually stimulating environment in which mid-career officers could be encouraged to prepare themselves for the challenge of command. He placed the raw material for a study of *the* naval career in a single volume, making it a convenient educational tool.

Recognizing that history would never secure an important place in the Greenwich curriculum until it was recognized as 'scientific' Laughton began by stressing that what little history the average naval officer knew was romantic, inaccurate and useless. He went on:

> I also find that an idea that the history of the past contains no practical lessons for the future, and is therefore a useless branch of scholarship daily gathers strength; and is, indeed, put prominently forward by those whose opinions on purely technical questions have a just claim to our respect.[14]

By contrast, he argued, naval history should be studied thoroughly, because it 'contained lessons of the gravest meaning'. It examined the way in which fleets had been collected and manned, the course of events leading to victory and defeat, as well as the principles of tactics. A thorough study would lead to the development of a coherent, written doctrine, to the lasting benefit of the service and its officers.

This history-based approach was in stark contrast to the technological obsessions that were already dominating naval thought. Although the paper was trying to make the case for a new, and apparently irrelevant, subject it was not without intellectual force and a strong, coherent theme. This was critical. Laughton had to clear the ground of the accumulated rubbish of half a century, and dig down to sound historical bedrock, before building a new, structured, doctrine on solid foundations. He stressed that it was unwise to look back to the easy victories of the Revolutionary and Napoleonic wars, secured against ill-manned and badly led opponents. Although he never used the word 'doctrine' which had a far narrower meaning in the 1870s, he was trying to develop a modern doctrine. This marked an enhanced role for history.[15] In Germany a similar pioneering approach was being applied to military history by Hans Delbrück, although in contrast to Laughton, Delbrück spent his career in a bitter battle with the German General Staff over the nature of

Frederician Strategy. His career should be an object lesson to all defence academics, particularly those who work in service education.[16] By contrast, Laughton worked with the Navy for sixty years without a single demonstration of ill-feeling, a fact that helps to explain both the success of his work and the subsequent oblivion that has descended on his name.

Laughton's historical approach was not confined to the age of sail or the Royal Navy. He used a lecture on the battle of Lissa of 1866, the only ironclad fleet action yet fought, to examine the education of the victor, the Austrian Admiral Tegetthoff. He demonstrated that Tegetthoff had educated himself throughout his career for the decisive moment. The example was used to push home the critical role of history in the higher education of the Navy:

> There is a certain tendency in the minds of those who are most earnest in the cause of naval education to confuse the means with the end, and to imagine that all that is wanted is a competent knowledge of such sciences as mathematics, physics, geography, astronomy, navigation even, or pilotage, gunnery or naval architecture. In reality, and so far as the duties of a naval officer are concerned, all these are but branches, however important, each in its different degree, of that one science, the art of war, which it is the business of his life to practise.[17]

The details of this art could be acquired by instruction, but the ability to use them, as required of captains and admirals, necessitated a different approach:

> Where the official instruction ends, the higher education really begins. From that time it is the man's own experience, and reading, and thought, and judgement, which must fit him for the requirements of higher rank.[18]

In the absence of personal experience, 'the wise man will learn from the experience of others.' This method could be applied to seamanship and navigation:

> so also will he learn the art of commanding ships or fleets from the history of his great predecessors.... But this is a higher and graver study than all that has gone before.[19]

For, unlike navigation and astronomy:

> the science of war is not one of mere rule and precedent, for changing conditions change almost every detail, and that too in a manner which it is often impossible to foresee.

The commanding officer who hopes to win, not merely to tumble into distinction, must therefore be prepared beforehand for every eventuality. The knowledge of what has happened already will not only teach him by precedent; so far as that is possible, it is easy, and within the compass of everyday abilities; it will also suggest to him things that have never yet been done; things in the planning of which he may rise to the height of genius, in the executing of which he may rise to the height of grandeur.[20]

This was the doctrine he was attempting to build. Because history, and only history, could contribute hard evidence to this process it was 'a study of real and technical importance'.[21] In the absence of personal experience the only way to learn the business of modern war was to profit from the experience of others, both in earlier ages and other navies. Only by such preparation would commanders be equipped to deal with the changing conditions of the next war, and develop the capacity to think at a higher level. This approach placed Laughton in the exalted company of the great strategic thinkers. History was only useful if it could produce lessons of direct relevance. Consequently Laughton devoted much effort to analysing the strategies of French sea power, from the battle fleet of Colbert to the commerce destroying cruises of Robert Surcouf. His critical analysis of existing accounts 'demythologized' the past, because only accurate history of the sort he engaged in could provide accurate lessons. A selection of his lectures, published as *Studies in Naval History* in 1887, was the first naval history textbook written for the College.

Laughton always stressed that while mathematics was the basis of junior-level officer *training*, history should be the basis of advanced level *education*. Despite his official position he repeatedly called for the closure of HMS *Britannia*, where 12-year-old boys were entered, in favour of taking them at 16 after a good general education. He could see that cramming advanced maths into young boys was of limited utility, and only compounded by repeating the process as sub-lieutenants at Greenwich when they were, hopefully, old enough to meet the challenge. To do so all over again on the senior course was absurd. In the twentieth century these ideas would be pursued by Herbert Richmond, but the original impulse came from Laughton.

In the course of his studies Laughton realized that the comparative analysis of secondary sources was an inadequate basis from which to develop doctrine. In 1879, with the support of Cooper Key, then First Sea Lord, he secured access to the Admiralty Records. The sheer scale of the archives, the raw material for doctrine development, persuaded him that the task of analysing and interpreting it would require more than the efforts of a single man. At the same time falling attendance on the voluntary courses persuaded the Admiralty in Easter 1885 to cut the Greenwich teaching establishment, and Laughton, on account of his long service and full pension. He regretted the loss of regular contact with the service.[22] However, the value of his doctrine studies ensured that he retained the history lectureship for several years. Appointed Professor of Modern History at King's College, London, he came into contact with leading professional historians, notably Samuel Rawson Gardiner, the proponent of German or 'scientific' history. Laughton realized that he could recruit other scholars into the field to speed up the process of providing the historical basis for doctrine.

His work had already secured him a following among British and American naval officers. Admiral Stephen B. Luce, a lifelong correspondent, relied heavily on Laughton's ideas to secure the United States Naval War College at Newport. Through Luce, and his published work, Laughton inspired Alfred T. Mahan, with whom he developed a fascinating intellectual relationship – one that has entirely escaped Mahan's biographers.

In the Royal Navy Laughton's closest friend was Admiral Sir Cyprian Bridge. The two men worked together both to develop the role of history in naval education, and educate the Navy in British strategy. Laughton and Bridge also spotted talent at Greenwich and recruited the naval intellectuals who feature in the debates of the late nineteenth century. He persuaded Philip Colomb, who also lectured at Greenwich, to adopt a historical basis for his strategic study *Naval Warfare* of 1891. Furthermore almost every First Sea Lord from 1879 to 1914 was a personal friend of Laughton and many, including Arthur Wilson and Prince Louis, were also former pupils.

It should be stressed that up to 1890 Laughton was working in an unfavourable environment. Britain took the Navy, and naval mastery, for granted: there was little public interest, aside from the odd 'scare' generated by the service to boost funding. All that changed in 1891 with the astonishing success of the Royal Naval Exhibition held at Chelsea Hospital. This was followed by Mahan's second 'Sea Power' book,[23] a breakthrough which first secured a wide audience for his views in Britain.

Laughton used the opportunity to marshal his friends, fellow scholars, serving officers, publicists and politicians to found the Navy Records Society in 1893. This was the culmination of his life's work, a society devoted to the recovery, analysis and publication of the naval past, in order to facilitate the development of doctrine. The Society was intimately linked to the Naval Intelligence Department (NID), then led by his old friend and co-founder Cyprian Bridge. At this time the NID was effectively the naval staff, and the Records Society formed the historical section of the NID. The link was maintained down to 1914 by men like Reginald Custance, Prince Louis of Battenberg and Edmond Slade. The subjects chosen for the majority of Records Society volumes were major campaigns, tactical thought, naval administration, strategy, blockade and the Navy in adversity. Volumes of particular relevance were made available to serving officers *of both* the Army and the Navy at members rates, and the Admiralty regularly made block purchases.[24] Laughton used the first two volumes, *State Papers Relating to the Defeat of the Spanish Armada*, to explode the old myth that the Armada had been scattered by the wind.[25] His demonstration that the Navy had defeated the Spanish threat was deliberate and timely, as the Army was, once again, arguing that Britain could be invaded despite the fleet. Using the funds provided by the Society Laughton recruited major scholars to work on naval history. His friend Rawson Gardiner began work on the First Dutch War, while Julian Corbett combined his own study of Drake with editing for the Society. The most important naval editor of the first generation was Herbert Richmond who used his 1913 study *The Loss of Minorca 1756* to work out his ideas on how to combine a strong Grand Fleet with the proper level of force on detached stations.[26] At the time Richmond, as Assistant Director of the Plans Division, was working on the contemporary aspect of the same problem.

THE ROLE OF NAVAL HISTORY IN THE ACADEMIC WORLD

By 1900 Laughton recognized that Navy Records Society Volumes, vital as they were for the development of doctrine, were not the most effective method of educating the naval mind. Before the past could be of any use junior officers needed a basic naval historical education. He addressed this glaring need with a textbook of naval biographies, with the assistance of Philip Colomb.[27] Only when junior officers understood their past, a past Laughton used to stress the role of the individual in the transmission of doctrine and experience, would they be ready for the study of tactics, strategy and administration. Then the historical record, worked up from the archival sources into accurate narrative histories and equipped with a full measure of 'lessons', could educate the entire officer corps. The task of producing the new advanced 'textbooks' required trained historians of real ability with the time and application to work on large bodies of primary source materials. There were very few scholars available with the skill to profit from the opportunity. The example of Corbett, an editor who developed into an analytical scholar, was one that Laughton would have wished to see emulated by others. However, the key to Corbett's ultimate success would be his relationship with the new Naval War Course. Having drawn the historians into editing Laughton recognized that anything more would require a secure grounding in the subject, which could only come from a proper university-level training in the methods of naval historical research. The happy chance that had thrown up a single Corbett would have to be replaced by a system to produce the trained intellects to continue his work. Such men would, if they were taken into naval education, become integral elements in doctrine development. Laughton attempted to establish a university department to teach the naval historians who would be needed to educate the growing Navy of the twentieth century, and work up the historical record as the basis for doctrine development. He was well aware that such work would have to be conducted outside the service. His career was proof positive that the Navy simply did not have the long-term perspective and intellectual commitment to support such an ambitious 'foundation' project. Unfortunately King's College proved to be no more supportive.

Recognizing the superior educational value of defeat Laughton began work on the problematic War of the Austrian Succession. The other difficult war of the eighteenth century, the American Revolution, had already been addressed by Mahan in his section of Laird Clowes' *History*.[28] Recognizing a new talent he passed the task to Herbert Richmond, who completed a three-volume study in 1914.[29] Mahan's study of the American War was finally published as a separate volume in 1913, while Corbett's last three pre-1914 historical studies continued this work in a new environment.

THE NAVAL WAR COURSE

After 1890, the short course of naval history which Laughton had provided was taken up by Admiral Philip Colomb, and from 1895 by Captain Henry May. As Laughton recognized, this was an inadequate base from which to develop doctrine. He made a telling contrast with the rounded programme of studies developed at the new United States Naval War College at Newport by his friend Stephen Luce and largely executed by Alfred T. Mahan. Luce provided Mahan with the time and space to produce lecture courses which, when published, revolutionized naval thought around the world. It did not, as many have argued, require the insight of a foreigner to write *The Influence of Sea Power Upon History, 1660–1783*. It required the creation of an environment where such studies were valued, suitable courses on which to develop and inter-link the basic themes of naval power, fleet tactics and strategy, and the appointment of lecturers who, when integrated with the active branch of the service, were capable of developing doctrine. Thereafter the process would be refreshed by the regular throughput of mid-career officers who could combine education with exposition, while the 'academic' role was enlivened by exchanges with universities and opportunities for fundamental thinking. However, having surpassed Greenwich with this impressive opening Newport soon proved that it was Luce and Mahan who had created the results rather than the system. After 1911 Mahan's strategy lectures continued to be read out with all the solemnity of Holy Writ. This was all the more absurd when Mahan had not rated them very highly in the first place.

History reached the heart of British doctrine development with the establishment of Lord Fisher's Naval War Course in 1900. Fisher, what-ever his faults, was a man of large mind and took a broad view of the needs of the service. He was not, it should be stressed, opposed to the use of history in naval education or strategy. What he objected to was the partisan and arrogant assumption that history was on the side of Lord Charles Beresford's 'Syndicate of Discontent', the conservative group of officers who opposed Fisher's reforms. Admiral Custance, the leading intellect of the Syndicate, made frequent, invariably obtuse, use of histor-ical examples to show that Fisher was wrong. It was to this that Fisher was referring when he complained that 'History is the record of exploded ideas.'

While Laughton disapproved of Fisher's nucleus crews and big battle-ships he must have taken satisfaction from the development of the Naval War Course, and particularly from the prominent role taken by Corbett. Fisher had long recognized that he could not hope to operate a staff system without a large pool of trained staff officers. He had the ability to pick out the best brains of the service and exploit them, but the task was becoming ever more demanding. Admirals had to be educated if they were to be efficient, and Fisher believed that until the Naval War Course was established this situation would not be improved.[30] He had urged the establishment of the course on the Admiralty when the Board visited Malta in 1900, with immediate results. The Course would provide the opportunity for a strategist of genius, a naval 'von Moltke' to develop war plans in isolation from the administrative and technical demands that dominated the work of the Sea Lords at Whitehall. The idea was Spenser Wilkinson's.[31] The Course would also act as an embryo Staff.[32] Because he was content to leave the development and delivery of the curriculum to others, notably the brilliant Captain Henry May, Fisher has rarely been given due credit for the War Course. The Course was linked to the American College; with Luce's work as a model Laughton's ideas, albeit at one remove, were critical to the new Course.

It was no accident that most of those involved in the delivery of the War Course were Councillors of the Navy Records Society. The War Course combined staff training, education and an active staff role. Fisher used Corbett, May, Charles Ottley, Slade, Maurice Hankey and George Ballard, among others, to develop plans that could be withheld or dismissed as 'exercises'. (It should be stressed that this 'brains trust' was entirely separate from the one that was used for technical questions, which included Jellicoe, Henry Jackson, Percy Scott and Reginald Bacon.)

When the course started in 1900 it was intended to provide an education in war-fighting and related issues for commanders and captains. Initially spread over eight months it was divided into two parts in 1903 to enable more officers to attend. More significantly it was compulsory from the outset, in marked contrast to the half-hearted and ineffective methods of recruitment adopted for the higher Naval College courses. This was the first full-time career path course for senior officers, but, as Richmond observed, those attending lacked the prior education to make the best use of the opportunity.[33] He, like Laughton, recognized the need for a textbook-based foundation course at Greenwich. After six years at Greenwich the course transferred to Portsmouth in 1906, and was expanded to include the special campaigns branch, which Fisher used, as the Ballard Committee, to plan for war with Germany.[34] In 1912 the Naval Staff Course for lieutenants, lieutenant-commanders and commanders was set up to provide trained staff officers.[35] By securing the course, providing it with the best brains in the service and the most able civilians, Fisher created a system to educate senior officers and provide the resources for staff work. In a period dominated by the need to win the naval race on a tight budget this was no mean feat and deserves higher praise than it is generally accorded. In addition it was critical to the creation of the first fully fashioned national strategic doctrine.

Julian Corbett's major texts *England in the Mediterranean*, *England in the Seven Years' War*, *The Campaign of Trafalgar* and *Some Principles of Maritime Strategy* were the published versions of his War Course lectures. They exemplify Laughton's view of naval history: well researched, well written, didactic and directed at officers undergoing higher-level education.[36] That Corbett's strategic ideas, first delivered to the War Course and then published in 1911, were of central importance to the development of BR1806 is suggestive. *Some Principles* was written at Fisher's request to provide a maritime strategic alternative to the 'continentalist' model pushed by the Army General Staff.[37] It has largely stood the test of time as a national programme, one that is increasingly relevant as Britain returns to an 'expeditionary' (read 'maritime') strategy.

Laughton's tactical opinions, also developed by Corbett, continued to have a significant impact on service doctrine. This could be seen not only in the heightened, if somewhat eccentric, interest taken in the tactics of Trafalgar, but more specifically in the work of Rear-Admiral Sir Reginald Custance. In 1902 Custance, then Director of Naval Intelligence (DNI), issued the fleet with a volume of old *Fighting Instructions* which he hoped would promote study and reflection by demonstrating underlying principles. Custance was trying to rebuild doctrine from historical material as an *alternative* to relying of the results of exercises because he believed the experience of the Army in South Africa had shown exercises to be a flawed source. Laughton and Custance persuaded Corbett to edit the material, used the Records Society to publish it and ensured that it was widely available. Subsequent disagreements between Corbett and Custance on the tactics of Trafalgar revealed a conflict over who should analyse the historical evidence and develop naval doctrine. As ever the big issue was the needs of the modern service, not the historical record; Custance's real target was Fisher, not Corbett.

The deliberately informal nature of the relationship between the War Course, the Admiralty and the development of plans enabled Fisher to make the best use of Julian Corbett. The more formal structures put in place by Churchill in 1912 could not incorporate Corbett effectively and he was left on the sidelines, although he used his time to write a confidential history of the Russo-Japanese war for the DNI. Only then did he realize just how much the development of doctrine and strategy would have been advanced by a thorough study of the wars of the nineteenth century, notably the 'Crimean'.[38] When Fisher returned to the Admiralty in 1914 Corbett was, once more, back inside the machine at a high level, but this role did not survive the resignation of his patron. The War Course had come too late to make a difference before 1914, for in the absence of John Fisher there was no one in authority, service or civilian, who understood the deterrent dynamic of British strategy. The opportunity went begging for want of a spokesman. Had the Admiralty asked the academics how the Navy had preserved the peace after 1815 and opened the relevant archives, they could have recovered the deterrent basis of

'Pax Britannica' without too much trouble. Fisher had learned the lesson as Flag Captain of the projected Baltic Fleets of 1878 and 1885, fleets that had deterred Russia.[39] Of equal importance, his active service had been dominated by littoral warfare, notably the suppression of shore defences in China and at Alexandria. The institutional recovery of this experience in a form suitable for doctrine development was precluded by the closure of the relevant archives to academics and the failure of the Admiralty to direct the effort. Even so the evidence for earlier periods was available to anyone who cared to look in the pages of Clowes' *History* and Laughton's work. That so little use was made of these pioneering efforts can, at least in part, be attributed to the stagnation of intellectual activity at Greenwich.

Consequently, the work of the Royal Naval College before 1914 was limited, dominated by technical issues and made little contribution to the development of naval thought. The failure to provide a course of study to meet Laughton's specification for a historically based *education* denied senior officers a vital opportunity. Fisher's Naval War Course demonstrated what could be done with enough impetus. However, it should be stressed that impetus was more important than structure, for without Fisher the Naval War Course also faltered.

INTER-WAR

At first the hard lessons of war seemed to have been taken to heart. When The First Lord of the Admiralty, Walter Long, introduced the 1920–21 *Naval Estimates* he stressed:

> In the interests of the future of the Service, great importance attaches to the selection and training of officers for the War Staff. A body of officers is required who have made a special study of the lessons of history and of war, and who are capable of sifting and applying the mass of evidence available.[40]

These officers would develop doctrine and keep that doctrine refreshed, avoiding the twin dangers of rigidity and irrelevance. History was vital to the process because, as the veteran naval writer Sir James Thursfield, one of the founders of the Navy Record Society, observed, 'history is the sole foundation for the construction of a sound and living common doctrine.'[41] He urged the Navy to take a closer interest in the work of the Records Society, a Society that had, after all, been established to serve its needs. The message is worth repeating.

History has always been the acid test of any theoretical analysis of war. It was only through mastering the details of wars, campaigns and battles, on a large scale, that broad principles of continuing import have been developed. Both Corbett and Clausewitz used their historical studies as the foundation for theory. Both wrote eight times as much history as theory, and it is to that balance that we should attribute the continuing value of their ideas rather than pathetically ascribing it to 'genius' in order to excuse ourselves the trouble of following so hard a road. Neither of them was ever satisfied with their theoretical work. They recognized that the process of strategic thought has to be a thing of life if it is to be of service.

By 1919, the leadership of the naval intellectuals had passed to Herbert Richmond who came to the College as President of the Revised Senior Officer's War Course (1919–23) anxious to improve officer education. He argued that the great commanders of the sailing Navy had studied the past beyond the living transmission of experience, and saw the foundation of the Vere-Harmsworth chair in Naval History at Cambridge in 1919 as an opportunity to make university-level naval history 'the foundation of knowledge of naval war'.[42] He wanted a Cambridge course to be compulsory for all naval officers, allowing civilian academics to open their minds to an understanding of 'the Navy as an Instrument of Policy'. These educated naval officers would develop doctrine, detailed plans and staff work. He repeated Laughton's old plea for a division between scientific training and historical education, and reused Laughton's favourite example, the central importance of the cultivation of intellectual development in the maturing of Nelson's genius. The process should, he believed, begin on the sub-lieutenants' course.[43]

Sadly the Admiralty made little use of the Cambridge course. The first professor, John Holland Rose, was not a naval historian. He had refused the position when it was first offered and wrote to urge Corbett to take it up, as he had 'that connection with the service that will give it life and strength'.[44] Sadly Corbett had neither the life nor the strength to take it up, and although he did continue to press for Laughton's department at King's College, his public reminders to the College hierarchy fell on deaf ears. Rose tried to broaden the study of naval history at Cambridge into the academic mainstream.[45] He was followed in 1934 by Richmond, who held the chair for two years. Since then the Vere-Harmsworth has become an Imperial History Chair which pays occasional lip-service to the original objects for which it was founded. There is still no university chair in Britain devoted to Naval History to the great detriment of the subject, the Royal Navy and the national interest.

The position at Greenwich was little better. A Professor of History was appointed in 1922, probably to avoid having to pay for officers to go to Cambridge, but Geoffrey Callender was a wholly inappropriate choice. Best known for *The Sea Kings of Britain* he had been a successful master at Osborne and at Dartmouth, but he had no pretensions to academic eminence, while his personal life made him an anathema to all 'right' thinking officers of the day. Although he paid lip-service to the doctrinal role of history Callender lacked the capacity for original thought or any analysis beyond the banal. Characteristically Richmond made no secret of his loathing for the new professor; having dismissed his work as 'rubbish' before the war, he refused even to speak to him after his appointment. 'You never saw such drivel as he pumps into [the students],' he lamented, and traced the problem to the Admiralty Adviser on Naval Education, an undistinguished Dartmouth headmaster. Richmond considered naval history was a valuable part of officers' professional education, and the opportunity should not be wasted on the type of antiquarian trifles that Callender espoused.[46] Equally Richmond recognized that Callender, by his mere existence, would demean the subject in the eyes of the academic community, destroying much of Laughton's legacy.

If the Navy was content to leave the provision of history to a man who reached his limit as a prep school housemaster it was scarcely surprising that the development of doctrine at Greenwich between the wars was severely circumscribed. The events of the war were subjected to endless reruns, but the old canard that technical progress had rendered the past irrelevant emerged once more. The easy and comfortable option of a single scenario in which the enemy, his fleet, his options and almost all variables had been reduced to certainty permitted an unhealthy concentration on a very limited range of issues. The fault was common in staff colleges at this time, but the Royal Navy, which had lost its pre-eminence to the Army after 1905, been ignored in the diplomacy of the 1914 crisis and then found itself saddled with a tedious and unrewarding war that hardly anyone inside the Admiralty had anticipated, needed to reconsider fundamentals more than most. The failure of formulaic military strategies in 1914 should have been a warning. There would be more unpleasant lessons in 1940 and 1941 before the continentalist illusion so effectively promoted by the General Staff between 1904 and 1914 was finally exploded.

Between the wars a posting to Staff College was widely regarded as a sure sign that a career had ended. Appointed President of the revived Senior Officers War Course in 1919 Richmond had hoped to move the Staff Course and War Course to a new building near Camberley, but on this occasion the pressure for economy condemned the Staff Course to a prolonged occupation, not of Bracknell Portakabins, but of the attics of Greenwich. Recognizing that there was still a fundamental cultural problem with the use of 'history', he argued that it should be studied not for its own sake but 'as a mental gymnastic'.[47] Richmond's revived Senior Officer's Course, and most of its staff and pupils, were cut by 'Geddes' Axe'. Richmond then served as President of the College in 1922–23, before returning to sea. The Naval Tactical School was hived off in 1925, while the Staff Course was largely supplanted as a centre for studying the higher direction of war by the inter-service Imperial Defence College in 1927, where Richmond, the first Commandant, made a major contribution to the development of common doctrine.[48] As Stephen Roskill discovered, the records of Greenwich's work down to 1939 were largely destroyed by the Admiralty after war damage and flooding.[49]

History was an important element of the Staff Course, working through a series of case studies, exploiting major texts and the Navy Records Society's volumes. The principles of the course were admirable and specific wars were examined in detail as a means of developing the students' awareness of principles.[50] Captain William James, Deputy Director of the Staff Course 1923–25 and Director 1925–6, was inspired by the task of providing history lectures to illustrate the principles of war. His first series, on the Seven Year's War, drew heavily on existing lectures and Corbett's book. He decided to write his own course for the following year, and like Laughton before him, saw the value of studying the American War of Independence, 'one that had not gone so well for us'. His book *The British Navy in Adversity* was the published version of the course.[51] However, James was an exception. The intelligent examination of the naval past, the basis for doctrine, made little progress between the wars. This was largely on account of the lack of depth and quality in the prior education of those officers attending. It was not insignificant that they were enjoined to work on their English before the course started. Richmond found that many had trouble spelling. Furthermore lieutenants were not taught strategy.[52] Callender's contribution, *The Naval Side of British History*, served the Navy best by prompting Corbett's son-in-law, Brian Tunstall, who worked in the History Department, to subject it to well-earned ridicule in *The Realities of Naval History*. Needless to say Tunstall did not stay at the College for long. This was particularly unfortunate because his intellectual weight and stimulating teaching might have begun the long overdue process of rebuilding the College's links with the universities rather sooner than was the case. That the relationship between the College and the universities would be critical to the success of the College had been a fundamental assumption of the Shadwell Committee in 1870; in the case of history it was an assumption without foundation before 1970. One hundred years is a long time to learn so simple a truth.

Another old problem resurfaced during the late 1930s. There were, the Admiralty argued, too few junior officers available for sea service to permit the continuation of the sub-lieutenants' course. It was closed in 1937. The historical education of naval officers would now end with the *Sea Kings* at Dartmouth. Little wonder Richmond doubted if those arriving at Staff College were able to benefit from what was on offer. He returned to Laughton's solution, 16-year-old entry. This was still too radical for the Admiralty, but was adopted post-war.[53]

POST-SECOND WORLD WAR

After the Second World War nuclear weapons, NATO and the Cold War provided the policy-makers with a host of reasons to ignore the past. They also resuscitated the continentalist illusion, which gained much credence, both historical and contemporary, from the advocacy of Sir Michael Howard.[54] When the Navy made a case, in the Staff and later Official Histories, they created a whole new set of myths, the sort of myths that Laughton had devoted his career to exploding. The Staff Histories, from which the 'Official History' was developed, were written to sell the case for a new Navy. To this end they argued, among other things, that the U-boat threat was 'never truly mastered'.[55] Having broken the enemy's will to fight, forced them out of the only potentially decisive theatre of operations, killed 75 per cent of their personnel and sunk an even greater percentage of their tonnage, it should be obvious that they were decisively beaten. However, the deception had purpose. Only the threat of a third battle of the Atlantic, waged by 300+ sophisticated Soviet submarines based on German designs, would persuade the governments of the 1950s to rebuild the fleet. In fact the 'advanced' Soviet submarines were short-ranged craft based on pre-war designs, intended for strategic defence against Western attack carriers. Down to 1956 Western intelligence knew they did not even have schnorkels, let alone the underwater performance of the German Type XXI of 1945, the first modern diesel-electric submarine. Furthermore the wartime record of the Soviet submarine service had been lamentable, and they were no better off the coast of Korea where they were sunk in short order by the Royal Navy. By dismissing the more distant past, keeping the relevant archives closed and employing Captain Stephen Roskill to write the public version of their work, the Naval Staff avoided having their ideas subjected to academic scrutiny. The Naval past was simply too important a business for historians.

Fortunately such attitudes were not universal. In the 1950s historical scholarship by the civilian staff at Greenwich was encouraged, leading to important work on major questions of contemporary import. But progress remained haphazard. Doctrine development remained a highly classified business dealing with war-fighting, from which civilians were necessarily excluded. Tactics were, as Laughton and later Mahan had always said, greatly affected by new weapons. Yet the same caveat did not apply to the study of principles, and has always been entirely irrelevant to the delivery of higher level education.

Even when history is studied there has been a tendency to confuse proximity with relevance. There is a widely held view that the only 'useful' history is that dealing with the Second World War and after. To follow this line of argument would be to build doctrine on too scant a foundation, leaving it fragile and inflexible, just as the old certainties have disappeared. What is needed now is a return to the first principles of national strategy, not a British 'Schlieffen Plan'. History can only help if it is studied in breadth, in depth and with understanding. The educational value of a case study of the development of the naval role within national policy, including relations with other states, is greatly enhanced by the availability of archival material from all relevant sources, unhindered by any 30-year rule. For example, and to return to where we began, the framers of doctrine for the next century would profit far more from studying why the Navy was not used as a deterrent in 1914 and why it was so ill-equipped for the coastal operations of 1914–15 than they will from re-examining the Gulf War. Similarly there is more of enduring import for the role of the Tactical Land Attack Missile in the history of the mortar vessel than in any operational use of the system to date. In 1907 Julian Corbett used the British experience in 1759 to demonstrate that the great art of strategy was to develop war plans that would force reluctant, inferior enemies to give battle at a time and place chosen by the British. As he said, 'the sublime moments in naval history have to be worked for.'[56] Yet the point passed almost unnoticed and had no impact on the war planning of 1914. Fisher, who understood these things far better than his fellows, was developing plans for offensive operations in the North Sea and Baltic that would have this effect. Only in this way could the High Seas Fleet be brought to battle when the Grand Fleet was ready. That Corbett and Fisher were right was demonstrated in 1918: with all other options closed down the Germans decided to send out their fleet on a forlorn hope. Only a mutiny prevented another Quiberon. However, there are more positive lessons to take from Greenwich to the new 'Joint' Staff College. Greenwich, in contrast to certain other establishments, has had a long and largely positive relationship with a department of civilian academics. The task for the future is to build on this experience and ethos, combining service and civilian expertise in the development of education and doctrine. The revival of Laughton's old link with King's College London in 1970 is an example of what can be accomplished. For close on thirty years a strong intellectual exchange has been conducted to the great benefit of all concerned. After decades of certainty the future is now uncertain. In developing doctrine to meet that future history remains central. No fighting service can look back on so long a record of victory, and the Navy needs to ensure that future leaders of the service not only recognize this, but understand how it came about. In the past the Navy has suffered because it did not examine the historical basis of its doctrine with the same professional standards that it has always applied to seamanship, tactics and technology.

In contrast to other staff colleges the Royal Naval College at Greenwich awaits its historian.[57] They will have more to say about the College's role in the development of doctrine. This chapter has emphasized the central importance of individuals as opposed to structures. Without Laughton the development of naval doctrine in the late nineteenth century would have been greatly retarded and he, it should be remembered, was the Professor of Meteorology. Julian Corbett, a classic English gentleman amateur, made a unique and timeless contribution between 1900 and 1914, while Herbert Richmond ensured that the legacy of the two men who fostered his historical awareness was not lost. Sadly Richmond's intellectual arrogance produced more opposition in six months than Laughton had engendered in sixty years. In no case was their contribution based on position. By contrast, the provision of a Chair in Naval History in 1922 was rendered worthless by a careless appointment. Fundamentally the College has provided a focus for the priceless interaction between sea officers and academics. Laughton's work with Cooper Key and Hornby, and Corbett's with Fisher, Henry May and Edmond Slade, are critical examples. This intellectual cross-fertilization has been the greatest contribution of the College to the development of naval power. The most effective doctrine development has always stemmed from the *regular* interchange of ideas and experience. To foster the process staff colleges have to sustain a highly motivated academic staff, combining teaching and research and working alongside serving officers on the staff and in the student body. Doctrine is a dialogue between the past and the present for the benefit of the future. For too long a technologically obsessed perspective has given undue weight to the present and ignored the fundamental issues. In the new century the balance will have to be restored, because history remains the foundation.

NOTES

1. Sir J. Thursfield, 'The Navy Records Society', *The Naval Review*, 1920, p. 401.
2. See my unpublished paper 'Deterrence', in M. Duffy (ed.), *Parameters of British Naval Power* (Exeter: Exeter University Press, forthcoming 1999), for a further discussion of this case.
3. Admiral Sir F. Dreyer *The Sea Heritage* (London: British Museum, 1955), p. 369.
4. A. D. Lambert, *The Foundations of Naval History: John Knox Laughton, the Royal Navy and the Historical Progression* (London: Chatham Press, 1998), ch. 2.
5. Admiralty Circular No. 28 14.3.1874 ADM 203/1.
6. J. R. Soley, *Report on Foreign Systems of Naval Education* (Washington, DC: US Government Printing Office, 1880), pp. 49–55, a work drawing heavily on Laughton's 1875 *RUSI* Lecture.
7. 'Admiral Ballard's Memoirs: Part IV', in *The Mariner's Mirror*, vol. 62, 1976, p. 249.
8. For a summary of Laughton's career, see A. D. Lambert, 'History, Strategy and Doctrine: Sir John Knox Laughton and the Education of the Royal Navy', in W. Cogar (ed.), *New Interpretations in Naval History: Papers from the Twelfth Naval History Symposium* (Annapolis, Md.: United States Naval Institute Press, 1997), pp. 173–87.
9. *Gun, Rum and Torpedo* (Portsmouth, Griffin & Co., 1873).
10. See A. Gordon, *The Rules of the Game: Jutland and British Naval Command* (London: John Murray, 1996).
11. J. K. Laughton, 'Naval Warfare', *The Edinburgh Review*, July 1885, pp. 234–64, quoting his notes of Hornby's lecture, p. 238.
12. J. K. Laughton, *Letters and Dispatches of Horatio, Viscount Nelson* (London: Longman, 1886), pp. vii–xx. Corbett's handling of the 'Nelson Memorandum' in 1905 was strikingly similar.
13. 'Naval Warfare', *The Edinburgh Review*, 1885, pp. 239–40.
14. J. K. Laughton, 'Scientific Education in the Royal Navy', *RUSI*, 1875, pp. 283–4.
15. Ibid.
16. A. Bucholz, *Delbruck and the German Military Establishment* (Ames, Iowa: Iowa University Press), 1985.

17. 'Tegetthoff: Experiences of Steam and Armour', in *Fraser's Magazine*, June 1878, pp. 671–2. Reprinted in J. K. Laughton, *Studies in Naval History* (London: Longmans, 1887), pp. 148–50.
18. Ibid.
19. Ibid.
20. Ibid.
21. Ibid.
22. Laughton to Stephen Luce USN 11.8.1889: Luce MS Library of Congress.
23. A. T. Mahan, *The Influence of Seapower upon the French Revolution and Empire* (London: Sampson Low, 1891).
24. The Admiralty purchased over 200 copies of Julian Corbett's two volumes of tactical material.
25. London Navy Records Society, 1894.
26. I am indebted to Prof. D. Baugh for this insight.
27. J. K. Laughton (ed.), *From Howard to Nelson* (London: Heinemann, 1899).
28. Sir W. Laird Clowes, *The Royal Navy: A History*, Vol. III (London: Sampson, 1898). J. K. Laughton (ed.), *Report on the Manuscripts of Lady Du Cane* (London: Historical Manuscripts Commission, 1905).
29. H. W. Richmond, *The Navy in the War of 1739–48*, 3 vols (Cambridge: Cambridge University Press, 1920), Vol. 1, Preface.
30. A. J. Marder, *The Anatomy of British Sea Power* (London: Knopf, 1940), p. 390, quoting Fisher.
31. H. S. Wilkinson, *The Brain of a Navy* (London: Constable, 1895). The arguments set out in this book were the basis of the Navy League, and were adopted by Beresford.
32. Fisher to Lord Selborne (First Lord) 29.7.1901, in A. J. Marder (ed.), *Fear God and Dreadnought*, vol. I (London: Jonathan Cape, 1952), p. 203
33. D. Schurman, *The Education of a Navy: The Development of British Naval Strategic Thought 186–1914* (London: Cassell, 1965), p. 127.
34. Ibid., p. 366. See also A. Offer, *The First World War: An Agrarian Interpretation* (Oxford: Oxford University Press, 1989).
35. A. J. Marder, *From the Dreadnought to Scapa Flow: Vol. 1 1904–1914: The Road to War* (Oxford: Oxford University Press, 1961), pp. 32–3 and 265.
36. D. Schurman, *Julian S. Corbett: 1854–1922* (London: Royal Historical Society, 1981), p. 33 for the role of Henry May and George Clarke in completing this process.
37. See my unpublished paper 'Deterrence', in Duffy, *The Parameters of British Naval Power*, for a further discussion of this issue.
38. J. Corbett, 'The Teaching of Naval and Military History', *History*, April 1916, pp. 12–19.
39. A. D. Lambert, '"Part of a long line of Circumvallation to confine the future expansion of Russia": Great Britain and the Baltic, 1809–1890', in G. Rystad, K.-R. Bohme and W. Carlgren (eds), *The Baltic in Power Politics 1500–1890* (Lund: Lund University Press, 1994), pp. 322–30.
40. 'The Royal Naval Staff College', *The Naval Review*, 1932, pp. 6–34 at p. 12.
41. Sir J. Thursfield, 'The Navy Records Society', *The Naval Review*, 1920, p. 401.

42. H. Richmond, 'The Place of History in Naval Education', *The Naval Review*, 1920, p. 9.
43. Ibid.
44. Holland-Rose to Corbett 6.1.1919, Corbett MSS National Maritime Museum.
45. J. H. Rose, *Naval History and National History* (Cambridge: Cambridge University Press, 1919).
46. B. Hunt, *Sailor-Scholar, Sir Herbert Richmond*, (Waterloo, Ontario: McGill University Press, 1982), pp. 126–9.
47. A. J. Marder, *Portrait of an Admiral* (London: Jonathan Cape, 1952), Diary entry 18.11.1919, p. 359.
48. Ibid., pp. 27–8.
49. S. W. Roskill, *Naval Policy between the Wars*, vol. 1 (London: Collins, 1968).
50. 'The Royal Naval Staff College', *The Naval Review*, 1932, pp. 6–34 for a positive view of the course.
51. W. James, *The Sky Was Always Blue* (London: Methuen, 1951), pp. 131–4. James became a prolific author and a Councillor of the Record Society. He attributed his interest to prolonged periods of illness which provided the time for reading and reflection. His career demonstrated that the time spent was not lost or wasted, and but for the Munich Crisis he would have taken command in the Mediterranean in 1938. See p. 265.
52. 'The Study of Strategy by Junior Officers', *The Naval Review*, 1932, pp. 2–4.
53. H. Richmond, *Naval Training* (Oxford: Oxford University Press, 1933). S. W. Roskill, *Naval Policy Between the Wars*, vol. II (London: Collins, 1976), pp. 341–2.
54. M. Howard, *The Continental Commitment* (London: Harmsworth, 1974). A work suffused with the realities of the age in which it was written, it provided a strong *ex post facto* justification for a British role in NATO dominated by the Central Front and the British Army of the Rhine.
55. S. W. Roskill, *The War at Sea*, vol. III, part II (London: HMSO, 1962).
56. J. S. Corbett, *England in the Seven Years' War* (London: Longmans, 1907).
57. Rear-Adm. E. W. Ellis, 'Royal Naval College Greenwich Centenary 1873–1973', in *The Naval Review*, 1973, pp. 330–40 is a brief résumé.

5 BR1806, Joint Doctrine and Beyond

Eric Grove

At the end of 1995 in a ceremony at the Royal United Services Institute in Whitehall the Royal Navy launched BR1806, *The Fundamentals of British Maritime Doctrine* (referred to henceforth as 1806).[1] This was the third of the single-service doctrine publications. The Army had led the way with *British Military Doctrine* first published in 1989 (with a Royal Navy assault ship on the cover) and reissued in 1996 (now with a Warrior Infantry Fighting Vehicle on the cover) as a capstone document to a number of Army doctrine publications.[2] The Royal Air Force produced their AP3000 in 1991. This was rapidly revised to take account the lessons of the Gulf War and re-emerged in its second edition form in 1993.[3] The Royal Navy was being left behind. This was not because the Navy had never had doctrine, as the First Sea Lord put it in his foreword:

> There has always been a doctrine, an evolving set of principles, practices and procedures that has provided the basis for our actions. This doctrine has been laid out somewhat piecemeal in various publications and there has never been a single official unclassified book describing why and how we do our business...[4]

The use of the number 'BR1806' was a self-conscious attempt to place it in the tradition of naval publications of a 'doctrinal' nature. This had been the number of the old *Naval War Manual* last issued in the 1960s but which had languished in classified bookstores rather than been widely disseminated or taught. The Navy's scepticism towards doctrine reflected an understandable reluctance to become too dogmatic in its professional approach and 1806 contains numerous cautions that doctrine must not be confused with dogma. Yet the lack of doctrine in the proper sense acted as an undesirable brake on the development of a proper professional culture in the service. It was difficult, for example, in the 1970s after the withdrawal from 'East of Suez' and before the development of NATO's Forward Maritime Strategy for Naval College lecturers to teach coherently and consistently on the role and functions of the Royal Navy. Sometimes there might be guarded references by visiting speakers to the development of NATO thinking[5] but there was no authoritative national framework of thought. Worse, when institutions such as the Royal

57

Navy's Maritime Tactical School undertook important studies on important matters such as the defence of merchant shipping, there was no easily available corpus of strategic and operational doctrine on which to draw – with sometimes disastrous results.[6]

Internal opposition to the development of doctrine remained significant throughout the evolution of 1806 but the process was carried through by a small team with the backing of successive Assistant Chiefs of Naval Staff and Directors of Naval Staff Duties. The original team were impressed with the advantages that the other two services gained from their possession of doctrine publications and sought to redress the balance. Moreover there was the key consideration that the development of joint doctrine was only a matter of time and that it was crucial that the Navy have a document 'on the table' when such development began. After an initial first draft the consultation process broadened to include a range of inputs. I was recruited to act under contract as academic author while Cdr Mike Codner, a highly intellectual officer (now at the RUSI) with experience of working at the US Naval War College at Newport, Rhode Island, became my principal Naval colleague. In order to make sure the work reflected as much of a consensus as possible, not only were revised drafts circulated but a major seminar was held at the Royal Naval College, Greenwich, at which a range of academics, including those from the Naval College's own Department of History and International Affairs, and interested service parties were asked to comment. Their contributions were most valuable and had considerable positive impact on the completed volume. As a result of this 1806 had, as its starting point, a firm belief in historical principles. Thus, included within 1806 was a statement that: '[d]octrine has its foundation in history; the study, analysis and interpretation of experience. It provides a shared interpretation of that experience which can be taught, in order to provide a common starting point for thinking about future action.'[7]

This definition had much in common with Sir Julian Corbett's definition of 'theory' in *Some Principles of Maritime Strategy*,[8] 'a common vehicle for expression and a common plane of thought'. Some, such as Donald Schurman, Corbett's distinguished biographer, confusing Corbett's right and proper warning against simple 'maxims' with the establishment of sound theory, would oppose the view that Corbett was a doctrinal writer but he was clearly regarded as such in his time.[9] Hervé Couteau Begarie revealed in discussion at the Conference 'Mahan is not Enough' held at Newport, Rhode Island, in 1993 that when French officers visiting the Grand Fleet asked about the Royal Navy's doctrine they were referred to 'Some Principles'. Certainly the strengths – and weaknesses – of that publication were reflected in the activities of the Navy in 1914–18. I had no compunction in asserting plainly in the box on 'Maritime Doctrine' in 1806 that Corbett 'provided the Royal Navy of the early Twentieth Century with its strategic doctrine'. It also allowed one to repeat Corbett's dire warning 'against slavishly following simple maxims and using them as substitutes for judgement. As he put it in his lectures "You might as well try to plan a campaign by singing Rule Britannia."'

Corbett's insistence that naval strategy was but part of a larger maritime whole and the consistent teaching of this basic doctrinal point by at least three generations of lecturers at the Royal Naval College, Greenwich, made it certain that 1806 should be regarded as the fundamentals of *maritime* doctrine. There are problems in this approach as it sometimes seems to make 'maritime' a single-service 'dark blue' word. But it does have the advantage of making the Royal Navy's doctrine basically joint. As 1806 put it:

> Maritime power is inherently joint in nature. It emanates from forces drawn from all three Services, both sea and land based, supported by national and commercial resources, exercising influence over the sea, land and air environments.[10]

This approach is fundamentally different from that of the US Navy which, typically, given inter-service relations in the USA, has been much more concerned to establish specifically *naval* doctrine.[11] It might also be added that the establishment of a complete command at Norfolk, Virginia, to produce doctrine publications contrasts somewhat with the small team created to produce 1806. The way the latter document was received in the USA probably demonstrates that the British approach was the more cost-effective.[12]

Perhaps because of its inherently joint nature BR1806 proved especially useful in the production in 1996 of *British Defence Doctrine* (*BDD*).[13] The dynamics of the creation of this document vindicated the architects of 1806. Not only were the authors of 1806 fully involved in its drafting (and the naval perspectives fully inputted) but Chapter 2 of 1806, 'General Concepts of Armed Conflict', proved a useful starting point for the authors of the new joint document – even if it did not prove possible to transpose all of its ideas directly into agreed joint doctrine.

There are two aspects of our Chapter 2 that are worthy of more extended discussion. The first is the deliberate attempt in 1806 to eschew simplistic concepts of 'war' as the primary purpose of military forces. Perhaps because Britain's naval forces have a long tradition of operation across a broad spectrum of operations, of which full-scale war-fighting has only been a part (albeit the most demanding part) it was decided to emphasize the broader term 'conflict' to cover situations where violence is used to achieve political ends. The presence or absence of conflict and the level of conflict, it was argued, are the controlling variables in determining the ways armed forces are used. Attempts to produce a well-ordered diagrammatic 'spectrum of conflict' soon fell victim to the complexities of reality but it was retained as a general concept 'to denote the full range of situations in which military forces may be called upon to operate, from stable peace to strategic nuclear war'.[14]

We then moved on in 1806 to define 'combat', 'hostilities' and 'war', the latter being 'combat that is intense, extensive and sustained over time'.[15] This definition was followed by a thoughtful dialogue box that briefly set out why 'war is difficult to define simply'. It pointed to the problem created by the outlawing of war by the United Nations Charter (a discussion sadly confused a little by a misprint of 1964 for 1945)[16] and the differing perceptions of combatants in 'wars'. We had to admit, however, that 'war', meaning sustained, extensive high-intensity combat is, nevertheless, an important doctrinal concept and that British Army and US Navy doctrine distinguished between war-fighting and operations other than war (OOTW).[17] A compromise between the 'conflict' and 'war' school was achieved in *British Defence Doctrine* but the greater flexibility of the former concept led to its adoption as the foundation of joint doctrine. The similarities between *BDD* and 1806 are clear.

A concept originated in 1806 upon which joint compromise was more difficult was the division of the three ways in which military forces are used:

1. *military* or combat governed use – in which combat is used or threatened or which presupposes a combat capability;
2. *constabulary* use or policing – 'where forces are employed to enforce law' and where 'violence is only employed for self defence or as a last resort';
3. *benign* use – where 'military forces contribute organized and self supporting formations with specific capabilities and specialist knowledge…, but the tasks are benign because violence has no part to play in their execution.'[18]

This trinity was developed from the older 'military/diplomatic/constabulary' concept outlined in my *Future of Sea Power*.[19] The division between 'military' and 'diplomatic' in the older categorization masked the fact that naval diplomacy was 'combat governed' in that, 'although under these circumstances combat may not be used or even envisaged, it is the combat capability of the forces that underpins their use.'[20]

At sea the Royal Navy often acts as a maritime policeman.[21] On land, however, the Army operates as an aid to the civil constabulary, not as a constabulary force in its own right. This is a distinction of politico-constitutional significance and it led to some controversy in the preparation of *British Defence Doctrine*. 'Khaki' opposition meant that this could not espouse the 'constabulary' role in the form the 'dark blue' had done. Nevertheless it is hoped that, although the next edition of 1806 will pay due attention to *BDD* as a 'capstone' document, the notion of 'constabulary' shall be retained as an important part of the explanation as to how military forces are used in the maritime environment.

One area where it is hoped lessons will be learned in the next edition is in the, in retrospect, mistaken inclusion of a detailed description of 'Security and Defence Policy' as it stood when the document was being drafted. This perhaps helped the document pass the scrutiny of the Ministry's officials but it was soon made somewhat obsolete by the evolution of the Conservative government's Defence Policy and it will look even more obsolete when the Blair administration publishes the result of the Strategic Defence Review (SDR). *British Defence Doctrine* also suffered a little from its rather inappropriate political foreword by the then Secretary of State for Defence but the more generally 'generic' nature of the *British Defence Doctrine* will be reflected in the next 1806. Doctrine, while grounded in national security and defence policies, should not be hostage to the political fortunes of the day. Happily, the nature of the SDR might well lend itself to a more broadly based agreed expression of national security policy that will last for at least the currency of the next BR1806.

BR1806 put the levels of command and planning for conflict into the now classical hierarchy of grand strategic, military strategic, operational and tactical, a process not without its problems in the maritime context. As is made clear in Chapter 6 on 'Planning and Conducting a Campaign or Operation', the primary focus of 1806 is on the higher three levels. The source of tactical doctrine is a classified document *The Fighting Instructions* for which the Maritime Tactical School at HMS *Dryad* is rightly responsible.[22] Clearly tactical doctrine should reflect doctrine at the higher levels and this has been reflected in the enthusiastic way in which HMS *Dryad* has taken to spreading the doctrinal word around the fleet. Indeed the creation of a Doctrine Cell at HMS *Dryad* has emphasized the seamless nature of the overall hierarchy of maritime doctrine.

This process is not without its dangers, however. The approach of the tactician, especially at the training level, tends to be highly structured.

This opens the way to overly dogmatic doctrinal articulation, exactly what we repeatedly argued against, with the Chief of Naval Staff's clear imprimatur, in BR1806. Throughout, 1806 sets out material from which the reader is expected to make choices – informed choices, but choices just the same. It came, therefore, as a considerable surprise to find 1806 accused at a seminar at Dartmouth in 1997 of having produced a fixed doctrine which potential enemies might be able to exploit and which therefore ought to be ignored by the sensible commander. This totally misunderstood the function of doctrine; indeed it flew in the face of what was stated in Chapter 6 of 1806 itself about planning even at the operational level:

> This document is not intended to provide detailed guidance on operational planning, nor to describe planning tools..., but to provide a logical train that will set the concepts discussed in earlier chapters in a practical context.

As with all other aspects of the 1806 the chapter was meant to guide and inform, *not* instruct.

Interestingly, this critique was put in the context of the book by Andrew Gordon *Conflict of Styles*[23] which sets out the conflict of tactical doctrine between Admirals Jellicoe and Beatty and its baleful results on 31 May 1916. What Gordon described was a conflict between two doctrinal styles, *not* a conflict between doctrine and some kind of inspired leadership working on intuition. The anti-intellectualism involved in the latter concept has been by far the greatest flaw in the Royal Navy's professional culture over the years.

It was for this reason that it was thought important to make the point about the continuity of doctrine quoted at the opening of this paper. Moreover, this was backed up by quickly invoking the sacred Nelson as an example of the successful creation and application of doctrine. In this we had the great example of Corbett who had mercilessly used the naval hero to help support his arguments. Thus, the introduction to 1806 reads:

> Nelson is well known for simple instructions such as his use of the signal 'close action' – usually interpreted as 'engage the enemy more closely' – and the sentence in his memorandum before Trafalgar that 'No captain can do very wrong if he places his ship alongside that of an enemy.' It is easy to be misled by the apparent simplicity of these instructions. In reality they reflected a confidence that his subordinates were completely familiar with contemporary Naval doctrine, amended sometimes by Nelson himself. Nelson, who was a great believer in delegation,

expected his subordinates to use their intelligence, seamanship and understanding of his intentions to do much between in outmanoeuvring their opponents. Importantly, he devoted much time and effort discussing with his Captains how he pictured forthcoming battles. As a result, they were able to take independent action in support of Nelson's objectives without further reference to him.[24]

This was what Beatty expected at Jutland, albeit sadly without communicating this to all his subordinates. The results of Jutland demonstrate the problems of not having a common doctrine, not those of the slavish application of doctrine. It was a weakness of the Fisherite Navy that its major doctrinal work, Corbett's *Some Principles*, was a civilian book without official status, and even it only came down to the higher levels of what would be later called operational art.

Corbett actually intended his book to be a more general national strategic manual and was dubious about its being rushed out with too great a 'naval' emphasis.[25] Certainly it did little to help the creation of the joint national maritime strategy that he longed for. We are perhaps luckier today. The combination of the publication of *British Defence Doctrine*, the creation of the Joint Service Command and Staff College and the formation of the Permanent Joint Headquarters at Northwood has the potential to create a more coherent and considered approach to the higher levels of planning for conflict. It was right that the *BDD* awaited the appearance of doctrinal statements by all three services as the perspective of each was important. However, it was perhaps equally right, and a belated vindication of Corbett, that the inherently joint nature of the maritime environment should make BR1806 such a key asset in the development of joint doctrine. The process of interactive revision of the current official doctrine publications should inexorably produce a more or less coherent national doctrine. Moreover, strategic logic dictates that doctrine must increasingly reflect the demands of joint, expeditionary (dare one say, maritime) operations.

NOTES

1. BR1806, *The Fundamentals of British Maritime Doctrine* (London: HMSO, 1995).
2. 'Design for Military Operations – The British Military Doctrine', *Army Code No. 71451*, revised edn 1996, first edn 1989.

3. 'Air Power Doctrine', *AP3000*, second edn 1993, first edn 1991.
4. BR1806, op. cit., Admiral Sir Jock Slater's foreword.
5. Admiral Sir James Eberle was particularly helpful in this, sharing his high-level professional perspectives with young officers in Annual 'Maritime Power Seminars' at Dartmouth.
6. The author remembers an MTS study on this subject in about 1979 which was based on a set of sources that did not include the crucially important (but then still classified) Staff History, *The Defeat of the Enemy Attack Upon Shipping*. The conclusions were weak to say the least.
7. BR1806, op. cit., pp. 12–13.
8. The latest edition of which I edited for the US Naval Institute in 1998 (London: Brassey's, 1998).
9. We disagreed on this point at a conference on the utility of history for modern armed services held a few years ago at the University of New Brunswick at Fredericton.
10. BR1806, op. cit., pp. 13–14.
11. See the various NDP publications.
12. See the review of 1806 in US Naval Insititute Proceedings.
13. *British Defence Doctrine*, Joint Warfare Publication 0–01, (London: MoD, 1996).
14. BR1806, op. cit., p. 32.
15. Ibid.
16. Interestingly this misprint was carried over by the unattributed extensive paraphrasing of 1806 in Maritime Doctrine for the Royal New Zealand Navy published in March 1997, p. 9.
17. BR1806, op. cit., p. 33.
18. Ibid., p. 34.
19. For my original see Eric Grove, *The Future of Sea Power* (London: Routledge, 1990), p. 234.
20. BR1806, op. cit., p. 34.
21. For a good recent description see Cdr Chris Lightfoot RN, 'Overseas Model and Experiences – UK and EU', *Policing Australia's Offshore Zones: Problems and Prospects*, ed. Chris Lightfoot (Centre for Maritime Policy, University of Wollongong, 1997).
22. Sadly the promised declassification of a version of Fighting Instructions seems not yet to have taken place.
23. Dr Andrew Gordon agrees with this assessment. (London: Leo Cooper, 1996).
24. BR1806, op. cit.
25. This is clear from recent study of Corbett's papers in the National Maritime Museum.

6 Constraints on UK World Power Projection and Foreign Policy in the New World Order: the Maritime Dimension

Michael Clarke

'Power projection' is back in fashion as the stability of the international order is threatened now more by the weakness of states than by their strength. The desire and ability to project power for policing, crisis management, conflict prevention and to obtain influence in the world order reflects a world freed from the imperatives of the Cold War and the ideological competition that it entailed. But the freedom of individual states to project power is now paradoxically constrained by the structure of international interdependence that finally finished off the Cold War and which has replaced it as the dominant trend in world politics. It is not fear of our adversaries or respect for the rules of a dangerous bipolar game that now constrains the major states from projecting their power so much as an awareness of how difficult it is, these days, to make such projected power effective in achieving our aims. This is particularly so for the United Kingdom, a state that has aspirations to a world role, a maritime and expeditionary tradition and the luxury now of a relatively stable international environment in which to operate.

The victory of liberal democracy over the forces of Soviet communism has allowed an unprecedented degree of discretion over how the UK should exercise its external policy. This has important implications for maritime policy. The UK is no longer driven by the imperatives of defending Western Europe against an overwhelming attack and thereby responsible for keeping Atlantic reinforcement routes open. Nor is it heavily burdened by the overseas responsibilities of Empire, or the immediate post-imperial role. Its responsibilities within the remaining Overseas Territories apply to less than 150 000 people.[1] The 1995 *Statement on the Defence Estimates* made the point that 92 per cent of the UK's trade (by volume) is transported by sea;[2]

65

but given that a significant proportion of UK trade is with European countries, the sea ways that really matter in this equation are the North Sea, English Channel and the Mediterranean. All these routes are relatively secure, are the mutual concern of many different states and (in the case of the UK) can all be circumvented by road and rail with the advent of the Channel Tunnel. The UK, in other words, is less constrained by its economic geography or its island status than at any time in its history. Nor, even, is the present government constrained by a lack of domestic political support. It enjoys a landslide majority within Parliament and is not faced – as even the 1945–51 Labour government was faced – with backbench dissent over defence policy and the relationship with the United States, the onset of the Cold War and much else besides. When the government asserts, therefore, that it intends to emphasize an 'ethical dimension' in its external policy and to give a more central place to environmental concerns, conflict prevention initiatives and peace support operations – all of which suggest more expeditionary operations – there is reason to believe that ministers mean it.[3]

Genuine constraints on external policy, however, come in more structural forms than is apparent from short-term policy initiatives. The present government has no choice but to express this unprecedented level of policy discretion within a thickening web of powerful structural constraints that affect all governments, in the developed and undeveloped world – with the partial exception of the United States – which serve to limit the capacity to project power overseas. This is not, however, necessarily all bad news for the United Kingdom. In some ways, the increasingly circumscribed structures of the international environment in which external policy is played out can work to the UK's advantage. The subtle realities of this proposition are evident in an examination of three particular dimensions of modern constraints: the international structure in which the UK exists; the resources it has to put in to external policy; and the domestic structure of policy-making in contemporary Britain. The trick for foreign and defence policy-makers – much easier said than done – is to discern the force and direction of major structural constraints and play to the strengths the UK still has within that framework. And certainly, the UK's maritime capacities – the ships and hardware, the quality of the naval personnel in both the maritime marine and the Royal Navy, plus the legacy and traditions of the UK as a maritime power – should be recognized as one of the country's strengths. It is a strength, however, that has to be exercised within the context of a rapidly evolving international system.

THE EMERGING INTERNATIONAL SYSTEM

The phenomenon that is most cited in the way we characterize the international system is 'globalization'.[4] Undoubtedly, this term expresses a genuine truth in our present transitionary age, but it does not capture the anomalies and contradictory processes that accompany it.[5] On the one hand it is certainly true that the increasing potency of the international market economy is characterized by growing homogeneity in economic and social interactions. The Bretton Woods economic system – and it did work as a formal system for the most part[6] – was dead by 1976 and could not be replaced by anything so organized. Instead, the international market has become the mechanism of economic discipline and regulation, based as it is on the knowledge and software revolutions, the declining real costs of transport and communication, the existence of a global, vernacular culture that creates converging patterns of consumer demands and the ability of all major companies to operate internationally. Thus, by 1990 travel and tourism had become the world's largest single industry, accounting for some six per cent of global output. The economic challenge of the traditional low-wage economies to the developed world had far less impact than originally expected, since low-wage production could only make a real impact when allied to high-value software efficiency gains and global marketing strategies – witness the phenomenon of the sports shoe industry since the mid-1980s. Nor is there any such thing as a purely national major car industry in Europe (apart maybe from the Saabs and/or Volvos); rather, there are European regions for Ford, General Motors, Toyota, Renault or Volkswagen that exist within a global automotive production network that supplies common designs and technical specifications throughout the world.[7] In a global sense, this has exacerbated the divisions between rich and poor, both within and between countries, while in Europe the economic map no longer bears much relation to the political map of the continent. The major economic regions of the continent almost all cut across the national boundaries of the major European countries. It is becoming increasingly difficult to speak meaningfully of 'national economies' in the European context.[8]

On the other hand, the 'globalized' economic system is also characterized by an increasingly diffused and fragmented political system. Political power is diffused both within and between states; the world is no longer noted for powerful, international 'isms' that unite nations at the political level. There are more states than ever before – some 190 – and more substate groups that claim autonomy or outright independence. And this phenomenon affects both poor and rich states alike. The

'Northern League' in Italy which claims to represent a nascent state of Padania, has echoes in the Basque country, Scotland or Quebec, just as significant, though for different reasons, as the political fragmentation that has afflicted South Eastern Europe or the Great Lakes region in Africa. The international market has exacerbated income inequalities to produce what has been called an 'elite international system' where local elites within poor states have common economic, and hence political, interests with powerful elite states, whilst all states are battling within themselves to maintain political cohesion.

The globalized twenty-first century, in some ways, is witnessing a 'crisis of the state', occasioned by the simultaneous growth of both economic homogeneity and political diversity. Governments are generally weaker in relation to their own populations. Even in the United States, it is possible to speculate that the US economy and society will remain dominant – maybe even become more dominant – in the next several decades, but that the US *government* will be weaker, unable to cope with multinationalism abroad and incapable of effective action at home through the operation of cross-cutting domestic vetoes which prevent incisive action.

It is not difficult to see that a number of less developed states are in a condition of crisis, hit often by violent domestic dissent, an international marketplace in which they cannot compete *as national economies*, often with levels of debt which not only provide no room for economic growth but condemn them to long-term economic failure, and operating under conditions imposed by the lenders that dictate short-term national economic policies. The result is that they have little political purchase on a world no longer divided into strategic camps. Though the once fast developing countries of East Asia and the traditional developed states of the Organization of Economic Cooperation and Development (OECD) did not suffer from the same economic diseases as the undeveloped, they have nevertheless exhibited, in their own context, many similar symptoms. The OECD states have been in a state of structural deficit since the oil crisis of 1973, measured in government expenditure over government revenues as a percentage of GDP.[9] They suffer an inability to deliver to their populations what has traditionally been expected of them as developed states. Within the OECD the tax base is diminishing as international companies manipulate their operations to garner the optimum tax levels, and the ratio of 'economically active' families has fallen from 5:1 in 1970 to 3:1 in 1990 and may reach 2:1 by the year 2010. Meanwhile, individuals with jobs are becoming more independent in the way they may choose to work for foreign firms; individuals with capital are more internationally minded in the way they invest it; individuals with leisure are more inclined to spend it in more than one country; and individuals with grievances are less inclined to accept the highest courts in the land as the final arbiter.

The international environment of UK foreign policy, therefore, especially in Europe, is uniquely constraining on the autonomy of national governments. Though the motives to project power have increased in this globalized economy that is characterized by political diversity, the effectiveness of doing so is now more in doubt than ever. In the maritime sphere, 'gunboat diplomacy' is no longer a discrete activity that can be conducted in a bilateral context. Even the simplest forms of contemporary gunboat diplomacy – such as attempts to enforce UN Resolutions against Iraq – are now highly complex and politically delicate. Modern technology has belied the predictions of George Orwell in his *1984*. Technology has facilitated 'smallness' as much as 'bigness' and put relatively more power into the hands of smaller governments in relation to bigger governments, and into the hands of individuals in comparison with governments of all sizes. The result has been characterized as 'a new medievalism' in world politics.[10]

THE UK'S FOREIGN POLICY RESOURCES

The constraints outlined above, however, are not necessarily all to the disadvantage of the United Kingdom. The country has some interesting resources with which to operate in this deeply interdependent environment. Its economic status as an actor in the world is far from simple. In an absolute sense, the UK is certainly no longer a pillar of the world economic order as it was in the 1950s when it was one of the state managers of the Bretton Woods system, sat at the centre of the 'Sterling Area' and (in 1954) accounted for around 19 per cent of the world's manufacturing exports and had an impressive merchant marine to facilitate its export position. In the 1990s the UK accounts for less than five per cent of world manufacturing exports and is between 15th and 20th in economic rankings when GDP is measured on a per capita basis or where manufacturing competitiveness is assessed. Nevertheless, the UK economy, in absolute terms, is still the sixth largest in the world with a GDP in 1995 of over $1014 billion.[11] It performs strongly in the oil, high technology and service industries. Service industries account for over 60 per cent of total British output (and about the same proportion of employment).[12] In 1996 the UK was second only to the US in the inward and outward flows of foreign direct investment.[13] And it still accounts for over half of all incoming US and Japanese investment in the European Union. Some 3000 major international companies operate in Britain as foreign subsidiaries with a marked concentration (some 26 per cent of the total) in electronics, computing, office equipment and chemical/pharmaceuticals. Over 2000 major UK companies operate abroad – almost half of them with divisions or subsidiaries in Germany alone.

Whichever selections of economic data are made, a generally consistent picture emerges of a UK that has a significant – if not a structural – role in the international economy, but that role is partly based on the depth of international economic penetration, balanced by the financial outreach, of the UK economy. It is a country that has a major stake in international economic growth and a liberal trading regime, a country that both benefits and suffers to a disproportionate extent from the booms and recessions of the world economy. Its trading patterns are similar to those of its major European partners, though a few percentage points more 'international' when flows of trade are examined. Its most high-value trade is in services and invisibles, but it also has a vigorous minerals trade position – based on the extent of North Sea oil – and a number of low-value, bulk trade relationships with more distant countries such as Russia, South Africa and the countries of West Africa and South America. The maritime dimension of the UK's economic status should be seen in this light.

Its broader diplomatic resources, too, conform to the same general pattern. In the 1940s and 1950s the diplomatic role of the UK as a core member of the United Nations with a permanent (P5) seat on the Security Council, powerful armed forces still based predominantly on a world-class navy that operated around the globe as a matter of course, the residue of empire and the emerging Commonwealth made it a structural diplomatic actor on a world scene dominated by the Cold War. Now, though considerably reduced as a maritime power, the UK emerges as a useful and respected diplomatic player that has the ability at least 'to make a difference' in world politics.[14] The Commonwealth remains a potential source of diplomatic influence (as well as implied defence commitments with the burgeoning of civil disorder in the developing world); the UK still retains a disproportionate voice in the management of the World Bank and the International Monetary Fund, based on its role in their foundation; and the country maintains a large diplomatic representation in the world – some 221 posts in 1997 – and a Foreign and Commonwealth Office (FCO) budget of just over £1 billion. In addition, the UK's military establishment now provides it with more diplomatic influence than at any time since the 1950s. The growth of peace support operations – involving a significant maritime element as essential infrastructure as in the case of the naval task group in the Adriatic to support UK operations in Bosnia – coupled with the accent on *political* effectiveness as a measure of *military* success, has highlighted the qualities of British Armed Forces more than the Cold War ever did. Maritime and air aviation operations in the Gulf since 1991 have highlighted the political sensitivity and the complex interactions between the use of force and the achievement of complex political objectives as never before. In this respect, the flexibility of the maritime element as a device for political signalling – 'presence' without threat that can quickly be transformed into a presence with a high threat, and with many gradations in between – comes into its own where operations have to be conducted in the context of deep interdependence. This has reinforced the UK's contribution to the UN, established its centrality – at least in defence matters – within the EU, and provided an important source of interaction with many different countries through training programmes, multinational exercises and military education within the UK. The closeness of the armed forces to those of the United States is also a tangible diplomatic asset, giving the UK a potential to help bridge the growing gap in security policies between Europe and the United States. Not least, the country enjoys the benefits of the English language as the international lingua franca – English is the official language of some 60 countries around the world – which gives it the opportunity (so far largely unrealized) to help educate future elites from all over the world, and to promote British attitudes and culture through the British Council, which operates in over 80 states, and the BBC, which broadcasts to over 120 million people outside the UK.

In a world order – and even more in a regional setting – dominated by deep interdependence, the UK's resources in external affairs are by no means slight. For the management of such interdependence requires the ability to deal with complex interactions, to deal informally with agents at supra-state, state and non-state levels, and to help build into various regimes as many elements of predictability and established convention as possible. Such requirements cannot be met without the physical resources to deploy military forces in distant theatres throughout the world: not just for military operations *per se*, but for technical assistance, training, support to the civil power and other functions which Maritime Doctrine defines as the 'benign application of maritime power'.[15] All this, in a word, tends to play to the UK's strengths. Its stake in the international economy and its diplomatic attributes can all be employed to best advantage in an interdependent context which – by definition – tends to be a great leveller on the more powerful. To put it crudely, therefore, one could say that the UK has a potentially more significant role to play within the full spectrum of interdependence – with all its multi-level interactions – than within the more uni-dimensional interactions between states alone.

The paradox, of course, is that any such role has to be played out in the general context of extreme restraint on the actions of government. European society is wealthy and technically innovative, but European governments cannot control their respective societies; at most they can influence them, and even that somewhat less than in the past. It is not surprising, therefore, that the government of the UK has far less control over the national economy than its predecessors of even 25 years ago. The fact that the first Chancellor of the Exchequer in the incoming Labour government of 1997 gave to the Bank of England the power to set interest rates was a spectacular recognition of the need to reassure the international financial markets that henceforth interest rates would only be determined by market forces themselves. The British government finds itself competing with other European governments to set fiscal and regulatory frameworks that will attract inward investment from major private companies; and an 8–10 dollar fluctuation in the price of oil can affect the balance of payments to a greater extent than any Chancellor can hope to achieve in even a 'big' budget. In the foreign policy field it is genuinely difficult to think of bilateral issues between states that are really significant; anything of real importance is invariably multilateral. This, inevitably, is reflected in the military sphere: UK military operations of any significance – particularly those classified as 'power projection' will, of necessity, be multinational and highly complex. For the international political requirements are normally that an operation should be legitimized by large sections of the international community which implies that many states have to send military contingents – 26 in the case of Bosnia – while the domestic political requirements are that an operation should not involve heavy casualties, which implies that high numbers have to be committed where there is any danger and that an all-arms approach will probably be adopted to provide the maximum back-up for forces. The maritime taskforce in the Adriatic that underpinned the Bosnia operation, for example, was as important for its casualty evacuation role as for any of its combat support.

The inescapable conclusion to be drawn from this paradox is that if UK governments can accept – even embrace – the context of extreme restraint on policy that the growth of deep interdependence involves, then the UK can play to its strengths in promoting 'management regimes' among its partners that can help shape the international environment in a way favourable to the country's longer-term interests.

This, however, is more easily said than done, since the implications, even if we consider only the armed forces, are considerable. It implies, for example, that the armed forces will be employed on joint and combined expeditionary operations that are only indirectly tied to tangible UK interests and which may be much more concerned with maintaining unity and influence among partners. This is likely to be difficult to explain adequately to public opinion. It would probably mean that UK defence policy should be more proactive than hitherto in promoting a European Security and Defence Identity, both in NATO and the general framework of the EU. At a deeper level, this notion also implies that the training of the armed forces would be affected: placing much greater emphasis on language training, for example, to allow UK officers to function more easily with other European forces; accepting the idea that the forces may have to perform more gendarmarie, monitoring and policing roles, both on land and sea, than they normally feel comfortable with; learning to operate regularly with non-military actors of all kinds as they contribute to a multi-agency approach to complex problems of disorder, or policing a regime of some sort; perhaps accepting, too, some sacrifices in the specifications of equipment to be procured, in the interests of greater interoperability among allies. Not least, while the close links with US forces are undoubtedly a card in the UK's hand in this situation, governments would not have to be frightened to *play it* – being prepared to diverge from the US – in cases where a bridging/managing role required the UK to throw its military weight behind its European allies. To be fair, UK defence policy has faced all these kinds of issue over recent years, particularly in Bosnia, but it may have to reconcile itself to a lot more of it if the country is to take a leadership role in conditions of deep interdependence.

The economic implications of this approach are even more far-reaching, but can be summed up in the idea that UK policy-makers would have to be a good deal more proactive in setting the agenda for regulatory and promotive frameworks that will help create international management structures – say, for regulating investment into the EU states, promoting a more efficient European defence-industrial base, or coordinating European and Atlantic arms sales guidelines to make them more consistent with arms control objectives. Indeed, in some analyses it is imperative to avoid transatlantic market *failure* – defined as the inability to sustain high quantitative growth through market integration – by having governments create tighter qualitative frameworks of public policy in their respective political, legal, social and ecological sectors. Deep interdependence, in other words, has the effect of creating a threat of economic failure as a penalty for governments who do not recognize the importance of embracing international constraints.[16] Whether or not such dramatic initiatives are unavoidable, the UK could achieve none of these objectives without strong multinational actions and the government could do no more than become an enthusiastic advocate of them. But some of the frameworks that the UK would try to promote might be unfavourable to UK companies or the attractiveness of the country to inward investment, and a delicate balancing act might have to be performed between protecting the interests of 'UK plc' and promoting longer-term interests in shaping the international economic environment.

As the UK has confronted the deepening webs of interdependence of the last quarter century and the greater constraints on policy that it brings with it, successive governments have reacted rather variably in the different sectors that interdependence affects. The early Thatcher governments kicked against the economic constraints but were forced to accept most of them by the mid-1980s.[17] The Major government was unable to handle the political problems that monetary constraints set on the country: European big businesses pushed towards the efficiencies of a single currency while national economic actors – rail operators, vendors, small businesses – feared its short-term economic costs, and the economic judgement became submerged within the political baggage that monetary union carries with it. In truth, fiscal policy throughout Europe is now so generally constrained by the market (and measures of market regulation) that the disciplines of monetary union would probably have a marginal effect on the economic autonomy of EU governments. But the fact remains that monetary union is a politically sensitive issue throughout Europe and the UK has not sought to take any lead in helping to manage this facet of economic interdependence. On the military side, the UK has been constructive in handling the growing 'Europeanization' within NATO and has taken a leading role in promoting the specifics of the Combined Joint Task Force initiative, the reform of NATO command structures, the development of multinational division force structures within NATO, not to mention the specifics of the Implementation Force (IFOR) and Stabilization Force (SFOR) deployments in Bosnia. On the other hand, the UK has been tardy in promoting more military interdependence outside the NATO framework, though it no longer opposes initiatives such as the Eurocorps or the EUROFOR. Nor does it take a particularly proactive role in helping to develop the International Atomic Energy Agency, which is a key player in managing the interdependent interests of the developed world in promoting nuclear materials' safety and as a key monitor of arms control agreements. The picture emerges of a country that can be surprisingly effective in promoting managed interdependence and limited power projection in those sectors in which it chooses to engage, but which invariably takes a short-term view of regime maintenance since it has not generally felt comfortable with the notion of interdependence. It is fair to say that at an operational level – particularly in the maritime sphere – the armed forces have seldom had any difficulty in operating multinationally in complex operations that are also politically delicate because they raise acute pressures of interdependence. Policing in the Gulf, for example, is an international interest that raises the danger of affecting world oil supplies if it is not performed with political sensitivity and high levels of international legitimacy. At the operational level, UK forces have repeatedly shown a high ability to engage in such operations. But at the political level, British governments have felt less comfortable with the requirements of regime maintenance beyond that of policing as such. When British diplomacy is 'on-board' in the service of an international regime, such as the banning of anti-personnel landmines or the enforcement of European border controls etc., it can be disproportionately effective, but Britain is seldom one of the moving forces in getting such international regimes started. The present government has made it clear that this will change in the future, but if it does, it will be going against the generally conservative trends of the past.

If a genuine shift of emphasis is under way, as the Labour government has indicated,[18] then the third dimension of foreign policy constraints become highly relevant – namely those embodied in the domestic structure of external policy-making.

THE UK'S EXTERNAL POLICY-MAKING

Domestic constraints on foreign and defence policy-making have become uniquely powerful over the last two decades. One phenomenon concerns the sensitive nature of public opinion – and hence political legitimacy – to external events. Politicians must address foreign and domestic audiences simultaneously since there is no possibility of tilting a speech in a 'foreign' or 'domestic' direction without the other audience simultaneously knowing about any significant shift in emphasis. Domestic pressure groups, such as the Freedom of Information Campaign, can operate internationally with easy linkage to sister groups in other countries, and genuinely international pressure groups – Amnesty International, Greenpeace, European Nuclear Disarmament, the Gay Rights Movement – have burgeoned in recent years. In 1996 Royal Dutch Shell was forced to change the plans it had made for dumping the *Brent Spar* oil platform at sea, not primarily because of the campaign against it in Britain, but rather because of the economic damage done to Shell's trade in Germany and the Netherlands, where environmental activism is stronger than in the UK. Or again, though McDonald's won its celebrated case in the English High Court against a small group of vociferous individual critics, the case did it enormous damage since critics of McDonald's from all over the world generated a complex on the Internet which pooled complaints, data and research most damaging to the reputation of the company to an extent that could hardly have been accumulated by even a major law firm. For UK governments it means that anti-arms trade campaigners can easily cross-check information offered by the government against other official data sources, publications and broadcasts are very difficult to ban, even on grounds of national security, it is more difficult to resist international moral and ethical trends such as those which affect women or homosexuals serving in the military, and traditionally national 'establishment' interest groups, such as the Confederation of British Industry, the Institute of Directors, the National Farmers' Union or the Trades Union Congress, increasingly see themselves as a component in an international – often European – movement of business leaders, trade unionists or farmers. The interest groups that presently try to represent British fisheries, for example, through a fairly national prism are becoming untypical.

The upshot is that governments have now to try to appeal both to internationalist pressures which take a domestic form *and* domestic demands that arise as a reaction to the forces of internationalism. Thus Amnesty International presses for more liberal asylum laws while tabloid newspapers reflect alarm that the opening of EU internal borders is leading to widespread abuse of the system. Or again, another example might be the Saudi dissident Al-Masari who conducted an international campaign against the Saudi authorities from London through the medium of the Internet and the fax machine. National and international pressure groups resisted his deportation from the UK on the grounds that this would be giving in to Saudi pressure on Whitehall, while Jewish groups were appalled at the anti-Semitic nature of all his other political campaigns. At the extreme, the difficulties that such issues pose have the potential to exercise effective vetoes over any governmental action and to reduce national politics to the simple business of electoral survival.

A second most significant phenomenon is the way in which the UK government remains predominantly structured by domestic categorizations which are trying to get to grips with this unprecedented level of internationalism. Thus, Whitehall deals with agriculture, education, trade, finance, environment, foreign and defence matters as the domestic scene has dictated the departmentalization of government. 'Security policy' or 'environmental policy' are abstractions that are meant to be addressed at the higher levels of coordination, essentially through the machinery of cabinet committees and Cabinet Office liaison. But the reality is that Whitehall's categories are becoming more anachronistic and in a tightly centralized cabinet system such as the UK's, the abstractions of policy are only given sporadic attention. Individual Whitehall departments 'take the lead' on issues as appropriate – the MoD on arms control, the FCO on EU security policy, the DTI on world trade issues – and the system 'coordinates' around that department with major directions being established at cabinet committee level, endorsed, if appropriate, by the full Cabinet. There has been surprisingly little experimentation with this system over the years that the international context has changed so dramatically. The Wilson governments of the 1960s made some attempts to reorganize the most strategic areas of government into 'super-ministries' such as the Ministry of Technology and the Department of Economic Affairs to boost the UK's economic performance, but the attempt was short-lived and not judged a success. Even the free-market reformist zeal of the Thatcher governments did not extend to bureaucratic reform; the Thatcher revolution was intended to be carried through in attitudes rather than structures. The Civil Service values its norms of professionalism so highly that it is naturally nervous of structural change that might undermine its essential quality and would rather be obedient to an 'attitude revolution' that can change – as it rapidly did after May 1997 – with the election to power of a different political party.

The result of all this has produced a third phenomenon, namely the concentration within Whitehall on efficient coordination. A mixture of elements such as the long-standing centralization of government, the role of the Civil Service, the business culture of British society and a tradition of general efficiency have made UK government genuinely good at policy coordination. The UK is certainly better at the preparation and coordination of external policy than most of its international partners. The danger, however, is that coordination absorbs so much bureaucratic energy that it militates against long-term thinking or real policy coherence. The British are very good at preparing for the next but one summit and asking the detailed questions necessary to make others' suggestions a practical reality. But the British are not good at defining clear international policy goals for the medium term or much beyond. At a time of rapid international change this makes the status quo orientation of the

UK seem like sheer conservatism to many of the UK's partners and (while accepting that a status quo power can be useful to have in all alliances) risks marginalization or self-fulfilling policy failure in an era when politicians are struggling to match their imaginations to the pace of international events.

The result of these three phenomena is that foreign and defence policy cannot be isolated in any significant way from domestic concerns and the penetration of international forces into the domestic environment. To a greater degree than ever before, external policy is just another area of policy with which governments have to deal and, since the barriers between policy areas are so porous, not deserving of greater deference than other aspects of policy. The British public is not noticeably 'maritime-minded' these days, and however cost-effective the exercise of 'sea power' may be, the fact remains that as individual platforms, ships are very expensive and represent a large number of eggs in a small number of baskets. Maritime planners have to make greater efforts to establish quite how maritime power projection can be consistent with the complexities of modern external policy. The case will not make itself as it appeared to do in the nineteenth century and for long periods in the twentieth.

Deep interdependence means that there is a great deal more to coordinate and that it is more difficult to maintain policy coherence within that coordinating function. Interdependence has long been noted for shortening governmental horizons while lengthening business and private horizons. In short, if the UK has some distinct advantages to offer in helping to manage a condition of deep interdependence, its executive machinery is not well-adapted to cope with the pressures. While the general skills of the operators are not in serious doubt – the Civil Service, the military, the leaders of finance and major industries, even the political leadership – the fact remains that the UK governmental machine has yet to come to terms with the forces of interdependence as they increasingly impact upon society.

CONCLUSION

The nature of the international environment, the general resources for the pursuit of power projection and the mode of governmental policy-making all interact in a courtly dialectical dance. It is dialectical, because each element has some capacity to shape the nature of the other two; and it is courtly because the elements interact with each other in a series of evolving conventions. The result at this juncture in the transition between two historical eras is that the UK government is highly constrained in the way it can pursue external policy in conditions of deep interdependence. But 'constraint' should be understood as a relative term. Aside from the United States – which might be described as only partially constrained – all the UK's partner governments suffer from a similar fate. Governments are weakening in relation to the economic and social forces surrounding them. If it wants to play a traditional role the UK could maintain a relatively high level of influence among partner governments themselves, like the butler amid the shipwrecked *nouveaux riches* who rises to the occasion among the survivors in a lifeboat. On the other hand, the UK could choose to be a significant, if not the central, player in an altogether bigger game where governments try to promote the underlying frameworks to manage contemporary interdependence in directions that are peaceful and prosperous.

The UK has an interesting set of resources to devote to this game if it so chooses, of which its military assets, and particularly its ability to engage in expeditionary military operations of all kinds, looms rather large. In this respect, maritime power projection will have a crucial role in maintaining the relevance and potency of such operations. Few other countries, even within the developed Western world, are so well-placed. But it is not a game that can be played casually or half-heartedly. If the UK wants to be as significant an actor as possible in this situation (and it is not automatic that any country has to want to be 'significant' – being simply 'comfortable' might be preferable), then it must try to use its external policy resources and its policy-making machine to best effect. But in so doing, they will be changed by the experience. That is the logic of a dialectical relationship. And though we may now be living in a profoundly post-Marxist world, Marx himself would certainly have understood this fact. The military, and particularly the maritime dimensions of the UK's military power, no less than the government, can help give the UK some added significance in the present international environment, but only if it accepts that it is likely to become more explicitly a part of the interdependence phenomenon itself.

NOTES

1. Of the remaining 13 Overseas Territories, Gibraltar and Bermuda account for around 100 000 of this population total.
2. *Statement on the Defence Estimates 1995: Stable Forces in a Strong Britain*, Cm.2800, (London: HMSO, 1995), para. 205.

3. On the ethical dimension in foreign policy see the FCO's 'Mission Statement', 12 May 1997, 'Statement by the Foreign Secretary', Foreign and Commonwealth Office, Verbatim Service, VS08/97, 12 May 1997. On environmental emphasis see Robin Cook's interview with the *Sunday Telegraph*, 22 June 1997, p. 5. An explicit statement on the importance of conflict prevention was made in the two government seminars on the Strategic Defence Review during July 1997, 'Strategic Defence Review – Seminars Held on 3 and 11 July 1997', Ministry of Defence (circulated document), 2 September 1997, pp. 7, 14.

4. Richard Falk, 'State of Siege: Will Globalization Win Out?', *International Affairs*, vol. 73, no. 1, January 1977, pp. 123–36.

5. See, for example, W. H. Reinicke, 'Transatlantic Economic Relations and the Globalization of the World Economy', in Centro Studi di Politica Internazionale, *Globalization in the Economy, Regionalization in Security?* (Rome: CeSPI, 1997).

6. R. Gilpin, *The Political Economy of International Relations*, (Princeton, NJ: Princeton University Press, 1987), pp. 131–4.

7. Only thirty years ago, even Ford would manufacture different designs and specifications for cars sold from Ford UK as opposed to Ford Germany, to satisfy two separate national markets.

8. The metropolitan economies of Europe have divided countries since the beginnings of industrialization in the nineteenth century: see N. Davies, *Europe: A History* (Oxford: Oxford University Press, 1996), pp. 764–5; but until the last thirty years, this did not promote high interdependence, and governments did not find that this diminished their authority to any significant extent.

9. See *Unsettled Times*, Report of the Chatham House Study Group (London: Royal Institute of International Affairs, 1996).

10. This notion was originally developed by Hedley Bull, *The Anarchical Society* (London: Macmillan, 1977), and has received more attention since then.

11. Official OECD figures.

12. M. Clarke, *British External Policy-making in the 1990s* (London: Macmillan/Royal Institute of International Affairs, 1992), pp. 44–52.

13. World Investment Report, quoted in T. Dodd, *The Strategic Defence Review*, House of Commons Library, Research Paper 97/106, 23 October 1997, p. 22.

14. This phrase was used by the Secretary of State for Defence at a public seminar in the Ministry of Defence, 5 November 1997, to describe the government's aim in promoting an internationalist foreign and security policy.

15. See BR1806, *The Fundamentals of British Maritime Doctrine* (London: HMSO, 1995), pp. 103–4.

16. Reinicke, 'Transatlantic Economic Relations and the Globalization of the World Economy', pp. 36–37.

17. See R. D. Putnam and N. Bayne, *Hanging Together: Co-operation and Conflict in the Seven-Power Summits* (London: Sage, 1987).

18. 'A Programme for Britain', Speech by the Foreign Secretary in Hamburg, 9 September 1997, Foreign and Commonwealth Office, *Verbatim Service*, VS12/97, 10 September 1997.

7 Gunboat Diplomacy: Outmoded or Back in Vogue?
Malcolm H. Murfett

Lord Palmerston once remarked that while diplomats and protocols were useful in themselves, in his opinion there were no better peace-keepers than well appointed three-deckers.[1] Palmerston's conviction that the Royal Navy was the key to British power projection overseas may be seen in his use of naval vessels to buttress British foreign and defence policy initiatives around the globe in time of peace. His chauvinistic truculence, therefore, found suitable expression in what was described as 'gunboat diplomacy'.[2] His dramatic naval initiatives, as popular at home as they were detested abroad, never failed to make a startling impact on those coastal states who were brought into confrontation with ships of the Royal Navy.

Although sophisticated technological advances have revolutionized naval vessels since those heady, imperialistic days of *Pax Britannica*, the principles that lay behind Palmerston's use of naval policy remain stubbornly familiar a century and a half later. Naval power continues to be used to defend a state's interests and bring influence to bear on other nations. Nowadays, of course, the pejorative term gunboat diplomacy is rarely used in articles and books written on the subject of the strategic deployment of sea power.[3] Avoidance of the term, however, does not constitute an absence of the application of this most durable of concepts.

Far from it. Sir James Cable has done more than most to make us aware just how tenacious a hold gunboat diplomacy still has on those who shape naval policy in the modern world.[4] His convincing work on this robust, practical concept has set a standard that other theorists, such as Edward Luttwak, Ken Booth and Eric Grove among others, have modified but not overturned.[5]

At this point it is appropriate to indicate in what direction this argument is set to go. It accepts the general scholarly consensus that gunboat diplomacy, for want of a better term, still exists. By examining why it continues to do so in the much changed political environment of the post-Cold War era, this chapter will demonstrate just what relevance this political application of naval power in peacetime has for us as we approach the dawn of a new millennium.

Most systems that last for many generations do so because they are successful in one form or another. Gunboat, or coercive, diplomacy is no exception to this general rule. Despite the vast changes that have taken place in the world since the mid-Victorian era, the coercive role that a navy – whether great or small – can perform in peacetime against a littoral state has survived virtually intact. Navies remain well suited as power brokers. Luttwak accounts for their long-established role as military-cum-political arbiters with his notion of active and latent naval suasion. He believes that perception is everything. Operational success in peacetime may not stem necessarily from the actual firepower of the naval vessel/s sent on any specific task by a particular state, but from the victim's assessment of the potential power of the state that has sent the vessel or fleet in question to do its bidding.[6] While this theory would hold valid for situations in which a more powerful nation asserts itself successfully against a smaller state, it hardly explains adequately why on some celebrated occasions smaller powers can triumph over far larger adversaries, as was the case when Iceland prevailed in its long-running series of Cod Wars with the United Kingdom in the 1970s.[7]

Cable, with the benefit of hindsight, has no difficulty in ascribing Iceland's success in the inhospitable reaches of the North Atlantic to the application of purposeful force.[8] This is one of four categories or modes of coercive diplomacy which he identifies – definitive, catalytic and expressive being the other types – any of which may be attempted by vessels ranging from a single ship to a multi-faceted amphibious fleet.[9] Nonetheless, Cable's definition of gunboat diplomacy refers, somewhat paradoxically, to a limited application of force short of war. Since nuclear-powered and armed aircraft carriers can hardly be seen as limited in any sense of that term, the definition needs further elaboration.[10] Essentially, limited in this context may not mean the actual force applied to a specific operation, it may not even mean acting with restraint, but it does mean that the naval action should succeed in gaining its objective short of war. This is an important distinction since the aim of any coercive diplomacy is to be successful in gaining a particular objective. That ultimate objective may indeed be compromised, or lost altogether, if the initial naval operation leads to war between the two adversaries. One need look no further than the Argentinian invasion of the Falkland Islands in 1982 to see the truth of this statement.[11]

In its crudest form, of course, gunboat diplomacy has been regularly employed over the years by governments who have wished to support their policy towards a foreign adversary with a practical demonstration of naval force. This might be construed as posturing or bullying, heroic or cynical, ill-advised or timely, but it has been embarked upon precisely because the ordinary process of diplomacy – the art of negotiation – has been found wanting in certain areas. If a state feels that it is getting nowhere in discussing a contentious matter with a foreign power, it has few viable options left open to it to resolve the matter to its satisfaction. It may appeal to an international body, such as the United Nations or the International Court of Justice, to resolve the matter. It might even be able, if the other power agrees, to rely upon some mutually acceptable third-party arbiter to make a ruling in the case. But if all else fails, and some nations do not even bother to explore any or all of these opportunities, a frustrated or aggrieved power may resort to naval action against a littoral state to cut the Gordian knot if it has the means to do so. More often than not the direct approach works. As states are acutely aware that coercive diplomacy achieves results, where intense discussion and judicious advocacy has failed to achieve a similar breakthrough, the likelihood is that direct action will remain a significant feature of statecraft in the foreseeable future.

Despite its popularity, a successful application of gunboat diplomacy can never be guaranteed in advance. Some operations may, however, begin with a distinctly greater chance of success than do others. One would imagine that a powerful nation has, all other things being equal, more likelihood of success if it confronts a minor power with limited and unsophisticated defences than would an assailant who wishes to employ gunboat diplomacy against an equally well matched victim. Another key determinant in the success or otherwise of a mission is the size, complexity and duration, as well as the financial, political and opportunity cost, of the naval action. Obviously the higher these figures are, the more dubious the outcome may be since a variety of military and political motives might arise to undermine public and government confidence in the venture. In other words, a swift seizure of the initiative would be seen as being infinitely preferable to a long-drawn-out, messy operation involving the possibility of countermeasures by the victim and a heightened state of tension between the various adversaries.

Gunboat diplomacy will again be more manageable if the environment in which it is staged is conducive to its use. Major problems have existed in the past when this situation did not apply. This point has particular resonance for those who remember the Royal Navy's unequal riverine encounters with the People's Liberation Army (PLA) mobile ground defence units along the Yangtze River in April 1949.[12] Launching limited

naval action in pursuit of a specific goal short of war is also more likely to
be successful when an assailant can reckon on its adversary being unable,
for whatever reason, to gather allies or other interested parties to support it in opposing any such naval operation. Success may also be more
easily facilitated if the type of action pursued is generally welcomed by
many of the states in the region who may either lend forces, provide supplies or take a benign stance to the operation once it has been mounted.

Sometimes the outcome of gunboat diplomacy is not so easy to predict. For instance, if a naval operation is launched to deter another state
from committing a particular act, the effectiveness of this mission will
almost certainly depend, in the last analysis, on both the nature of the
deterrent and the victim's assessment of the assailant's overall intentions. If the former assumes the latter will be prepared and has the means
to go to great lengths to support its coercive diplomacy, the deterrent
may actually work. If that equation were to come out differently, however,
the victim might decide to issue a challenge of its own that would call the
entire operation into question. Moreover, if the victim thinks that the
naval operation is no more than an expensive bluff, the deterrent mission
will almost certainly be doomed to failure. In those cases where bluff is
not an essential ingredient, however, and where an assailant embarks
upon punitive action, such as a bombardment, or a naval demonstration
(whether singly or as part of a task force) to get a message across to its
adversary, the nature of this communication is unlikely to be misunderstood by the victim even though success in the venture is still far from
assured. If one considers the often fraught nature of the operation in
peacetime, a decision by an assailant to establish a naval blockade and
impose economic sanctions upon its victim may be viewed as a measure
of its deep frustration with and enmity towards its adversary. Apart from
taking a great deal of time to work, economic sanctions are a constant
legal minefield, an economic liability and a high-cost political offensive.
Painful experience has shown that most sanctions policies rarely succeed
in practice. This sobering realization dawned on the British government of
Harold Wilson some thirty years ago when it attempted to use a blockade-
cum-sanctions policy (the ill-fated Beira Patrol) to bring down the errant
Rhodesian Front leadership of Ian Smith.[13] Needless to say its efforts
foundered on some ingenious methods of 'sanctions busting' by Rhodesia's friends and neighbouring states.[14]

Another hazardous and unpredictable example of gunboat diplomacy
concerns the defence and protection of a state's interests, property and
citizens abroad. If the nature of the problem is confined geographically
within a disputed territory or a foreign state, the chance of success may

be a little higher than it would be if the investments and personnel were scattered over a wide area. Nonetheless, even in the best-case scenario this type of naval intervention is likely to be very difficult to orchestrate successfully. Guard ships need regular replenishment and relief and remain a visible irritant to those whose territorial waters they infringe. If a humanitarian mission to evacuate a state's nationals from a foreign country is launched by an assailant, the chance of overall success may be higher since withdrawal may provide the alienated victim arguably with some political kudos and maybe, therefore, less reason to interfere with the rescue effort. Other interventionist roles, such as landing marines to try and bring peace to a war-torn country, may pose insuperable difficulties, as the international community discovered to its cost in Somalia in the post-1992 period.[15] Much can happen, therefore, to disrupt the best laid plans of foreign intervention and/or evacuation procedures and their success is problematic at the best of times.[16]

Before turning to other types of operations that have been launched under the guise of coercive diplomacy, it might be prudent to dwell a little on the great imponderables – the classic variable factors – that may arise during the exercise of these limited naval actions. Variable factors are crucial to the success or failure of any mission. Many cannot be either dismissed or assessed accurately beforehand. Even if the defences of a state are well known by an adversary, it may be difficult to gauge just how well or ineptly these defensive units may perform under pressure. Will, for instance, a victim's air defences prove to be too difficult to contain for the assailant's naval vessels? No matter how efficient a state's intelligence-gathering facilities may be, or how lucid its military appreciations are, the difference between reality and illusion, exaggeration or underestimation, is actually worked out on the spot and can be a very sobering experience for all concerned when these calculations and premises prove to be false or at best unreliable. Even in the most perfect conditions the most elaborate and functional of plans can go badly awry. An unforeseen contingency, for example – sudden illness or accidental misfortune – can wreak havoc or seriously disrupt any plan that has not taken the possibility into consideration. Luck, therefore, may be said to play a part, and an infinitely variable part at that, in any military operation. Heretical though this may be to those blessed with actuarial skills, what makes luck all the more frustrating to commanding officers is that it cannot be quantified accurately in advance.

Despite these reservations and shortcomings, gunboat or coercive diplomacy continues to be used in furtherance of international disputes. One of the reasons why it still has relevance in the modern world is because it can be used on a wide variety of occasions to achieve certain tangible results. Its cosmopolitan appeal is shown in the almost bewildering number of enterprises that it has been employed to resolve. It has, for instance, often been used to score political points against a foreign power. Throughout the 1980s, for example, the United States deliberately challenged a unilateral claim made by Libya that the Gulf of Sidra (Sirte) lay in its territorial waters. US warships made repeated violations of the disputed area and in 1981, 1986 and 1989 serious incidents took place in the Gulf as a result of these provocative acts by carriers of the Sixth Fleet.[17] Provocative acts of gunboat diplomacy by the Americans have not been solely confined to their potential or actual enemies. Since August 1985 they have sent several ships through the disputed North West Passage to contest the Canadian claim to sovereignty over the waterway.[18] Another device favoured by the US Navy has been its insistence on stationing fleet units in a particularly important foreign region, for example the Mediterranean, where its presence may cajole, deter and/or provoke its potential enemies, while encouraging, motivating and supporting its own allies and friends. Sometimes American naval operations in peacetime have taken on a more definitive nature than even these purposeful or expressive acts have done. In October 1983, for example, President Reagan sanctioned Operation *Urgent Fury* which was designed to bring about the fundamental overthrow of Maurice Bishop's New Jewel Movement in Grenada which he and his administration violently disliked.[19] On other occasions, the threat of the use of force has been sufficient to achieve the same results as President Kennedy discovered when a powerful US naval demonstration, including the carriers USS *Franklin D. Roosevelt* and USS *Valley Forge*, finally convinced the Trujillo family to yield power in the Dominican Republic in November 1961.[20]

Gunboat diplomacy has also been used to maintain international peace or prevent a war from spreading and enveloping other states in a given region. Ships of interested third parties may be used to prevent an aggressive state from embarking upon or succeeding in its intended seaborne invasion of another power to which it is opposed. Warships may also be used to protect mercantile vessels from the attentions of predatory states and to keep waterways open to international traffic.

Naval vessels, converted from their original use, have also taken on more shadowy roles in the past, specifically in the realm of electronic surveillance and intelligence-gathering activities.[21] Nowadays, satellites provide a far more comprehensive picture of what is happening in a particular country. Nonetheless spy ships, as the South Koreans discovered in 1996, can have many uses and have not gone out of fashion in Pyongyang.[22]

While there clearly is a sinister side to some aspects of gunboat diplomacy, not everything carried on its name is negative. One might, for instance, mention some of the maritime constabulary duties which are usually reserved for a state's coastguard but which may also find a place under the heading of coercive diplomacy. These tasks involve combating the menace of international piracy and terrorism, detecting and preventing both the traffic of illegal immigration and the smuggling of controlled narcotics and/or contraband goods, let alone dealing with problems of countering environmental pollution at sea. No less an authority than Sir James Cable seems to think that even these tasks may be seen to fall within the ambit of gunboat diplomacy.[23] Once again, of course, it is a definitional problem. If these illegal acts can be attributed to a particular state or group of states, then the classic definition of gunboat diplomacy may be seen to hold. For under these circumstances, those states wishing to stop these illegal activities would be able to direct a limited naval operation against those sponsoring or condoning these acts. Whether states can either individually or collectively organize an effective response to these problems remains to be seen, however. Even if such a naval initiative was mounted, the success or failure of the mission might well depend upon the level of operational sophistication achieved by the perpetrators of these acts and the level of state corruption that protects these criminals from being apprehended and brought to justice.[24]

By examining the past we may provide ourselves with a key to understanding the present. Whether we shall be able to predict the future unerringly, however, is much less certain. As Professor Geoffrey Till observed in 1982 in his *Maritime Strategy and the Nuclear Age*: 'History provides insights and questions, not answers.'[25] Nevertheless, predictions are what policy-makers and ministerial officials require, so let us try to visualize what problems are likely to emerge in the short to medium term that might be resolved by gunboat or coercive diplomacy.

One familiar naval operation that has been used in the past and almost certainly will be revived in the future is that brokered by a state seeking to promote its rights to a certain disputed area of territory. One need look no further than the divisive problem of the Spratly Islands to see at least four nations – China, the Philippines, Taiwan and Vietnam – currently vying for the right of sole ownership to this island chain in the South China Sea. Sino-Vietnamese enmity, scarcely absent at the best of times, has already resulted in naval action over the ownership and administration of the Paracel Islands in the same South-East Asian region and may well do so again in the future.[26] On a much smaller scale even ownership of small fishing shoals in the South China Sea is bitterly contested between rival powers and provides irresistible opportunities for a range of publicity seekers and/or political extremists to make some provocative gesture in these disputed areas – action which is calculated to infuriate those states who also have a claim to the shoal in question.[27]

If we stay in the Asian region and move northwards the whole question of the Taiwan Straits is pregnant with possibilities. While one would not expect a Chinese thrust from the mainland within the short term, particularly in view of continued American support for Taiwan, the relationship between Taipei and Beijing will have to be monitored closely and is likely to offer various opportunities for gunboat diplomacy in the future.[28] In the East China Sea a dispute concerning China, Japan and Taiwan over the fate of the Senkaku (Diaoyu) Islands remains a lively and extremely sensitive issue to all three governments.[29] In North-East Asia gunboat diplomacy has been no stranger to the Korean peninsula and the endemic crisis between Seoul and Pyongyang looks likely to offer renewed instances of it in the near future. Further north the Kurile Island chain remains an object of contention between Russia and Japan. This dispute is also unlikely to disappear off the strategic map of Asia in the foreseeable future.

It is in the Pacific that one of the most startling developments of recent times has taken place. Under the Third United Nations Conference on the Law of the Sea (UNCLOS III) a new Law of the Sea Convention was established in 1982. This has revolutionized an island state's control over the ocean around it. By extending territorial waters to 12 nautical miles (nm) (22 km), exclusive economic zones (EEZs) to 200 nm (360 km), providing rights to areas even beyond the EEZs and by developing an archipelagic concept that places ownership of the sea's resources even more firmly under their control, the potential significance of island communities has grown enormously in the past fifteen years.[30] As Anthony Bergin points out in *Naval Power in the Pacific*, Kiribati, with 690 square kilometres of land area, now controls 3.5 million square kilometres of the sea. The Marshall Islands, whose land area is a mere 181 square kilometres, now has a fishing zone of 2.1 million square kilometres.[31] As the economic resources of these island states improve, the temptation for interference will grow from those powers with envious eyes on the financial returns they could make if they incorporated any of these minor states into their own sphere of influence. Watch this space might be an appropriate message to all concerned.[32]

Elsewhere in the same ocean where the waters of the South-Eastern Pacific meet the cold murkiness of the South Atlantic, Chilean ownership of the islands of Picton, Lennox and Nueva in the Beagle Channel, settled by agreement with Argentina in November 1984 and ratified by both countries in May 1985, has never been popular in Argentina and could be subject to naval exploitation as it was about twenty years ago in January 1978.[33] Whether the historic, national quest for the Falkland Islands or South Georgia will tempt a post-Menem administration in Buenos Aires to reveal some expressive display of its concern for these territories is difficult to gauge. Definitive force was used and found wanting under General Galtieri and the military junta and is unlikely to be tried again while the British retain troops on the islands. Yet the potential marine, mineral and energy resources of the seas around the Falklands and particularly Antarctica will almost certainly make this inhospitable region a magnet for many of the world's leading powers. In those situations where financial incentives are vast, so is the potential for trouble between states. Gunboat diplomacy may well be seen in one form or another in this region more frequently in the early years of the next century as the race to exploit the continental riches of Antarctica becomes more pronounced.

In European waters, the momentous break-up of the Soviet Union and the deleterious effects this has had upon its former fleet are already well known.[34] Whether the Russian or Ukrainian fleets will exercise any restraint upon small or medium powers in the region is less certain. All the while the two superpowers were active in the Mediterranean, states in the region were likely to think twice about engaging in significant naval actions against their foes. Regional powers, freed from the shackles of superpower rivalry, may not be so inclined to exercise self-restraint in future. If one looks at the situation pessimistically it would be possible to predict a more turbulent future in the Mediterranean, Adriatic and Aegean. Plans hatched by states with a singular purpose in mind, which once might have been shelved, may now be implemented. While it would be foolish to discount this possibility altogether, the continuing strong presence of the US Fleet in the Mediterranean gives cause for hope since it is likely to retain some form of deterrent effect upon all but the most mercurial of powers. Even so it would be very rash of anyone to conclude that coercive diplomacy will not put in an appearance in the familiar Eastern Mediterranean trouble spots from Cyprus to the Holy Land, or elsewhere, such as along the coast of the Maghreb. Equally, and as unfortunately, the littoral states of Africa and the Middle East always seem to be prime targets for naval action of some kind. It is a sad fact in the post-Cold War world that serious disagreements and disputes between independent states show no sign of abating. No region is devoid of such problems or crises but some areas appear to be more prone to them than others for a host of reasons that lie beyond the scope of this present essay.[35]

At this juncture it would repay us to remember that states do not have to resort to definitive force to articulate their demands. Depending upon the circumstances of an international dispute, the leaders of an aggrieved state may judge it sufficient for one of their ships to do little more than make its presence felt in the area by showing the flag in foreign waters. Such simplicity is alluring to developing states with small naval forces at their disposal. Despite the fact that the number of naval powers in the world now exceeds 130, there are many who do not have the economic or military resources to indulge in some full-scale offensive against a foreign power.[36] If the stakes are high, more rigorous action may be required but this type of operation is bound to become more complex and costly as a result.

In the years to come a number of navies will have the capacity to mount such high-profile amphibious operations against a determined foe. Apart from the United States and some of the traditional European naval powers, several countries are looking to acquire aircraft carriers and sophisticated weapons systems so as to improve their overall fleet potential and enable them to cater for just this type of operation in the future. China, India, Iran, Japan, South Africa, South Korea and Turkey may be seen to fall into this category. States whose economies have developed rapidly in the recent past, such as Indonesia, Malaysia and Thailand, may also ultimately aspire to join the ranks of the more advanced naval powers.[37] It is interesting to note that the last has just commissioned its first aircraft carrier. Below the medium powers are a motley collection of states, some with high-quality ships and trained personnel that could adopt coercive measures against a neighbouring power relatively easily, others with obsolete craft and inexperienced crews that may be pushed into gunboat diplomacy without necessarily gaining the same results.

Judging from the foregoing analysis, it appears that gunboat diplomacy has stood the test of time. It retains its attraction and utility for states and may be said, therefore, to be neither outmoded nor back in vogue. In reality, it is starkly present in the modern world and shows little sign of being ignored in the future. Gunboat, or coercive, diplomacy predated Palmerston and has survived his demise. It looks destined to be a feature of our international society for a long time to come.[38]

NOTES

1. L. W. Cowie, *From the Peace of Paris to World War I* (London: Nelson, 1996), p. 122.
2. Gunboat diplomacy was essentially a supportive feature of Palmerstonian foreign policy. For a closer examination of what this meant in practice, see Jasper Ridley, *Lord Palmerston* (London: Panther, 1972), pp. 174–6, 315–17, 394, 484, 486–7, 491, 500, 513–15, 624, 728. Cowie quotes from a contemporary of the great Victorian statesman to underline the utility of gunboat diplomacy at this time: 'Generally when Lord Palmerston speaks of diplomacy, he talks also of ships of war.' Cowie, op. cit., p. 122.
3. George Robertson, the current British Secretary of State for Defence, has now begun to refer to 'Defence Diplomacy' as an alternative word for the old practice.
4. James Cable, *Gunboat Diplomacy 1919–1991: Political Applications of Limited Naval Force* (London: Macmillan, 1994).
5. Edward N. Luttwak, *The Political Uses of Sea Power* (Baltimore, Md.: Johns Hopkins University Press, 1974); Ken Booth, *Navies and Foreign Policy* (London: Croom Helm, 1977); Eric Grove, *The Future of Sea Power* (London: Routledge, 1990); Harold J. Kearsley, *Maritime Power and the Twenty-first Century* (Aldershot: Dartmouth Publishing, 1992).
6. Luttwak, op. cit., pp. 1–38.
7. H. Jónnsson, *Friends in Conflict* (London: C. Hirst, 1982). Eric Grove, *Vanguard to Trident: British Naval Policy Since World War II* (London: Bodley Head, 1987), pp. 300–3.
8. Cable, op. cit., pp. 199–200, 202–3.
9. Ibid., pp. 15–64, 100–15.
10. Ibid., pp. 7–14. It is noteworthy that Cable does not include the activities of submarines as platforms for gunboat diplomacy. 'A warship equipped only with nuclear missiles cannot use or threaten limited force. Other submarines spend much time peering and prying around foreign naval bases. If this is just reconnaissance and training for a potential war, it is not gunboat diplomacy.' Sir James Cable, 'Gunboat Diplomacy's Future', *US Naval Institute Proceedings*, August 1986, p. 38.
11. David Brown, *The Royal Navy and the Falklands War* (London: Leo Cooper, 1987); Martin Middlebrook, *Task Force: The Falklands War 1982* (Harmondsworth: Penguin Books, 1987); Geoffrey Till, *Maritime Strategy and the Nuclear Age* (New York: St. Martin's Press, 1982), pp. 239–56; Eric Grove (1987), op. cit., pp. 356–84.
12. Malcolm H. Murfett, *Hostage on the Yangtze: Britain, China and the Amethyst Crisis of 1949* (Annapolis, Md.: Naval Institute Press, 1991).
13. Cable (1994), op. cit., pp. 107–8; Grove (1987), op. cit., pp. 300–1.
14. Ben Pimlott, *Harold Wilson* (London: Harper Collins, 1992), pp. 375–6, 378–81, 398, 452, 455–8, 725–6.
15. *Keesing's Record of World Events*, vol. 39, 1993, pp. R20–1; vol. 40, 1994, pp. R24–5; vol. 41, 1995, p. R30; vol. 42, 1996, p. R29.
16. Robert S. Wood, 'Intervention and the Use of Force to Achieve Limited Regional Objectives to Restore Order', in Peter T. Haydon and Ann L. Griffiths (eds), *Maritime Security and Conflict Resolution at Sea in the*

Post-Cold War Era (Halifax, Nova Scotia: Centre for Foreign Policy Studies, Dalhousie University, 1994), pp. 199–205. For a glimpse into the future, see the article by the US Marine Corps, 'Commentary on OMFTS' [Operational Maneuvers From The Sea], *Marine Corps Gazette*, July 1996, pp. 13–15.

17. Mahmoud G. Elwarfally, *Imagery and Ideology in US Policy Toward Libya, 1969–1982* (Pittsburgh, Pa.: Univ. of Pittsburgh Press, 1988), pp. 173–5; P. Edward Haley, *Qaddafi and the United States Since 1969* (New York: Praeger, 1984), pp. 227, 262, 275–8; Stephen Howarth, *To Shining Sea: A History of the United States Navy, 1775–1991* (London: Weidenfeld & Nicolson, 1991), pp. 545–6; Cable (1994), op. cit., pp. 206, 209, 211.

18. In the first instance, *Polar Sea*, a US Coastguard icebreaker, entered the North West Passage on 2 August 1985 on passage from Greenland to Alaska. See *Keesing's Contemporary Archives, Record of World Events*, vol. XXXI, 1985, Nov. 1985, pp. 33983–4; Cable (1994), op. cit., pp. 151, 209.

19. M. Adkin, *Urgent Fury: The Battle for Grenada* (London: Leo Cooper, 1989); Robert J. Beck, *The Grenada Invasion: Politics, Law, and Foreign Policy Decisionmaking* (Boulder, Colo.: Westview Press, 1993); S. Davidson, *Grenada* (Aldershot: Gower, 1987); P. M. Dunn and W. Watson (eds), *American Intervention in Grenada* (Boulder, Colo.: Westview Press, 1985).

20. J. Barlow Martin, *Overtaken by Events* (New York: Doubleday, 1966), chapter 4; Cable (1994), op. cit., p. 190.

21. Cable (1994), op. cit., pp. 195, 197, 201, 205, 208. See also J. R. Hill, *Maritime Strategy For Medium Powers* (London: Croom Helm, 1986), pp. 92–6; Grove (1990), op. cit., p. 55.

22. *Keesing's Record*, vol. 42, no. 9 (Oct.1996), pp. 41272–3.

23. Cable (1994), op. cit., pp. 147–57; Michael Pugh and Frank Gregory, 'Maritime constabulary roles for non-military security', in Michael Pugh (ed.), *Maritime Security and Peacekeeping: A Framework for United Nations Operations* (Manchester: Manchester University Press, 1994), pp. 74–101.

24. Hill, op. cit., pp. 99–107, 122–7.

25. Till, op. cit., pp. 224–5.

26. M. S. Samuels, *Contest for the South China Sea* (London: Methuen, 1982); Cable (1994), op. cit., p. 211.

27. According to a Reuters report from Manila carried by the *Sunday Times* on 11 May 1997, the latest of these incidents took place on 30 April 1997 at Scarborough Shoal some distance off the west coast of Zambales province on the island of Luzon. China issued a diplomatic protest against the activities of Filipino fishermen who had not only driven off two Chinese fishing vessels from these disputed waters but had then compounded matters by hoisting a Philippine national flag on the shoal.

28. An example of the US commitment is evident in the position taken by Newt Gingrich, Speaker of the US Congress, in 1997. Gingrich confided to the international press that he had indicated to his Chinese hosts that the United States was more than an innocent bystander in the China–Taiwan struggle. He is alleged to have stated to Wang Daohan, the former Mayor of Shanghai and an influential figure in relations between the mainland and Taiwan: 'We understand that in principle you will not renounce the right to use force. We want you to understand that we will defend Taiwan.

Period.' *International Herald Tribune*, 31 March 1997. He backtracked a little from this provocative position a few days later. See *International Herald Tribune*, 2 April 1997.

29. Another twist to this ongoing drama was provided by the landing of a radical Japanese MP on one of the disputed islands in the Senkaku chain on 6 May 1997, an event faithfully recorded for posterity by the ubiquitous camera crew. See *International Herald Tribune*, 7 May 1997.

30. Anthony Bergin, 'New Developments in the Law of the Sea', in Hugh Smith and Anthony Bergin (eds), *Naval Power in the Pacific: Toward the Year 2000* (Boulder, Colo.: Lynne Rienner, 1993), pp. 65–82.

31. Ibid., p. 67; Gert de Nooy (ed.), *The Role of European Naval Forces after the Cold War* (The Hague: Kluwer Law International, 1996), pp. 105–84.

32. An interesting insight into the problem facing smaller naval powers in the Asia-Pacific region is set out in Sam Bateman's 'The Functions of Navies in the Southwest Pacific and Southeast Asia', in Smith and Bergin (eds), op. cit., pp. 129–43.

33. *Keesing's Contemporary Archives*, vol. XXIV 1978, 24 Mar. 1978, pp. 28890–1; *Keesing's Record of World Events*, vol. XXXI (1985), pp. 33517–18, 33579; Cable (1994), op. cit., p. 204.

34. Captain Richard Sharpe has reminded us, however, of the old adage: 'Russia is never as strong as it looks; Russia is never as weak as it looks.' See his foreword to *Jane's Fighting Ships 1996–1997* (Coulsden: Jane's Information Group, 1996), p. 17.

35. For a discussion on this point see, for example, S. P. Huntingdon, 'The Clash of Civilizations', *Foreign Affairs*, Autumn 1996, pp. 617–37.

36. The International Institute for Strategic Studies, *The Military Balance 1996/97* (London: Oxford University Press, 1996).

37. Since this chapter was written, a severe recession in East and South-East Asia has blighted the economies of Indonesia, Malaysia, South Korea and Thailand. What effects this recession will have on defence priorities is unclear at this stage.

38. Cable (1986), op. cit., pp. 38–41.

8 International Peace Support Operations from a Maritime Perspective
Michael Pugh

INTRODUCTION

Given a reversal in the fortunes of United Nations-authorized international peacekeeping operations since the number peaked in 1994, it is an appropriate aim of this chapter to review the politics and strategic value of peace support operations. The chapter begins with the UN's discovery of the maritime dimension and achievements since 1989. It moves on to the credibility crisis precipitated by the problems that enveloped recent UN-authorized operations and the pre-eminence of nationalism in US defence policy. It ends with an assessment of the institutional interests invested in peace support operations. Much of the UN's experience of maritime peacekeeping, and the 'nuts and bolts' of the operational aspects, have been addressed elsewhere and will not be recounted here.[1]

First, however, it is important to offer a brief comment on terminology in view of the confusion of vocabulary currently used to describe international operations. The term 'peace support operations' (PSOs), borrowed from UK and NATO land doctrine, is used to encompass a range of intercessions usually authorized by the United Nations – from monitoring to enforcing embargoes and imposing stability on parties who have signed a peace agreement. 'Peacekeeping' is used here in a narrower, specific sense to refer to the traditional role of blue berets in interpositioning by consent between sides that were previously in violent conflict. The more general designation, 'peace support operations', is actually more useful for the maritime environment than 'peacekeeping' because it gets away from the restricted connotation of interpositioning with consent – a less relevant concept at sea than on land.

REDISCOVERY OF THE MARITIME ENVIRONMENT

In the period since Mikhail Gorbachev came to power in the Soviet Union in 1985, use of the maritime environment for impartial international operations has been discovered, or more accurately rediscovered, by UN member states. They were made aware of the potential during the Tanker War in the Persian Gulf in the 1980s when merchant shipping had to be protected and escorted against attacks by Iran and Iraq. Credit for highlighting the issue should go to the former Soviet Deputy Foreign Minister, Vladimir Petrovsky, and his superior, Eduard Shevardnadze. From the time of the controversy in 1987 over reflagging Kuwaiti oil tankers, the two Soviet officials suggested the extension of UN peacekeeping activities to the sea. They proposed the creation of standing UN maritime task forces to protect and convoy merchant shipping in war-affected zones, and to undertake the conduct of 'good order' and constabulary functions such as ensuring freedom of navigation and dealing with criminal activities and environmental pollution at sea.[2]

Petrovsky's concept may well have been an artifice, primarily intended to offset the new Western build-up in the Persian Gulf during the Iran–Iraq war. It made little headway in the UN, partly because of obvious financial and practical impediments that bedevil all proposals for standing UN forces, and partly because the Western allies were determined not to countenance any such move towards an independent UN capability or to allow their naval predominance in the Gulf to be challenged. Despite the failure of Petrovksy's more ambitious ideas, however, they certainly gave an impetus to the study of maritime contributions, both actual and potential, to peace support operations.[3]

Clearly, too, the end of the Cold War provided a political context in which expansive internationalism could thrive and an economic context in which expensive navies could be made to dwindle by politicians and officials looking for a peace dividend. In these circumstances, maritime establishments explicitly incorporated PSO into the inventory of maritime operations and maritime doctrine.

THE EBB AND FLOW OF INTEREST

In fact, Petrovsky and Shevardnadze had merely *rediscovered* the UN's potential for action at sea, foreshadowed during the League of Nations era.[4] The UN conducted its first maritime operation in the eastern Mediterranean in 1948. A powerful task group of US warships, led by the aircraft carrier USS *Palau*, and a French minesweeper was sent to support the Palestine Truce Commission and the UN Truce Supervision Organization with coastal patrols and the transport of materiel and personnel.[5] Subsequently, between 1962 and 1963, the UN Temporary Executive

Authority in West Irian operated nine vessels provided by the Netherlands and crewed by Pakistanis during the Dutch transfer of power to
Indonesia. Outside the UN, but operating on traditional peacekeeping
principles, three Italian minesweepers have monitored freedom of navigation in the Strait of Tiran under the provisions of the Egypt–Israel
Peace Treaty of 1979. Other maritime operations have included the
Royal Navy patrols off Mozambique in the 1960s to implement a UN
sanctions mandate to prevent oil reaching Rhodesia, and many humanitarian rescue missions such as the rescue of expatriates fleeing the
Yemen in 1986.

Most operations of this kind were considered to be variations in rou-
tine conducted by all navies and maritime establishments rather than
requiring some kind of special status. They have now been swept up,
recategorized, conceptualized, moulded into frameworks and elevated
to doctrinal status. No one suggests that the actual work itself is really
very different from what global navies have always done. New labels
cannot disguise the fact that the fundamental objectives of maritime
forces change little: defence, deterrence, merchant ship protection, maintenance of free navigation and good governance at sea. In peacetime,
these require the habitual tasks of patrolling, monitoring, poise, exercising, the establishment of good command, control and communications and interoperability (both joint and multinational), and so on. One
might be forgiven for wondering whether peace support in the maritime
environment is an artificial notion, designed by academics to keep themselves in business, coining new terms and phrases to create a new club of
expertise. Even if maritime peace support operations merit the attention
lavished on them, how special are they?

In assessing the contemporary situation we have to acknowledge that
peace support operations no longer command the headlines as they did
in the early 1990s. Moreover, the scepticism with which Petrovksy's ideas
were originally greeted appears to have grown. Even the concept of peace
support operations, let alone any proposal for UN standby forces, has its
share of critics.

First, there is doubt about whether the concept of maintaining international peace and security through the UN *per se* is basically sound.
Attacks on the notion come from two main directions. Die-hard real-
ists argue that there are better alternatives such as national defence or
collective security through alliance systems. Radical internationalist critics argue either that the UN simply reflects the hegemonic manipula-
tions of global resources by the most powerful members of the Security
Council or, from a postmodernist perspective, argue that the UN is

part of a moral mission to impose particular, Western, values on societies that may, for example, even choose to be governed by alleged war criminals. The controversy is inherent in the deep-seated and contested views about how the international system works or should work. It does appear to be the case, nevertheless, even in the United States, that both popular, intellectual and governmental support for the UN system is surviving over both ultra-nationalist and radical internationalist critiques.

Second, scepticism about mainstream assumptions gained momentum as a consequence of the UN's credibility crisis after perceived failures in Somalia, Rwanda and Bosnia. The perception is probably not fully justified, given that lives were saved and conditions ameliorated in some of these operations, even if more could have been done. Furthermore, states tend to resort to the UN only for the most intractable disputes, and its credibility is at the mercy of inconsistent support from the major powers who ultimately determine how it performs. In this respect, 'the faults and weaknesses of the UN lie not in the Charter, nor in the Organization, but in the defects of its most powerful members.'[6] Almost by definition, the odds on success are long. Even so, the flaws in the Organization's performance cannot be denied and it was an easy target for Congressional hostility in the United States to which Bill Clinton had to kow-tow in his bid for re-election in 1996.[7]

But it is also important to note that scepticism about peace support operations has been uneven, with the United States taking the most extreme stance among the Western democracies. Elsewhere, doubts were voiced, but without them impeding a trend towards the institutionalization of PSO concepts or hindering renewed efforts to make PSOs work more effectively. It will be suggested here that vested interests have emerged and have had a significant influence on developments. In this respect the situation is very different from the past. Unlike, say, the period between the two world wars when support for collective security had a populist strand (in the UK the League of Nations Union had a million members in 1933), or in the Cold War period (when worldwide campaigns for a nuclear freeze and disarmament had a similar appeal), no one is organizing huge rallies for peace support operations. There is no need: policy-making elites and military establishments are taking PSOs seriously. So, too, are the private-sector defence and security suppliers, for whom the UN represents US\$30 billion worth of contracts annually.[8]

First, however, we should acknowledge the military conservatism in the United States where resistance to PSOs has been strongest.

US EXCEPTIONALISM

As the only remaining superpower, the United States enjoys the luxury of choice about whether or not to take a lead in world affairs. While the State Department and President Clinton's foreign policy advisers attempted to maintain a multilateral, interventionist approach, the Defense Department under Les Aspin and the military under Chairman of the Joint Chiefs of Staff, Colin Powell, pulled in another direction. Basically, the American military remain uncomfortable, both about the risks of getting caught up in long and drawn-out low-intensity wars of limited US interest that remind them of Vietnam,[9] and about the absence from the PSO agenda of the concept of 'winning'. Intervention in intra-state conflicts is messy, a quick exit strategy is usually a delusion and stabilization rather than winning is the objective.

US defence policy is predicated on preparation for the 'near simultaneous' use of decisive force in two major inter-state regional wars. Decisions about intervention are to be taken in the light of criteria laid down in the National Military Strategy of January 1992 and keenly fostered by Colin Powell, then Chairman of the Joint Chiefs of Staff.[10] Subsequent pronouncements – from the Bottom-up Defense Review of 1993, to the notorious presidential directive PDD-25 of May 1994 and statements by Powell's successor, John Shalikashvili – reinforced the article of faith that while localized intra-state contingencies were the more likely, they would be a distraction from the role of US 'warriors' in fighting and winning 'the nation's wars'.[11] This was mirrored in the US military's reluctance to get involved in the conflicts in Rwanda, Haiti, Zaire and Bosnia, the relegation of PSOs to the designation 'Operations Other Than War' (OOTW) and a determination that resources, training and preparation for such interventions should trail well behind preparation for high-intensity, inter-state wars.[12] 'We do deserts, we don't do mountains,' said Shalikashvili apropos of Bosnia.

To some extent, the US Navy and the US Marine Corps can afford to be less dogmatic about this head-in-the-sand approach. Their roles are less compromised by the prospect of casualties in civil wars than the Army or Air Forces because few warlords have the wherewithal to threaten navies and Marines are rewarded for innovation in OOTW situations.[13] Indeed the naval doctrine *From the Sea* (1992) contained the explicit assumption that projecting force ashore in complex emergencies would be a growing role relative to fighting inter-state naval battles at sea. Nevertheless, according to a 1995 US General Accounting Office (GAO) report *Peace Operations: Effects of Training, Equipment and Other*

Factors on Unit Capability, PSOs were having a significantly deleterious impact on the US Navy. The GAO noted that the demand for 'peace operations' in the Caribbean required the Navy to call on non-deployed ships and crews. This extracted people from basic training for an average of 30 days, reassigned ships from other operations and disrupted maintenance schedules.[14]

COMING TO TERMS WITH THE REAL WORLD

The smaller military and naval establishments in other countries have been more willing than the US defence establishment to come to terms with peace support operations, though they have also warned that such operations should not determine defence policy or force structures. Indeed they have attempted to make PSOs relevant by integrating them more effectively into mainstream roles. Thus doctrinal revision in the UK, NATO and among some military advisers in the UN has attempted to adapt principles of war to peace support operations and locate PSOs in a military spectrum of activities with combat readiness a pervasive requirement.[15] UK naval doctrine distinguishes between threatening and benign environments, and acknowledges that peace support operations are capable of being in both.[16] Whatever the flaws in these doctrines, and they can be seen as dangerously lacking in political nuance, they at least recognize that the real world is unstable, not because of distinctive threats to 'the nation's peace', but because of diffuse threats from complex emergencies that require international rather than national responses. Similarly, the creation of a European Maritime Force (EUROMARFOR) by France, Spain, Portugal and Italy, although more a political gesture to do with alliance politics than a force of significance, at least acknowledges that the most likely challenges to southern Europe's security will be from large numbers of refugees from the poor and volatile parts of the Mediterranean or from the internal collapse of states such as Albania.

The Powellite view, however, as reflected in the GAO report on the US Navy, ignored key factors about the post-Gulf War world.

First, it offered a limited view of what constitutes national interests in the absence of major threats to national survival. Ivo Daalder has been properly critical of the ultra-nationalism that failed to recognize that diffuse instabilities might have an impact on US interests. If the impact is limited, the involvement can be as well.[17] Indeed, the Haiti mission itself could hardly be said to have fallen outside even the restrictive PDD-25 criteria for US involvement. Some observers argue that the UN Security Council was manipulated so that an embarrassing influx of Haitian refugees to the United States could be defined as a threat to international peace and security.[18]

Second, spreading the burden multilaterally has distinct advantages and this was amply demonstrated during the war in the former Yugoslavia. The North Atlantic Treaty Organization (NATO)/Western European Union (WEU) operations in the Adriatic could perhaps have been undertaken by a large naval power alone, but the effort would have been considerable. It is true that the Yugoslav crisis gave rise to disarray in the Western Alliance. It was also the case that operations *Sharp Fence* and *Maritime Guard* in the Adriatic displayed elements of duplication and rivalry between the WEU and NATO until the forces combined (ripples of which are evident in the operation by WEU Mediterranean states with regard to Albania). It is also true that participating states produced a hierarchy of commitment, German and Spanish ships being exempted from enforcement. In the end, however, these combined operations provide an impressive example of robust enforcement and integrated multinationalism at sea, in large measure a tribute to the professionalism of the participants.[19]

Third, we should roast the familiar canard that peacekeeping is 'not work for warriors' or 'not proper soldiering'. Appalling incidents from operations in Somalia have certainly indicated that a 'warrior culture' and poorly motivated or wrongly trained soldiers are disastrous for effective peacekeeping and humanitarian operations.[20] PSOs do require a particular ethos, as emphasized by the Argentine maritime squadron in the UN's Central American operations.[21] But PSOs are not inherently antithetical to the cultural well-being of military establishments. In the symbolism, ritualism and *esprit de corps* of Ireland's Defence Force the role of peacekeeping takes pride of place. Of course, armed forces have to generate their pride and reputation where they can, and no doubt neutral Ireland has to take the UN seriously in default of anything else. This merely tells us that armed forces have different priorities and cultures. The point is that PSOs are not incompatible with a military/naval culture *per se*, but accord fully with the Western rationale for defence forces as institutions for the controlled use of violence.

Fourth, the GAO's argument that peace support operations are an opportunity cost, consuming resources that would otherwise be denied to war preparations, misses the point that peace support operations may be 'the opportunity'. From this point of view, the GAO's report could appear to be a plea for keeping navies permanently tied up to save money.

But the *entire* cost of UN peacekeeping operations in 1996 amounted to less than the estimated cost *increase* of the Eurofighter[22] (though the additional costs of Caribbean operations were proportionately large for the US Navy alone). No doubt larger defence expenditure can be justified by a 'two-front, inter-state war' policy, but while waiting for the big and winnable war to turn up the US military runs the risk of redundancy.

Fifth, it can be argued that unit capability *includes* peace support operations, and that such operations are not distractions even though they require additional training and flexibility among armed forces. In the maritime context, PSOs offer significant 'spillover' and transferability because the actual tasks are not unusual for the most part. Mats Berdal argues that 90 per cent of peace support operations involve overwhelmingly familiar skills such as seamanship, navigation and communications.[23] Many of the roles and skills in PSOs are also transferable to preparation for war: poise and non-strategic deterrence, power projection, protection of shipping, support to joint operations, sanctions enforcement and blockade, amphibious operations, maritime air reconnaissance, tactical maritime aviation and helicopter support, evacuation and medical support, minehunting/sweeping and so forth.[24] Obviously, the political environments of PSOs vary markedly, requiring a range of skills. Some environments will be relatively benign, placing a premium on minimum force, transparency, neutrality and impartiality. Others will entail options to use force to impose a UN mandate. But in general, there will be no designated enemy and in states with internal wars factional access to ships, aircraft and shore-based missiles or gunnery is likely to be limited or, as in the case of Serbia, maritime operations will not have a high priority. The activities and targets of warlords are more likely to be on land.

VESTED INTERESTS IN THE JAZZ OF MILITARY STRATEGY?

There now seems to be a sufficiently strong commitment to peace support operations on the part of key military establishments to suggest the emergence of 'interests'. Powell's policy never prevented the setting up of a Peace Support Under-Secretary's Office in the Department of Defense, the training and education of forces in PSOs at Carlisle Barracks, Maxwell Air Base and elsewhere, or the incorporation of PSOs in doctrine for OOTW. Somewhat against the Powellite doctrine, an aide to the US Army Chief of Staff once described PSOs as 'the jazz of military strategy'.[25] Perhaps he meant that PSOs were exciting because they entailed creative improvization, a range of traditional and modern styles and interesting multilateral combinations. In any event, the tune in the United States may be modulating with blue notes. A version of policy has emerged since Clinton was re-elected in late 1996, known as 'Preventive Defense', that calls for more emphasis on multilateralism and early involvement in PSOs if key allies are agreed.[26] Another straw in the wind is Clinton's nomination for Chairman of the Joint Chiefs of Staff, General Henry Shelton, who led the US forces in Haiti and was praised by the President for his expertise in unconventional warfare.[27]

Obviously, maritime forces act according to the dictates of political masters. All the same, naval establishments have 'interests' which they can promote in tendering advice and lobbying. Are interests in maritime PSOs cosmetic (as a form of lip-service to a political fashion), welcomed for opportunistic reasons (to enhance the effectiveness, status and future prospects of naval establishments) or supported ideologically (as a commitment to the values of PSOs)? Some of each is probably involved.

Naval establishments have to redefine the irreducible demands of national defence in ways that do not give undue attention to roles that might be transient. Sceptics might argue that there is therefore something cosmetic about UK naval doctrine in BR1806, heading up Chapter 1 with a section on the UN. However, the justification in BR1806 is far from cosmetic. It makes four points about the context of national defence:

- the world in which the UK operates is less predictable;
- the pattern of global politics has changed;
- violence anywhere in the system can damage global security;
- UK security concerns need to be addressed in a multinational context.[28]

Even if a commitment begins as cosmetic, it can become institutionalized if PSOs are regarded as part of the bread and butter activities of maritime forces. Whatever one thinks of the strategic logic, there is little doubt that PSOs present additional opportunities:

- to show what maritime forces can do, thereby contributing to maintaining a profile in politics and the media;
- to provide operational experience;
- to help maintain a fleet in being;
- to provide tests of procedures, equipment, personnel and integration with allies; and
- to reinforce trends towards 'joint' and 'combined' operations.

Of course, problems of overstretch will arise. But in the absence of direct threats to national security, manifestations of overstretch can also be used as ammunition against treasuries and other government departments.

Finally, we should not altogether discount 'attitudinal' commitments that may grow from experience of such operations. All military establishments that were caught up in the Cold War have had to re-examine their politics, in the sense of having to live without a 'clear and present danger'. Furthermore, national forces are said to gain credibility through supporting 'good' (i.e. charitable/humanitarian) causes.[29] Military establishments might be expected to be dubious about international 'good causes', especially when they become frustrated by UN rules, procedures and bureaucracy or, for example, when embargoes are not selective in the populations targeted. But it is salutary to record comments made by UK personnel who had participated in the 1996 Angolan logistic support group deployment which required sealift. One senior officer confessed that he had acquired an appreciation of the possibilities of ameliorating suffering under the UN's emblem. He was, he suggested, in danger of being accused of becoming a 'left-winger'.[30]

CONCLUSION

To sum up, there is evidence of the institutionalization of peace support operations, in spite of the downturn in the credibility of UN-authorized interventions. This is affecting maritime as well as land-based forces in a number of ways.

- In the UN system, there is certainly a greater awareness of maritime support functions. Naval personnel serve in the Military Advisor's Office where they are in a position to influence the Department of Peace-Keeping Operations (DPKO). However, apart from a Norwegian maritime input, there is little by way of maritime elements in the existing UN Standby Arrangements.
- Perhaps the greatest scope for institutionalization, however, lies in franchising coalitions of the willing and able: the NATO/WEU operations in the Gulf and Adriatic; the Southern European force in Albania.
- PSOs are an area of common ground for the North Atlantic Cooperation Council and the Partnership for Peace programme. Numerous naval exercises are now listed under peace support.[31]

- In key establishments, PSOs have entered military and naval doctrine. There is even a case for arguing that through the Army Field Manuals *Wider Peacekeeping* and *Peace Support Operations*, the UK has captured the international debate about PSO doctrine. It has taken a lead which others, including the United States and NATO, have followed.[32]
- There are also growing private-sector interests in taking on functions previously conducted by the state, including base management in theatre during operations. These interests are bound to have more of an impact on land operations than at sea, but maritime forces may not be completely immune from the trend.[33]

We are unlikely to witness a reordering of priorities in the United States so that preparation for war is classified as War Operations Other than Peace Support (WOOPS). But peace support operations may be sufficiently central to maritime operations to encourage naval establishments to demonstrate their synergy with what are regarded as more traditional national and alliance defence roles. They can also be sufficiently different from warfare roles to justify acknowledgement of the special training, doctrinal and ethical implications. Although the demand for PSOs is bound to fluctuate, there is today much greater acceptance of PSO concepts and of the need to integrate them into the culture of defence establishments so that the jazz may also become music to maritime ears.

NOTES

1. See also the forthcoming Defence Studies (RN) publication edited by Eric Grove, *The Dynamics of Sea Power*, 1998.
2. *The Times*, 24 September 1987, p. 1; Vladimir Petrovsky, speech at seminar on Problems of UN Peacekeeping Operations, Salzburg, 4 August 1989 (official Austrian text); USSR, 'The United Nations in the Post-Confrontation World', UN Doc. A/45/626, S/21869, 12 October 1990.
3. Others were thinking on similar lines, and the foremost authority on peacekeeping research in the UK, Alan James, had a short maritime section in a survey of peacekeeping operations in *Peacekeeping in International Politics* (London: IISS/Macmillan, 1990).
4. After the First World War, UK and French naval forces had been involved in plebiscite supervision in Schleswig-Holstein in 1921.
5. Frank Uhlig, 'The First United Nations Force', *Proceedings*, US Naval Institute, February 1951, p. 201.

6.   Lord Caradon, cited by Anthony Parsons, *From Cold War to Hot Peace, UN Interventions 1947–1995* (Harmondsworth: Penguin, 1995), x.

7.   Michael MacKinnon, *Fairweather Friend? The Clinton Administration's Policy Towards the UN and Peace Support Operations* (London: Frank Cass, forthcoming 1999).

8.   See Rhys Dogan and Michael Pugh, *From Military to Market Imperatives: Peacekeeping and the New Public Policy*, Plymouth International Paper No. 8, International Studies Centre, University of Plymouth, 1997, p. 14.

9.   See 'The Weinberger Criteria', *Annual Report of the Congress: Fiscal Year 1987* (Washington, DC: Department of Defense, 1986), pp. 78–82.

10.   *National Military Strategy of the United States* (Washington, DC: USGPO, January 1992); Colin Powell, 'U.S. Forces: Challenges Ahead', *Foreign Affairs*, vol. 71, no. 5, Winter 1991/92, p. 38. Powell had also assisted in drafting the criteria originally laid down by Caspar Weinberger, US Defense Secretary, in 1984. These referred to: the use of force as a last resort; the need for clear political objectives; a clear end-point to military intervention; force to be used decisively; having vital US interests at stake; and assurance of continuing public support. The last two are implied but not included in Powell's 1992 criteria.

11.   Les Aspin, *The Bottom-Up Review: Forces for a New Era* (Washington, DC: DoD, September 1993); *The Clinton Administration's Policy on Reforming Multilateral Peace Operations*, PDD-25 (Washington, DC: Department of State, May 1994); 'Shalikashvili. Focus on Warfighting not Peacekeeping', *Defense Daily*, 2 September 1994.

12.   Ivo H. Daalder, 'The United States and Military Intervention in Internal Conflict', in Michael E. Brown (ed.), *The International Dimensions of Internal Conflict* (Cambridge, Mass: MIT Press, 1996), pp. 461–88.

13.   Cindy Collins and Thomas G. Weiss, *An Overview and Assessment of 1989–1996 Peace Support Publications*, Occasional Paper No. 28, Thomas J. Watson Jr. Institute for International Studies, Brown University, RI, 1998, p. 90.

14.   'Peacekeeping Hampers Ship Maintenance, Other Schedules', *Navy News and Undersea Technology*, 13 November 1995.

15.   Unattributable presentations by, and discussions with, participants at *Aspects of Peacekeeping*, Conference at the Royal Military Academy Sandhurst, 22–24 January 1997. See Michael Pugh, *From Mission Cringe to Mission Creep? Implications of New Peace Support Operations Doctrine*, Defence Study No. 2/1997 (Oslo: Instituut for Forvarsstudier, 1997).

16.   BR1806, *The Fundamentals of British Maritime Doctrine* (London: HMSO, 1995).

17.   Daalder, op cit., pp. 485–6.

18.   This has been described as a 'broad-stroke return to the Bush-era approach of a tactical use of the UN only as a tool serving unilateral U.S. interests': Phyllis Bennis, *Calling the Shots: How Washington Dominates Today's UN* (New York: Olive Branch Press, 1996), p. 97. See also, Justin Morris, 'Force and Democracy: UN/US Intervention in Haiti', *International Peacekeeping*, vol. 2, no. 3, Autumn 1995, pp. 391–412.

19.   After 17 April 1993 when the UN Security Council extended the Adriatic mandate to prohibit all merchant ships from entering the territorial waters

of Serbia-Montenegro except on a case-by-case basis or in the event of emergency, no ship was able to break the embargo. From then until 1 October 1996 when the embargo operations were terminated, 74192 merchants ships were challenged; 5951 were boarded and inspected at sea; 1480 diverted and inspected in port; and 6 ships were caught attempting to break the embargo. This intensive effort by 14 NATO/WEU members involved nearly 20000 ship days at sea, over 7000 maritime patrol aircraft sorties and over 6000 AEW sorties. NATO/WEU Operation *Sharp Guard*, IFOR Final Factsheet, 2 October 1996, http://www.nato.int/ifor/ifor.htm. See also Eric Grove's chapter in John B. Poole and Richard Guthrie (eds), *Verification 1995: Arms Control, Peacekeeping and the Environment* (Boulder, Colo. and Oxford: Westview Press for VERTIC, 1996).

20. Incidents of murder and mistreatment in Somalia involving Canadian, Italian and Belgian troops have been the subject of investigations, and a Canadian Airborne Regiment was disbanded. 'Peacekeeping "torturers" on trial in Belgium', *The Guardian*, 23 June 1997, p. 14.

21. Capt. R. E. Schroeder, '"Operacion Gaucho" en Centro America', *Puestos de Maniobra*, vol. 3, no. 4, September 1991, pp. 18–21.

22. Neil Cooper, *The Business of Death: Britain and the Arms Trade* (London: I. B. Tauris, 1997).

23. Mats Berdal, *Whither UN Peacekeeping?*, Adelphi Paper No. 281 (London: IISS, October 1993).

24. Lt-Cdr D. N. Griffiths (CN), 'Maritime Peace Support Roles and Capabilities', unpublished paper.

25. Bennis, op. cit., citing Lt-Col Doug Coffey, p. 103.

26. Collins and Weiss, op. cit., p. 93.

27. *The Guardian*, 18 June 1997, p. 16.

28. BR1806, op. cit., p. 18.

29. At one stage it was believed that: 'White House and Pentagon strategists alike believed that the image of a kinder, gentler military, prepared to keep the peace as well as prepared to wage catastrophic war, would have a better chance of winning public support for keeping the military's budget intact when all other public spending faced slash-and-burn cuts.' Bennis, op. cit., p. 102.

30. BBC TV, 'Mission Angola', *Defence of the Realm*, 1996. Of course embracing an 'ideology of compassion' carries its own dangers: of peddling moral virtues and paternalism, often with an emphasis on technical fixes. Barbara E. Harrell-Bond, *Imposing Aid: Emergency Assistance to Refugees* (Oxford: Oxford University Press, 1986), pp. 16–17.

31. See, for example, North Atlantic Cooperation Council, 'Report to Ministers by the Political-Military Steering Committee/Ad Hoc Group on Cooperation in Peacekeeping', Noordwijk-aan-Zee NACC Meeting, 31 May 1995.

32. See Michael Pugh, 'The Politics of Peacekeeping Doctrine', in Knud Erik Jorgensen, *European Crisis Management after the Cold War* (The Hague: Kluwer Law International, 1997), pp. 153–70.

33. See Dogan and Pugh, op. cit.

9 Maritime Power in the 1990–91 Gulf War and the Conflict in the Former Yugoslavia
Tim Benbow

During the Cold War, the need of the major Western powers for maritime forces was clear.[1] They were confronted by a superpower adversary which, although primarily continental in outlook, also maintained large submarine, maritime air and surface naval forces capable of threatening the sea communications on which the NATO countries depended. With the demise of the USSR, there is no longer any navy capable of offering a significant challenge to Western use of the oceans; with no plausible opponent, it could be argued, there must be scope for significant reductions in British and American naval forces. For example, one respected American analyst wrote a recent article arguing that the United States should spend less on its navy, on the grounds that:

> The threats that carrier battle groups and a large attack submarine fleet were built to confront no longer exist. With the demise of the Soviet navy, there is no significant naval fleet in the world other than the U.S. fleet. Nor could one emerge quickly.[2]

In reality, however, the purpose of a navy is not only to fight an opposing navy – that is a means to the end of making use of the sea. In both Second World War and Cold War NATO plans, the defeat of opposing naval, submarine and air forces was required in order to use the sea to transport reinforcements and supplies and to project military power ashore. Moreover, during the Cold War period, although the central focus for both the US Navy and the Royal Navy was the possibility of conflict with the USSR, they saw frequent action in regional conflicts of various sorts, in which their contribution was in projecting power and supporting forces ashore rather than fighting an opposing fleet.[3] The size and shape of the navy needed by a state depends on what it seeks to do at and from the sea, not solely on the threat posed by potentially hostile fleets.

The relevant question about navies after the Cold War is therefore not whether there is an opposing navy they may have to defeat but, rather, are there any important roles which they can efficiently fulfil? This issue can be investigated by examining the two major regional conflicts in which the Western powers have been involved since the end of the Cold War – the 1990–91 Gulf War and the conflict in the former Yugoslavia. While some caution is needed in drawing lessons from them, together they form a significant part of the experience on which planning and force structures will be based. It is therefore important to have an accurate account of the roles played in these two conflicts by different sorts of forces; yet while land-based air power has been lauded, the contribution made by maritime power has been generally neglected. The Gulf War tends to be portrayed as having been fought primarily by land-based aircraft, with ground forces completing the victory. On the other hand, Western forceful intervention in the former Yugoslavia is seen as having been initially conducted by ground forces supported by air power, but as succeeding only when air power took the lead; in neither case did naval power play more than a marginal role. In fact, these pictures of the two conflicts are caricatures.

This chapter outlines the role of maritime forces in each of the conflicts.[4] It argues that even though both the Gulf War and the Western intervention in the former Yugoslavia represented difficult tests for maritime power and were by no means unusually favourable for its exercise, in each navies performed a number of vital functions for which other forces could not have substituted.

THE GULF CONFLICT, 1990–91

Accounts of the Gulf conflict tend to give greatest prominence to land-based air power. Several analysts even saw in it the fulfilment of the claims of the interwar air power thinkers. One USAF officer concluded that Douhet 'was right all along.' Indeed:

> This is the essence of Douhet's concepts: air power so powerful that it alone could defeat an enemy. It happened in Desert Storm. ... Perhaps the key question remaining from Desert Storm is, 'Did we need a ground operation at all?'[5]

For Luttwak, Alexander de Seversky was also rehabilitated: 'at least it may be said that after 70 years the old promises of "Victory Through Air Power" were finally redeemed in 1991 in the skies of Iraq'; and 'the final ground offensive of Desert Storm was not offensive at all but rather an almost unopposed advance.'[6] Luttwak concluded that, although it appeared to be conducted by balanced forces, Desert Storm 'was in fact an air war that might have ended with Iraq's surrender in a few more weeks, but which was concluded by a ground advance that turned out to be almost administrative in character.'[7] Colonel John Warden, the principal intellectual mentor of the air campaign, subsequently claimed that '[Iraq] lay as defenceless as if occupied by a million men. For practical purposes, it had in fact become a state occupied from the air.'[8] This debate is not of merely historical interest: the proclaimed success of air power in the Gulf has given rise once again to suggestions that US strategy should rely far more on air power. A 1993 RAND study recommended that although the other services would continue to be necessary, their funding should be cut to fund modernization of the US Air Force.[9]

It is true that Coalition air power enjoyed a great deal of success in Desert Storm. The 38-day aerial campaign rapidly gained air supremacy and seriously degraded Iraqi command, control and communications, thus facilitating the other objectives of the air campaign and greatly assisting the land offensive. It inflicted serious damage on various strategic military and political targets; wore down the strength of the Iraqi armed forces by restricting its flow of supplies, attacking armoured vehicles and artillery and damaging Iraqi troops' morale; and, finally, prepared the way for the advancing Coalition land forces. It thereby established the conditions for the ground campaign to succeed at low cost. Although this is less than is sometimes claimed on behalf of air power, it clearly played the leading part in Coalition strategy and made a major contribution to the military success it achieved. However, a number of caveats must be acknowledged to avoid drawing unwarranted conclusions from this one, idiosyncratic case.

First, although the list of successes is impressive by the standards of any previous conflict, air power did not achieve quite all that some of its more enthusiastic proponents had predicted before the conflict or have claimed since. Even though 20 per cent of aircraft sorties were directed against Iraqi Scud missiles, the air campaign had little success against them (and the success it did enjoy depended on the support of Special Forces). Iraq's weapons of mass destruction programmes were not set back as badly as was initially thought, as has been evident from the subsequent tribulations of the UN weapons inspectors.[10] Similarly, estimates of equipment destroyed by the air campaign were reduced after the war and the contribution to victory of some of the 'strategic' attacks, such as those on Iraq's oil industry, was at best uncertain.

Second, the air campaign of Desert Storm took place in such uniquely favourable conditions that any attempt to draw broadly applicable conclusions would be highly dubious. Coalition air forces were supported by an abundance of well equipped ports and air bases with fuel easily available; the enemy refrained from attacking these vulnerable and lucrative targets and so conceded a build-up period of several months in which stockpiling of supplies and weapons, acclimatization, training, intelligence gathering and planning could continue unhindered. Moreover, while NATO forces were free of Cold War concerns and thus available to be redeployed, both the forces and their support facilities were still at Cold War levels and locations; as McCausland noted, since the war many of the US overseas bases used to support the operation have been closed down.[11] The Allies enjoyed a technological superiority of at least one or two generations over an opponent who sought the classic, armoured war for which NATO land and air forces had spent 45 years planning and training. In this case, however, their task was made very much easier by the desert terrain (which left the Iraqis in the open, with long and exposed supply lines yet minimized the risk of collateral damage), by the weather of the theatre (which was worse than usual for the region, but far better than might be expected in Europe or Korea), and by Iraq's strategic and tactical shortcomings, not least of which was in presenting the would-be intervening states with the most favourable political conditions imaginable for domestic and international backing, host nation support and approval for overflight of aircraft for the initial build-up (and for basing for the tankers which supported them) and for a long and intensive air campaign. These circumstances were so flattering to air power that they resemble an ideal case which would have attracted scepticism if offered as a planning scenario.

Finally, the air campaign was not independent of the land and maritime campaigns. The presence of Coalition forces on the ground compelled the Iraqi army to take up positions that made it vulnerable to air attack, rather than, say, pushing into Saudi Arabia. Moreover, a land campaign was necessary to force Iraq out of Kuwait, which could not have been achieved by air strikes alone. Further, the pre-advance bombardment of Iraqi positions was not solely conducted by air strikes, but also by intense artillery and helicopter attacks. Eliot Cohen, the director of the Gulf War Air Power Survey, concluded: 'Although ground action necessarily consummated the final victory for coalition forces, air power had made the final assault as effortless as a wartime operation can be.' He also noted that the Republican Guard lost nearly a quarter of its armour to air attacks (some front-line units lost more) and that overall, its armour was destroyed 'in roughly equal proportions by air and ground action'.[12] In Desert Storm, land and air forces supported each other.

THE MARITIME CAMPAIGN

John Keegan recognized the crucial importance of ground forces but displayed a different though widespread oversight when he wrote: 'A brief but dramatic air and ground war has been fought in the Gulf.'[13] The general lack of attention that has been given to Coalition naval forces is extraordinary. Part of the reason may be that when analysing a conflict it is easy to fall into the trap of focusing on combat operations, to the exclusion of what went before and afterwards. Thus, with the Gulf conflict it is easy to concentrate on Desert Storm but more revealing to look at the crisis as a whole, including the initial response to Iraq's invasion, the build-up of Desert Shield, Desert Storm itself, and then the aftermath and post-crisis activity. Maritime power played an important role in each stage.

The aim of the initial Coalition deployment of military forces in response to the Iraqi invasion of Kuwait was to contain the conflict, and particularly to prevent a further advance into Saudi Arabia and hence keep free the ports and air bases needed for subsequent reinforcements. Naval forces played a leading role in this initial deployment, along with light ground forces and quick-reaction air forces: an hour after the start of the Iraqi invasion, one carrier group was ordered to the Gulf of Oman and another to the eastern Mediterranean.[14] Most importantly, carrier air power arrived in the theatre ready immediately for combat and with its own logistic support,[15] and was from then on available to supplement the growing number of aircraft based on crowded airfields ashore. McCausland concluded that the value of naval forces 'in presenting Iraq with a real, self-sustaining threat from the onset cannot be underrated'.[16] Friedman suggested that without their availability, Saudi Arabia would have been taking a huge risk in allowing in Coalition forces, given the size of the Iraqi army on its border.[17] Maritime forces therefore played a central part in establishing a force capable of deterring an Iraqi push into Saudi Arabia, which would have had a grave effect on Coalition strategy.

After the initial deployment, heavier forces were brought in to assure the defence of Saudi Arabia and were later reinforced to provide an offensive option. Although some lightly equipped troops and combat aircraft could arrive by air, the heavier forces and the materiel and personnel of their vast logistic tail could not: 95 per cent of cargo came by sea.[18] This vast effort had to be protected, although in this case the level of threat was low and, in practice, sea communications were not challenged. Iraq's navy was small, lacking large warships or submarines, but it did have 13 missile boats with Styx anti-ship missiles and six captured

Kuwaiti boats with Exocet missiles. Its maritime capability also included 400 air-launched Exocet missiles and 50 aircraft capable of using them (as they had against tankers and USS *Stark* during the Iran–Iraq war), together with 50 Silkworm anti-ship missiles and seven mobile launchers, and large numbers of mines.[19] There was some concern that Coalition shipping in the Mediterranean might be vulnerable if Libya should make its verbal support of Iraq more tangible. Hence in September 1990 the NATO Naval On-Call Force Mediterranean was activated and in January 1991 the carrier HMS *Ark Royal* and her escorts were deployed there to free an additional US carrier to move on to the Gulf.[20]

The other naval role in this early phase was the enforcement of the economic embargo on Iraq, carried out in cooperation with land-based maritime patrol aircraft, which proved the easiest forceful measure for the Security Council to authorize. Sanctions had some economic impact and indirect military utility; also important was their diplomatic value in showing that options other than force were being pursued and in giving the opportunity for various states to contribute forces to the coalition. In all, Coalition forces comprising 165 ships from 19 navies patrolled nearly 250 000 square miles of ocean, challenged more than 7500 merchant ships, boarded and inspected 964 and diverted 51; warning shots were fired in 11 interceptions but none required disabling fire.[21]

Accounts of the conflict which begin with the air campaign therefore omit the vital precursor stages of responding to the Iraqi invasion, defending Saudi Arabia and building up for offensive operations. Naval forces also had a central role in Desert Storm itself. First, they had to maintain sea control. The Iraqi navy was quickly rolled back and eliminated, largely by helicopters from British destroyers and US carrier aircraft. A couple of attempted Iraqi air attacks were easily countered, though more dangerous was a Silkworm attack on the battleship USS *Wisconsin*, in which a British destroyer, HMS *Gloucester*, shot down the missile and carrier aircraft then destroyed the launcher. More troubling was the threat from mines which, in spite of the considerable effort which went into countering them, damaged two US ships.[22]

Naval air power also played a prominent part in the air campaign. The precise statistics about this are the subject of much inter-service wrangling, but maritime aircraft made up about a quarter of the aircraft in the theatre and undertook about a quarter of the offensive air missions. Whereas sending carriers into the Persian Gulf had previously been thought too dangerous, at the height of Desert Storm four operated there. Naval aircraft also contributed to air defence, securing the Coalition's eastern flank, and took part in operations at sea. As in previous conflicts, land- and sea-based aircraft had their own advantages and disadvantages and proved to have complementary capabilities: air power is not synonymous with Air Force! One novel aspect of the naval contribution to the air campaign was the use of 288 Tomahawk cruise missiles, fired from submarines and surface ships. These provided a force multiplier for the air campaign, being used against heavily defended targets in daylight (when Stealth fighters could not operate) or against air defences prior to the arrival of manned aircraft.

Other maritime tasks in Desert Storm were more traditional exercises of naval supremacy, including the bombardment of targets ashore by warships and the amphibious demonstration in the Gulf which tied down several Iraqi divisions to guard against an attack that never came. This feint assisted in the deception operation which was so important to the success of the land campaign, but it could have gone ahead in earnest had the ground campaign run into difficulty (or indeed had there been less time for preparation). Naval helicopters were used to support both warships in the Gulf and forces ashore by transporting supplies.

Undoubtedly, in any future major regional conflict, ground forces supported by land-based air power and cruise missiles would again play the principal part just as they did in the Gulf War, but maritime forces would have a critical role in stabilizing the initial situation, securing command of the sea, protecting the movement into the theatre of the heavier land-based ground and air forces, and then contributing to the war ashore.

The value of maritime power can also be seen in other operations in the Gulf, both before and after this conflict. During the Iran–Iraq War the major naval powers maintained forces in the Gulf, and when merchant shipping came under attack they were able to assist. When a different threat arose with the laying of mines, a combined European operation was arranged to sweep them, while the US Navy took more active measures against the Iranian forces responsible. In July 1990, shortly before the invasion of Kuwait, Saddam Hussein's bellicose language prompted the United Arab Emirates (UAE) to ask for American help to guard against air attack. The US response was to deploy two tanker aircraft to support UAE fighters, and to push three of the US warships in the Gulf to the north to act as a radar picket to provide early warning of an attack.[23] This response was appropriate yet also unobtrusive and hence unlikely to escalate the situation. After the 1991 war, naval responsibilities continued with the removal of Iraqi mines laid during the conflict, continued presence in the region, contributions to the reinforcement of Kuwait in the face of periodically renewed Iraqi

threats, and the use of naval aircraft and cruise missiles for the enforcement of no-fly zones over Iraq and for a series of strikes against air
defence sites and other targets. The unambiguous nature of Saddam's
aggression and the threat to other regional states of the 1990 crisis had
ensured the availability of abundant host nation support; in several subsequent crises this was restricted or not available, enhancing the importance of naval forces which do not require permission to go about their
business.[24] The Gulf War was not a typical conflict: subsequent forceful
diplomacy directed against Iraq may well prove to be more characteristic
of the post-Cold War period. Moreover, Saddam's strategic errors are
clear for all to see, so even a future major conflict might not resemble the
Gulf War. It therefore needs to be taken into account in addition to the
Gulf War – as does the second of the two case studies of this chapter.

THE INTERVENTION IN FORMER YUGOSLAVIA

The Western intervention in the former Yugoslavia is worth examining
because it poses such a contrast to the experience in the Gulf, and
because it seems more representative of post-Cold War conflict. Major
regional warfare such as that precipitated by the Iraqi invasion of Kuwait
is likely to be less common than more unconventional conflicts such as
those seen in Somalia, Haiti and Rwanda. The Yugoslavia crisis was
characterized by mainly unconventional, irregular warfare and a combination of intra- and substate violence. As a result, the political circumstances which facilitated international action in the Gulf crisis were
lacking and there was an absence of consensus within and between the
states with the capacity to intervene over the desirability and objectives
of any external intervention. These factors made Yugoslavia far less conducive than the Gulf to decisive military action.

Western action was initially confined to diplomacy, given some degree
of bite with the much contested arms embargo and the imposition and,
later, the enforcement of economic sanctions and a no-fly zone. Such
steps were inevitably slow to have an effect, and that effect was modest.
Having an impact in a territorial conflict such as this one required
ground forces but when they were eventually deployed, the underlying
domestic political will and international agreement were limited. Hence
commitment was delayed and then constrained in its objectives and
means, which resulted in yet more disagreements within the states that
contributed to the UN Protection Force (UNPROFOR), and between
these states and others which had not committed troops in Bosnia.

One suggestion often heard from those advocating a more assertive approach against the Bosnian Serbs – as in the US 'lift and strike' proposal – was that the West should make use of air power, which had clearly won many converts in the Gulf War. Here, it seemed, was a low-cost, limited commitment means to end the conflict, which would take full advantage of the formidable qualitative superiority of the Western powers over any or all of the local factions. Allied aircraft would be operating from familiar and secure bases within easy reach of the theatre, and the accuracy of modern air power was such that no target could be immune from destruction. Surely if the states concerned were not prepared to repeat what they had done on behalf of Kuwait, it simply demonstrated their venality and vacillation? Thus many voices which had previously been sceptical about the utility of air power suddenly discovered a deep faith in its capabilities.

Air power was not the panacea it was sometimes claimed to be, since it was as constrained in the former Yugoslavia as it had been flattered in the Gulf. The nature of the conflict was not at all conducive to a decisive air campaign; potential targets were unsuitable, consisting mainly of snipers, light infantry, small and mobile mortars and artillery, and irregular forces with little in the way of support needs or logistical infrastructure. Added to this was the unfavourable terrain, which was rough, mountainous or urban, and the weather which was a serious constraint,[25] particularly with the restrictive rules of engagement and exacting requirements for target identification that applied. As if all this were not enough, the nature of the conflict produced divisions in the international community on the desirability of air bombardment, let alone its objectives. Any such action could not have been quickly decisive, and would have carried costs, since it would have been accompanied by the withdrawal of UN peacekeepers and a consequent probability of an escalation in the fighting, in addition to fracturing the fragile Security Council consensus. Yet even small-scale air strikes risked provoking retaliation against civilian targets, attacks on peacekeepers or taking them as hostages. This conflict was not one in which air power alone could provide an easy or cheap solution.

Nevertheless, air power played several roles in the former Yugoslavia. Some of these were less glamorous than air strikes but perhaps more useful, particularly the use of helicopters and transport aircraft to carry relief for Sarajevo and to provide UN peacekeepers with supplies and mobility. Most attention, however, was devoted to the more coercive functions. Operation *Deny Flight* began in April 1993 (replacing Operation *Sky Monitor*) after UN Security Council Resolution 816 authorized the enforcement of the no-fly zone. The value of this ban was widely questioned, given the frequency with which breaches were ignored, although on 28 February 1994 four out of six Serb aircraft which had attacked a Bosnian government munitions plant were shot down. *Deny Flight* also involved providing close air support for UN forces and wider air strikes as requested. These were threatened to protect 'safe areas' or to enforce exclusion zones for heavy weapons. There were few suitable targets for wider air strikes; air defence sites could be hit to send political signals to the Bosnian Serb leadership, as well as reducing the threat to NATO aircraft, but the destruction of other targets, such as a few tanks or SAM batteries, could not have a great effect on any of the parties. Command and control centres and concentrations of vehicles were far more rewarding targets for air attack than dispersed forces or smaller weapons, but these could only be effective as part of a wider campaign rather than as one-off punishment strikes. However, the restrictions described above limited the use of air strikes, and up to August 1995 there were only nine attacks, for which the targets included air defence radars, a tank, an airfield, a tracked anti-tank gun and an ammunition dump.[26]

Eventually, however, the long-awaited wider air campaign did occur in the form of Operation *Deliberate Force*, which began on 30 August 1995.[27] During this two-week campaign, some 3500 strike and support sorties, together with 13 cruise missiles and Rapid Reaction Force artillery fire, targeted air defence sites, command and control facilities, ammunition depots, lines of communication (especially bridges) and heavy weapons. Since this air campaign was closely followed by the Dayton peace agreement, many commentators have been tempted to exaggerate its effect and independence; its actual impact demands careful scrutiny. First, the direct effect of the bombing on the Bosnian Serbs was open to doubt and its perceived success declined as the campaign went on. *The Economist* commented: 'NATO has demonstrated its awesome capability to inflict aerial damage on military targets. Whether such damage can break the will of a stubborn, cornered people, is another matter.'[28] Two weeks later, after the suspension of the operation, the same journal concluded that 'NATO has damaged but not smashed the Bosnian Serb war machine', and that many of its heavy weapons in particular had survived.[29] More importantly, the air campaign did not stand alone but was just one strand among many in a broader policy which came together to put pressure upon the Bosnian Serbs to make some concessions. The long economic embargo had convinced the leadership of the rump Yugoslavia to cut support for its allies and to nudge them towards peace (although the prospect of a disastrous defeat for them could have reversed both this position and the acquiescence of Russia). Furthermore, the Bosnian Serbs were militarily over-extended on the ground, demoralized by an earlier Croatian offensive and were now faced by resurgent Croatian and Bosnian government forces which had somehow managed to rearm themselves in spite of the arms embargo and had in March 1995 been pushed into alliance by the West. Without their military advance, it is highly questionable whether *Deliberate Force* alone would have been sufficient to compel the Bosnian Serbs to relinquish so much territory. Meanwhile the existence of a powerful Rapid Reaction Force reduced the effect of their habitual response against Sarajevo. These factors, together with the air campaign, produced a background in which US-led diplomacy could succeed when, after two weeks of air strikes, the Bosnian Serb military commander, General Mladic, was refusing to pull back his heavy weapons and 'NATO was running short of suitable targets.'[30]

THE MARITIME CONTRIBUTION

Given the nature of the conflict and the political and military constraints on Western strategy, there were basic limits on what military power in any form could achieve. Unconventional conflicts of this sort are not suitable for decisive intervention with air power, and unappealing for large-scale ground operations. In some ways the limitations of naval power are even more obvious: there is little apparent role for maritime forces in an intra-state campaign taking place solely on land, in which neither side has a significant navy or a grave vulnerability to the interdiction of its maritime trade. In practice, however, the naval contribution was both substantial and significant.

The first task which fell to the navies of the intervening powers was to monitor and then enforce the economic embargo imposed by the United Nations. In July 1992 both the Western European Union (WEU) (Operation *Sharp Vigilance*) and NATO (Operation *Maritime Monitor*) began to monitor the embargo in the Adriatic. In November 1992, UN Security Council Resolution 787 authorized the enforcement of sanctions and the blockade commenced, again with forces participating under both the WEU (*Sharp Fence*) and NATO (*Maritime Guard*). This system was rationalized in June 1993 when the two operations were combined to form Operation *Sharp Guard*, under the command of NATO COMNAV-SOUTH. This effort involved 19 699 ship days at sea and, offering a good example of cooperation between naval and land-based maritime air forces, 7151 maritime patrol aircraft sorties and 6174 AWACS sorties.[31] There was considerable leakage in the sanctions regime, both across land borders and through the Danube, although the latter was tackled in April 1993 when the WEU sent ten launches to operate there. The effect of sanctions is notoriously difficult to specify and limited when the target has cooperative neighbours, but at the very least they had a significant impact on the economy of Serbia, and splitting that state from the Bosnian Serbs was a fundamental aim of the UN approach.

The basic task for the intervening navies was therefore to maintain local sea control in the Adriatic, which was difficult in such enclosed and congested waters.[32] Still, the proximity of Italy facilitated operations, providing host nation support for naval and land-based maritime aircraft. There was a potential threat from the navy of the rump Yugoslavia (for example, on 1 May 1994, Yugoslav Navy ships unsuccessfully challenged *Sharp Guard* forces engaged in diverting an oil tanker which was seeking to break the embargo),[33] or from its land-based aircraft or coastal anti-ship missiles which were within range of some of the naval operating areas. Any of these threats could have been used in practice, especially in the event of an escalation ashore, but as in the Persian Gulf, the evident capability of the naval forces in the Adriatic would have had a considerable deterrent effect.

A second naval contribution was air power. Even though the theatre was so close to NATO air bases, there was still a role for carrier aviation. At the start of the conflict, aircraft carriers were able to reach their stations quickly, without the need to arrange political approval for land basing; throughout the conflict they were able to provide a platform for aircraft which were immune to the political objections which occasionally affected those based ashore in Italy, Hungary or Greece.[34] The mobility of carriers was another definite advantage, because it allowed them to move to find suitable weather for flight operations; as Grove noted, this was particularly useful when aircraft based in Italy were grounded by fog.[35] The mobility of maritime forces also allowed them to be swiftly dispatched elsewhere when other crises emerged (with a US aircraft carrier being temporarily diverted to the Gulf or an amphibious group to Somalia). Carrier aircraft took part in the whole range of aerial missions – monitoring and enforcing the no-fly zone, providing close support for UN forces and participating in Operation *Deliberate Force*. They also provided a capability for search and rescue of downed pilots, as when US Marine Corps special operations forces successfully extracted an F-16 pilot.

The aircraft carriers of medium navies played a prominent role, with both the UK and France deploying them in the Adriatic; the fact that prior to Operation *Deliberate Force*, the principal naval participants were Britain and France represents yet another way in which this conflict provides an interesting contrast to the Gulf War. The UK maintained one carrier on station at one hour notice or less for action for three years, and it contributed greatly to air operations.[36] The aircraft carrier's Sea Harriers not only operated as fighters but also as photo-reconnaissance, close support and ground attack aircraft. Due to the low level of submarine threat, the anti-submarine helicopters normally carried were moved to Royal Fleet Auxiliaries and replaced by transport helicopters.

A further aspect of the maritime contribution to the campaign ashore deserves a separate mention. As part of Operation *Deliberate Force*, 13 cruise missiles were launched from a US cruiser against Serb air defence targets near Banja Luka in northwest Bosnia. They were used because of their proven accuracy and ability to function even in poor weather, and the fact that they avoided the danger to pilots which flying in such high-risk areas would involve.[37]

The other tasks of maritime forces in the Adriatic were in support of the forces ashore. Fewer ground units were transported by sea than in other cases because of the proximity of US forces in Germany, the availability of overland rail routes and the willingness of Hungary to allow passage and marshalling – though sea lift was still of use, particularly for British and French forces and their supplies. Naval units also provided ongoing support to forces ashore with intelligence gathering and surveillance, transportation and supply, and a contingency force for reinforcement or partial or total extraction if events deteriorated. Moreover, at sea they were invulnerable to guerrilla attacks or to hostage takers, and had less impact on local political sensitivities. Unlike land forces, they could be held in position and used without needing any additional consent. This is generally referred to in naval doctrine as poise or, as one of the commanders of the British task group in the Adriatic put it, 'the Navy holding itself ready to support the land battle at short notice in whatever way the Land Force requires and when, where and how it requires it.'[38] Warships offered several advantages for this kind of multinational effort, being easy to commit and, due largely to NATO experience, to integrate with other ships (as seen in *Sharp Guard*, or when a Dutch frigate operated as a part of the British task group), and also able to be held back as a national insurance policy in case forces ashore needed reinforcement or evacuation.[39] Thus, while some US, British and French warships in the Adriatic were part of the sanctions enforcement effort, others were kept under direct national command, capable of either providing support for the multilateral forces at sea or UNPROFOR ashore, or of acting unilaterally.

Maritime power alone was not decisive and indeed could not have been in such a conflict, yet neither could economic sanctions or air power. Maritime forces allowed external powers to pursue some of their objectives at an acceptable level of risk and cost, and were required for the support of the other forces which were committed. Besides, the circumstances of the conflict more seriously constrained the utility of air power and this is likely to be repeated in future conflicts: for example, there were few suitable targets for air strikes in Somalia or Haiti, and in both of these the role of air power was limited to supporting land forces. Air power, particularly that possessed by the United States, has a formidable capacity for destroying specific targets. The problem, as has been shown on many occasions, lies in applying this to achieve political objectives, particularly in unconventional conflicts. What air power can do without ground forces is limited; it cannot, for example, ensure the safety of aid convoys, protect safe areas, or defend cities against sniper and mortar fire. The role of ground forces is circumscribed in conflicts such as that in the former Yugoslavia, where the interests of intervening states are only indirectly affected, and by the limited willingness of public opinion to accept casualties.[40]

The role played by navies in the former Yugoslavia was less visible than that of land or air forces, but that does not make it insignificant. It was by necessity a joint campaign, and maritime forces made a number of contributions to the economic embargo and the no-fly zone, in supporting troops ashore and conducting air and missile strikes.

CONCLUSION

The two conflicts examined in this chapter were very different from each other but taken together they offer some useful conclusions for the post-Cold War use of force. First, air power (including missiles) can be immensely effective in the right circumstances, but these rarely arise and even when they do it is unlikely that air power alone can achieve significant political results. Secondly, maritime power plays a greater role in conflicts of varying kinds than is often acknowledged. Its main limitations include relatively slow speed (though this has proved less of a hindrance in practice than might be supposed) and the fact that ships offer high value, politically symbolic targets. Nevertheless, navies have other compensating advantages. Like air power, what they can achieve by themselves is limited, but maritime forces have much to contribute to joint operations because of their access, mobility, independence of host nation support and the breadth of military capabilities they embody, particularly naval aviation. Their role may often be that of supporting other services, but there seems to be less resistance to accepting this in navies than there has historically been in air forces.

Navies are needed both for operations at sea (which are either important in their own right such as sanctions enforcement, or to achieve sea control as a precursor to subsequent action) and to project power and influence ashore. Both of these conflicts demanded heavy ground forces; this necessitated large-scale sea lift, which has to be protected. Naval forces also offer mobile platforms for rapidly developing capabilities such as longer-range missiles, unmanned aerial vehicles and improving C4I systems. The value of a navy is not confined to one of superpower status, as shown by the contribution of so many navies in both the Gulf conflict and the former Yugoslavia. (This is true even for such sophisticated capabilities as cruise missiles, which the UK has decided to fit on some of its submarines.) The need to be able to secure control of the sea remains, and with the proliferation of advanced weapons is a demanding task. Yet the emphasis of naval doctrine has shifted towards maritime operations – that is, influencing events on land from the sea – and towards the littoral instead of the deep oceans. This is less of a shift for navies than might be assumed. The experience of the US Navy during the Cold War was more regional than its doctrine, while the importance of maritime strategy has long been recognized by the Royal Navy. Indeed, Admiral Nelson, its great hero, was no stranger to combined operations: well before his death in one of the greatest ever fleet engagements, he lost an eye and an arm in land battles.[41]

This chapter began by arguing that the utility of a navy does not depend on the existence of a powerful hostile fleet, but rather depends on what roles naval forces can perform. The experience of maritime operations in the Persian Gulf and the Adriatic suggests that navies have much to offer in the post-Cold War period. This is reflected in the comment of a British Minister of Defence to a meeting of the Cabinet Defence Committee:

> The tasks which might fall to the Navy cannot be judged by reference solely to the strength of potential enemy fleets. For example, it might well become necessary to make a display of force in the Persian Gulf or on the Dalmatian Coast and the Navy would be called upon for this purpose.[42]

This statement, dating from 1947, was offered in response to a suggestion from the Chancellor of the Exchequer that without a naval threat, the case for expenditure on the Royal Navy was diminished! Much has changed over the past fifty years but the failure to appreciate the role of navies, it seems, has remained.

NOTES

1. This chapter has benefited from the comments of Robert O'Neill, Adam Roberts and Guy Challands.
2. W. E. Odom (Lieutenant-General, US Army (ret.)), 'Transforming the Military', *Foreign Affairs*, vol. 76, no. 4, July/August 1997, p. 61. Hobkirk made a similar point about the Cold War period, describing the US Navy's post-1945 emphasis on large carriers as 'puzzling to many', because 'the Soviet Union has never posed a surface threat for which carriers would be the answer.' M. D. Hobkirk, *Land, Sea or Air? Military Priorities, Historical Choices* (London: Macmillan for RUSI, 1992), p. 194.
3. The one conflict in which there was an intense struggle for sea control was the Falklands War of 1982. This example still supports the argument, because the UK task force sought control of the local sea and air in order to project power to retake the islands.
4. Maritime forces are defined in UK doctrine as 'Forces whose primary purpose is to conduct military operations at or from the sea.' BR1806, *The Fundamentals of British Maritime Doctrine* (London: HMSO, 1995), p. 223.
5. J. F. Jones (Lt-Col., USAF), 'Giulio Douhet Vindicated: Desert Storm 1991', in *Naval War College Review*, Autumn 1992, pp. 97, 99, 101. See also P. S. Meilinger, (Colonel, USAF), 'Giulio Douhet and Modern War', *Comparative Strategy*, July–September 1993, pp. 321–6.
6. E. Luttwak, 'Victory Through Air Power', *Commentary*, vol. 92, no. 2, August 1991, pp. 28–30.
7. E. Luttwak, 'Air Power in US Military Strategy', in R. Shultz and R. Pfaltzgraff, *The Future of Air Power in the Aftermath of the Gulf War* (Maxwell AFB, Ala.: Air University Press, 1992), p. 30.
8. J. A. Warden (Colonel, USAF), 'Employing Air Power in the Twenty-First Century', in Shultz and Pfaltzgraff, op. cit., p. 75. For his view of the theoretical basis of air power, see *The Air Campaign: Planning for Combat* (Washington, DC: National Defense University Press, 1988).
9. C. Bowie et al., *The New Calculus: Analysing Airpower's Changing Role in Joint Theater Campaigns* (Santa Monica, Calif.: RAND, 1993). This report was the result of a project funded by the US Air Force.
10. After the war, the UN Special Commission reported that it had found no evidence of any mobile Scud launchers being destroyed by aircraft, and of fixed launch sites, 12 were destroyed, 14 slightly damaged and two untouched; J. McCausland, *The Gulf Conflict: A Military Analysis*, Adelphi

Paper No. 282 (London: Brasseys for International Institute for Strategic Studies, 1993), p. 35. As Atkinson noted in 1993, UN inspectors had discovered 100 Scud missiles plus production facilities and 19 mobile launchers, 70 tons of nerve gas and 400 tons of mustard gas; and while the air campaign had targeted three nuclear facilities, the UN found 20 and were still looking. R. Atkinson, *Crusade: The Untold Story of the Gulf War* (London: Harper Collins, 1994), pp. 495–6.

11. McCausland, op. cit., p. 61.
12. E. A. Cohen, 'The Mystique of US Air power', *Foreign Affairs*, vol. 73, no. 1, January/ February 1994, pp. 111–22. Cohen acknowledged the unusual features of the war and the difficulties which might arise in using air power under different circumstances.
13. J. Keegan, *A History of Warfare*, (New York: Knopf, 1993), p. xi. It is also noteworthy that the special issue of *Survival* about the conflict (vol. XXXIII, no. 3, May–June 1991) included articles on the strategy of the war, the air campaign, the land campaign and technological aspects of the war, but nothing on the maritime campaign.
14. Department of Defense (US), *Conduct of the Persian Gulf War: Final Report to Congress* (Washington, DC: US Government Printing Office, April 1992), p. 19.
15. The logistic tail of land-based aircraft, often overlooked, is significant: in terms of personnel alone, 'each twenty-four plane squadron also required more than fifteen hundred engineers, technicians and armourers': Schwarzkopf, op. cit., p. 312.
16. McCausland, op. cit., p. 9.
17. N. Friedman, *Desert Victory: The War for Kuwait* (Annapolis, Md.: US Naval Institute, 1991), pp. 87–8.
18. Ships carried 3.5 million tons of dry cargo and 6 million tons of fuel; by contrast, 500 000 tons were moved by air: Department of Defense (US), *Conduct of the Persian Gulf Conflict: An Interim Report to Congress* (Washington, DC: US Government Printing Office, July 1991), p. 3.2–3.3.
19. McCausland, op. cit., p. 37; C. Craig (Captain, RN), *Call For Fire: Sea Combat in the Falklands and the Gulf War* (London: John Murray, 1995), p. 166.
20. McCausland, op. cit., p. 19; IISS, *Strategic Survey 1990–91* (London: Brasseys for IISS, 1991), p. 64; Friedman, op. cit., p. 317.
21. *Final Report to Congress*, pp. 53–60.
22. UK forces played a significant role in this aspect of the campaign; the US Navy was seen as having underestimated the danger from mines (see Craig, op. cit., *passim*) but has devoted considerably more effort in this direction since the war.
23. N. Schwarzkopf, *It Doesn't Take a Hero*, (London: Bantam, 1992), pp. 292–93.
24. See, for example, 'Royal Navy Still Rules the Waves', *Daily Telegraph*, 20 March 1997, which describes Sea Harriers from HMS *Invincible* joining the enforcement of the no-fly zone without any need for permission from Gulf states; 'Saudis and Turks Limit Tornado Missions', *Times*, 14 November 1997, about the reasons for the deployment of a British carrier; and 'UK "Ready to Fight Saddam"', *Guardian*, 17 January 1998, which notes that although it would be quicker to deploy RAF Tornados than carrier

aircraft, the former would need permission from the host state for raids on Iraq: 'In the current climate this would not be forthcoming.'

25. For example, during *Deliberate Force* (of which more below) bad weather forced the cancellation of over 40 per cent of the sorties planned for 13 September; AFSOUTH Information Sheet, *Operation Deliberate Force*, 6 November 1995.

26. Further strikes against SAM sites and a command post were carried out after the suspension of *Deliberate Force*. In total, between 12 April 1993 and 20 December 1995, *Deny Flight* involved over 100000 aircraft sorties, including over 23000 no-fly zone fighter sorties and 27000 close air support and air strike sorties. NATO AFSOUTH, *Operation Deny Flight – Final Fact Sheet*, 21 December 1995.

27. The details about Operation *Deliberate Force* are largely taken from AFSOUTH Information Sheet, *Operation Deliberate Force*, 6 November 1995; and IISS *Strategic Survey 1995–96* (London: Oxford University Press for International Institute for Strategic Studies, 1996), especially pp. 73–4, 126–37.

28. *Economist*, 2 September 1995.

29. *Economist*, 16 September 1995.

30. *Economist*, 13 January 1996; it also notes that both General Rupert Smith and his aides accepted that the Holbrooke diplomatic mission and pressure from Serbia were crucial to the peace deal.

31. In total, 74 192 ships were challenged; 5951 were inspected at sea and 1480 were diverted and inspected in port; six were caught trying to break the embargo. IFOR Final Fact Sheet, *NATO/WEU Operation Sharp Guard*, 2 October 1996.

32. For an account of the difficulties involved, see J. J. Blackham (Rear-Admiral, RN), 'Maritime Peacekeeping', *RUSI Journal*, vol. 138, no. 4, August 1993, pp. 18–23.

33. IFOR Final Fact Sheet, *NATO/WEU Operation Sharp Guard*, 2 October 1996. According to the IISS, *Military Balance 1992–93* (London: Brasseys for International Institute for Strategic Studies, 1992), the Serbia-Montenegro navy consisted of 5 submarines, 4 missile-armed frigates, 12 missile craft, 12 torpedo craft and 30 patrol vessels: pp. 87–8.

34. For example, Italy rejected a US request for basing for Stealth fighters: *Economist*, 16 September 1995.

35. E. Grove, 'Navies in Peacekeeping and Enforcement: The British Experience in the Adriatic Sea', *International Peacekeeping*, vol. 1, no. 4, Winter 1994, pp. 462–70 at p. 464.

36. In 1995 the Ministry of Defence stated that six Sea Harriers from HMS *Illustrious* had flown over 2200 sorties, nine Jaguars 2600 sorties and six Tornados 2100. *Statement on the Defence Estimates 1995*, Cm. 2800, May 1995, pp. 50–1.

37. Transcript of Press Briefing by Group Captain Trevor Murray, Chief Air Operations, AFSOUTH Headquarters, 11 September 1995.

38. Blackham, op. cit., p. 19.

39. Grove viewed the presence of British and French carriers as 'a key condition of the deployment of national forces in an enhanced peace-keeping role' because of their ability 'to bring national firepower to

bear in certain extreme circumstances': op. cit., p. 469. See also Black-ham, op. cit..

40. Luttwak noted that although air power or sea power alone can achieve much at little risk to life, 'Bosnia, Somalia and Haiti remind us that the typical great power business of restoring order still requires ground forces', and fear of casualties restricts their use. E. Luttwak, 'Where are the Great Powers?', *Foreign Affairs*, vol. 73, no. 4, July/August 1994, pp. 23–9. He considers further the effect of Western reluctance to risk casualties in 'A Post-Heroic Military Policy', *Foreign Affairs*, vol. 75, no. 4, July/August 1996, pp. 33–44.

41. Although he also famously stated that 'A ship's a fool to fight a fort'.

42. DO (47) 20th Meeting, 18 September 1947, CAB 131/4, Public Record Office, London.

10 The Measurement of Naval Strength in the Twenty-First Century

Norman Polmar

As we enter the twenty-first century, a number of significant factors will affect the world's navies. Among these factors are several new technologies, the proliferation of advanced weapons among Third World countries, the severe reduction of the Soviet-Russian fleet, the euphemistic 'downsizing' of the US Navy and the reshaping of US defence policy.

PERSPECTIVE

Close to the Royal Naval College at Greenwich, long the site of the navy's intellectual cornerstone, was the earliest headquarters of the British Admiralty, the Gun tavern on the Green at Deptford. That tavern was the headquarters of Lord Howard of Effingham, the Lord High Admiral of Queen Elizabeth's reign. Some historians believe that tavern was the place later called 'Her Majesty's House at Greenwich'.[1]

During the reign of Elizabeth, England's warships were largely influenced by Henry VIII's decision to build specialized ships for military purposes and by the experience of English 'pirates'. Warships were counted as men-of-war carrying so many cannon. This chapter will not recount here the various types of cannon employed except to say longer ranges for cannon were highly sought in this period. Beyond sailing warships, the Spanish, Russian and other navies of the era contained many galleys intended for operating in coastal areas where ships under sail could not easily manoeuvre.

As warships developed in the seventeenth, eighteenth, and early nineteenth centuries, the principal criteria for measuring warships and hence navies was a warship's firepower: how many guns, how many decks of guns, throw-weight of their shot and, subsequently, the calibre of their guns. By the late 1700s, the era of Nelson, ships-of-the-line or battleships mounted 100 guns or more; ships carrying 20 to 48 guns were called frigates, while those ships carrying fewer than 20 guns were designated as sloops-of-war in the Royal Navy and corvettes in the French Navy.

The introduction of steam propulsion and steel to warship construction in the 1800s enabled ships to mount rifled guns in rotating turrets. The new centre-line turret with two large guns could successfully challenge the broadside batteries of warships with larger numbers of smaller guns. Thus gun calibre or bore diameter became the principal measurement of major warships, more important in most instances than the number of guns carried.

By the early 1900s the calibre of battleship turret guns had reached 12 inches (304 mm), generally in two turrets, supported by a number of intermediate and medium calibre guns. This philosophy culminated in ships such as the *King Edward VII* class of 1903 armed with four 12-inch, four 9.2-inch (234 mm) and ten 6-inch (152 mm) batteries and the American *Connecticut* class of 1904 equipped with four 12-inch, four 8-inch (203 mm) and 12 7-inch (178 mm) batteries. However, the use of a mixed battery presented significant fire-control problems and led to the construction of the *Dreadnought* of 1906 equipped with a uniform main battery of ten 12-inch guns. This design epitomized two trends both of which were designed to increase throw-weight. The first trend was to maximize the number of heavy-calibre guns. Thus the Brazilian battleship *Rio de Janeiro* ordered in 1911 had no less than 14 12-inch guns in seven turrets while the American *Pennsylvania* class of 1913 and Russian *Gangut* class of 1915 mounted 12 12-inch guns in four triple turrets on displacements of 31 400 and 23 370 tons, respectively.[2]

The second trend was to increase the calibre of individual guns still further. In this the British tended to be the market leaders progressing to 13.5-inch (343 mm) guns in the first 'super' *Dreadnoughts* of the *Orion* class ordered in 1909 and 15-inch guns (381 mm) in the *Queen Elizabeth* class ordered in 1912.[3] The Germans responded moving from 11-inch (279 mm) to 12-inch and subsequently 15-inch.[4] The USA and Japan likewise responded moving from 12-inch to 14-inch (356 mm) calibres. With one exception they took the lead during the First World War, moving to 16-inch (406 mm) guns in 1917.[5] The exception was the British 'light battle cruiser' *Furious*, a white elephant, which took to sea in 1917 equipped with two single 18-inch (457 mm) guns. The forward gun was rapidly replaced by a flying-off platform, a harbinger of the coming change in the 'main battery' of warships.[6]

As mentioned above, battleship firepower grew again during the First World War with the Japanese and United States navies adopting the 16-inch gun. By the early the 1920s the 'big three' navies, American, British and Japanese, had become embroiled in a mini-arms race. With 16-inch gun battleships and battlecruisers under construction all three began to consider moving towards larger calibre weapons in the order of 18-inches. These plans were, however, thwarted by the agreements reached at the Washington Conference of 1921–22, albeit temporarily. [7]

As the international situation deteriorated during the 1930s, a new wave of battleship and battlecruiser building began, reaching its pinnacle with the Japanese super-battleship *Yamato*. Completed in 1941, this giant displaced 62 000 tons and carried nine 18.1-inch (460 mm) guns – the largest gun battery ever mounted in a warship. [8] Both the *Yamato* and her sister ship *Musashi* were sunk in 1944–45 by US Navy carrier-based aircraft. Indicative of the changing nature of maritime strength referred to above was the conversion of a sister ship into an aircraft carrier while in the course of construction.

The achievements of aviation in the Second World War and the use of atomic bombs against Japan in 1945 ushered in a new era for naval forces. [9] Within a decade of the end of the war guided missiles and nuclear propulsion were taken to sea by the US Navy, soon followed by the Soviet Navy and other fleets. Admiral S.G. Gorshkov astutely characterized the change in the measurement of warships when he wrote:

> We have had to cease comparing the number of warships of one type or another and their total displacement (or the number of guns in a salvo or the weight of this salvo), and turn to a more complex, but also more correct, appraisal of the striking and defensive power of the ships, based on a mathematical analysis of their capabilities and qualitative characteristics. [10]

His 'mathematical analysis' took into account a variety of warship features but 'firepower', be it guns, missiles or aircraft, remained a critical measurement of warship effectiveness in the Cold War era.

A NEW APPROACH

This assessment would suggest that in this post-Cold War era we must develop a new method of measuring naval strength. In the same manner that the Industrial Revolution led to steam-powered, steel-hull warships, and the nuclear-missile revolution led to the naval forces of the Cold War era, the so-called 'information era' that we have now entered demands new criteria for measuring the effectiveness of navies.

This chapter proposes that a new approach to the measurement of naval strength and effectiveness must begin with what can be called 'core factors'. These are:

1. Space – a navy's ability to effectively employ satellites and other space systems for navigation, ocean surveillance, targeting, communications and other functions.
2. C3I – a navy's effectiveness in employing advanced, computer-based systems for Command, Control, and Communications as well as for Intelligence collection and processing.
3. People – well-trained and motivated officers and enlisted men and women who can man the fleet and provide the vital command and support services ashore.

These three core factors will become the keys to measuring the effectiveness of major navies, more important, arguably, than the numbers of guns, missiles, aircraft or even warships in a fleet. Without the active use of space, without effective C3I and without suitable personnel a major navy cannot be effective regardless of the number of ships or their theoretical firepower. Without these core factors it is reduced, at best, to a coastal defence force of questionable effectiveness. To understand the relationship of these core factors with regard the Russian Navy, this chapter will briefly review a hierarchy or structure for considering naval forces (see Figure 10.1).

NAVAL MISSIONS

Naval missions will depend upon the nation's political and economic stature and its geographic location. Using the contemporary Russian situation as an example, this would suggest the following as principal naval missions for the Russian Navy in the first part of the twenty-first century:

1. *Coastal defence*. Russia has a lengthy maritime border which requires surveillance and patrol, to monitor and, if required, stop intrusions by foreign naval forces.
2. *Strategic deterrence*. Strategic missile submarines provide an effective and highly survivable strategic defensive force. Certainly a mixed force of land-based missiles, especially when one considers the wide expanses of Russia, as well as missile submarines appears to offer the optimum nuclear deterrent force.[11]
3. *Forward presence*. The use of warships to represent Russian political-military interests in the Third World. In many respects this will be the most important role for the Russian Navy in the early twenty-first century. The focus of such operations will be different than during the Cold War, when Third World operations were peripheral to

the superpower confrontation between the Soviet Union and the United States.

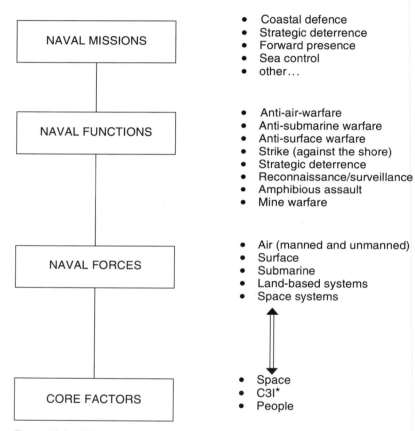

Figure 10.1   The measurement of naval strength in the twenty-first century
*C3I = Command, Control, Communications and Intelligence

Because of its importance, it is necessary to expand on the forward presence of naval forces. First, the deployment of a warship overseas has none of the political burdens of sending ground troops or air forces, as no foreign bases or permissions are required. Second, a warship can engage easily in exercises with Third World navies, building friendship and support. Third, a warship can appear and withdraw from an area with little explanation to anyone. Finally, a warship can be a passive observer, or can engage in 'gunboat diplomacy', the use or threat of use by limited naval forces, or can participate in a conflict. An Englishman, Oliver Cromwell, reputedly said, 'A warship is the best ambassador.' *Most* types of warships are useful for political presence. As British diplomat and political scientist James Cable observed, 'In time of peace a superior warship on the spot can achieve results not obtainable in other ways and without regard to the purpose for which the ship was built.'[12]

However, nuclear-propelled surface ships have increasing political liability in the forward presence role. Growing concern for nuclear accidents make such ships less and less welcome in a large number of ports. But other major warships with conventional propulsion – aircraft carriers, cruisers, destroyers – are most suitable for this role. Indeed, the proliferation of advanced weapon technologies to the Third World (many from Russia) increasingly will require that more capable warships be employed in the forward presence role.

NAVAL FUNCTIONS

The conduct of naval missions requires the performance of various naval functions. The principal functions are:

- anti-air warfare;
- anti-submarine warfare;
- anti-surface warfare;
- strike (against shore targets);
- strategic strike (deterrence);
- reconnaissance/surveillance;
- amphibious assault;
- mine warfare.

The Soviet-Russian navy has demonstrated a high degree of competence in all of these warfare areas, especially during the later stages of the Cold War. It is questionable, however, if a high level of competence is now being maintained by the Russian Navy in all of these areas.[13] Reductions in the time ships spend at sea, the amount of flight time for naval aviators, the availability of munitions for training, the lack of maintenance funds and numerous other constraints are seriously degrading these capabilities.

In time, certain capabilities will be depleted beyond realistic effectiveness. It is unlikely that the Russian naval high command will wish to see any of these functions disappear completely. If some naval functions must be deleted, it could be suggested that amphibious assault – an offensive function – could be given up in the interest of maintaining the others. Very careful management of resources will be required to ensure that at least a minimal capability is retained in each naval function, both for actual operations and as the basis for possible future rebuilding of the Russian Navy.

NAVAL FORCES

Naval functions are performed by naval forces which are:

- aircraft (manned and unmanned);
- surface ships;
- submarines;
- land-based systems;
- space systems.

The Soviet-Russian Navy has put to sea impressive ships and aircraft, and has developed impressive weapons and sensors. Again, it is expensive to maintain this broad spectrum of naval capabilities. Naval aviation, especially with conventional carrier aircraft, is particularly expensive. Although aircraft carriers are useful in a number of naval roles and are excellent ships for political presence, one must question the viability of an aviation force that, for the foreseeable future, will have but one aircraft carrier, the *Admiral Kuznetsov*.[14]

In this regard, if the United Kingdom and France are to remain major naval powers, it will require the British government to fund the two follow-on aircraft carriers envisaged as replacements for the current three ships of the *Invincible* class,[15] and for the French government to facilitate the construction of a second carrier, of either nuclear or conventional propulsion, to serve alongside the *Charles de Gaulle*. Indeed, a single ship may be a 'symbol' of naval power, but one or more similar ships are required to enable one or more always to be either on station or available for immediate deployment.

For the devastated Russian economy the solution to sea-based aviation will be much more complicated. The high cost of carrier aviation makes the practicality of maintaining a single 'flat-top' a highly doubtful means of preserving sea-based aviation. One cannot help but speculate on the efficacy of keeping a single ship like the *Admiral Kuznetsov* as opposed to developing a force of several smaller V/STOL carriers,[16] probably in size between the British *Invincible* class (20 600 tons full load) and the US LHA/LHD classes (40 500 tons).[17]

From a viewpoint of naval missions and naval functions, it is unlikely that surface ship or submarine programmes can be further reduced by the Russian Navy (except in the amphibious category). Indeed, the Soviet-Russian excellence in undersea craft indicates that this category of warship design, development, construction and operation should be preserved at all costs.

Furthermore, land-based forces and air assets are also important to navies. For example, in Britain the Royal Air Force controls land-based maritime aircraft as well as the nation's fixed-wing Airborne Early Warning (AEW) aircraft. In the United States the Navy operates the land-based maritime patrol aircraft, as in the Russian Navy. However, land-based forces have naval roles that are much broader than only aircraft. There are, of course, the land-based C3I systems.

From a Russian viewpoint land-based, long-range or 'strategic' missiles are also considered when one addresses naval operations. Their potential use against naval forces is highly significant. While little has been said about this aspect of Russian naval forces, there is ample evidence that at least from the early 1960s, when the classic work of Marshal V. D. Sokolovskiy, *Military Strategy*, was published,[18] the Soviets had considered the use of land-based ballistic missiles against surface ships *and submarines*. For example, in a then classified article published in October 1961, Admiral V. A. Kasatonov, later the First Deputy Commander-in-Chief of the Soviet Navy (1964–72), wrote:

> The essence of the problem is to create effective means for the distant destruction of submarines from the air which will make it possible to employ for their destruction the most effective modern means of destruction – missiles with nuclear charges launched from submarines, aircraft, and ships and possibly also from shore launching mounts.[19]

In this and possibly other areas land-based forces may be able to support effectively naval operations to a far greater degree than at present. This use of land-based assets under naval control can be increasingly effective as warships become increasingly expensive (on a relative basis.)

Further, space activities will be increasingly important in naval operations. Again, the Soviet-Russian expertise in this area must be continued and exploited for naval use. Of particular significance is the detection and targeting of surface ships by satellites, and possibly the detection and targeting of submarines.[20] A final note on future Russian naval activities: An analysis undertaken by the author of this chapter into areas of Russian defence spending and research efforts in the post-Cold War period have indicated only three 'growth' areas: developments in military use of space, tactical aviation and submarine/anti-submarine warfare.

CORE FACTORS

The use of space activities, it should be noted, is addressed as both a component of naval forces and as one of the core factors that is part of the foundation of a modern navy. These core factors, as described earlier in this chapter, are:

- space;
- C3I;
- people.

No modern navy can operate without the extensive use of space, nor without competent and comprehensive C3I systems. Virtually all naval activities are heavily dependent upon these core factors. One only has to look at the developments in the field of the Global Positioning System (GPS) to understand the impact of space on military operations. A receiver the size of a packet of cigarettes can provide the precise time, indicate north and give one's location to within a couple of metres.

Computers and satellites have already revolutionized naval command, control and communications. The trends in reliance on these advanced systems *and* their potential vulnerability will only continue at an increasing rate. And satellites and unmanned aerial vehicles are similarly having a major impact on the 'I' or intelligence part of the C3I equation.

Within a year or two the US Navy could have a Mach 1-plus aerial vehicle that can be launched from a submarine torpedo tube or destroyer's vertical launch cell, streak more than 500 miles, slow and provide real-time aerial photography that can be relayed (via satellite) back to the submarine or task force commander.[21]

In many respects, the most difficult of the core factors is people, the key to the effectiveness of the future navies. And it is here that cause for pessimism lies. Many national and naval leaders would prefer to invest in new weapons or even in keeping older weapons operational than they would in recruiting higher quality people, properly training them and paying the costs of retaining them in active service. Further, with the end of the Cold War and the employment opportunities for people with a high technological aptitude (the 'teckies'), the personnel problems are being further exacerbated.

The challenges for naval and political leaders as we approach the twenty-first century are considerable. This chapter therefore argues that to build an effective navy for the twenty-first century, one must employ new measurements for judging fleet effectiveness.

NOTES

1. Leslie Gardiner, *The British Admiralty* (Edinburgh: William Blackwood & Sons, 1968), p. 15.
2. Richard Hough, *Dreadnought: a History of the Modern Battleship* (Cambridge: Patrick Stephens, 1984), p. 239, 246 and 257.
3. Ibid., pp. 56–7 and 124–30.
4. Ibid., pp. 60–1 and 131.
5. The US *Maryland* class of 1916 and Japanese *Nagato* class. Ibid., p. 247 and 254.
6. The *Furious* was designed to mount two 18-inch guns in single-gun turrets. Her two near-sister ships, *Courageous* and *Glorious*, were each completed with two twin turrets mounting 15-inch guns. The trio was the result of Churchill–Fisher proposals for more extensive naval operations against the Germans in the North Sea and Baltic. The *Furious* initially had her forward 18-inch gun removed to allow for a flying-off platform to be installed. After this the after 18-inch gun was removed in 1917 and a separate flight deck installed amidships to allow aircraft to land on. She retained her centre-line superstructure. Subsequently, a full flight-deck was installed on the ship. The *Courageous* and *Glorious* were also converted to full-deck aircraft carriers.
7. Stephen Roskill, *Naval Policy Between the Wars, Vol. 1: the Period of Anglo-American Antagonism, 1919–29* (London: Collins Clear-Type Press, 1968), pp. 204–33.
8. The largest US battleships were the four ships of the *Iowa* class, completed in 1943–44; they had a standard displacement of 45 000 tons and carried nine 16-inch (406 mm) guns. These ships were in intermittent active service until 1992! The planned *Montana* class was to have carried 12 similar 16-inch guns. Peter Padfield, *The Battleship Era* (London: Rupert Hart-Davis, 1972), pp. 262–5.
9. To get a feel of the new era in maritime warfare see Eric Grove's comparison of the planned postwar (1947) and prewar (1938) deployments of the Royal Navy. Eric Grove, *Vanguard to Trident: British Naval Policy since World War II* (London, The Bodley Head, 1987), p. 25.
10. Admiral of the Fleet of the Soviet Union S. G. Gorshkov, 'Navies in War and in Peace', *Morsky Sbornik*, no. 2, 1972.

11. The relatively high cost and relative limitations and vulnerabilities of manned bomber aircraft in the strategic role severely reduce the viability of these aircraft.

12. James Cable, 'Political Applications of Limited Naval Force', *The Soviet Union in Europe and the Near East: Her Capabilities and Intentions* (London: Royal United Services Institution, 1970).

13. Richard Scott, 'Which Course Will Russia's Navy Steer', *Jane's Navy International*, October 1996, pp. 18–21.

14. The *Admiral Kuznetsov* has not been to sea since her brief Mediterranean cruise in 1996. She is in an Arctic shipyard, awaiting funds for completion of an overhaul.

15. See Martin Edmonds (ed.), 'British Naval Aviation in the 21st Century', *Bailrigg Memorandum 25* (Lancaster: Centre for Defence and International Security Studies, 1997).

16. V/STOL stands for vertical/short take-off and landing aircraft.

17. The *Admiral Kuznetsov* has a full-load displacement of 67 500 tons. Specific benefits provided by these smaller V/STOL ships were twofold: first, they were slightly larger than the US LHA/LHD helicopter carrier-V/STOL carriers and had much heavier weapons and sensors; and second, the fleet of four vessels meant that operational capability was not impaired when individual ships were in refit.

18. Vasilii Sokolovshy, *Soviet Military Strategy*, 3rd edn, ed. Harriet Scott (London: Macdonald & Jane's, 1975).

19. Admiral V. A. Kasatonov, 'On the Problems of the Navy and Methods for Resolving Them', noted by Capt. Harlan Ullman, USN, 'The Counter-Polaris Task' in Michael MccGwire et al. (eds), *Soviet Naval Policy: Objectives and Constraints* (New York: Praeger, 1975), pp. 585–600. An excellent exposition on the use of land-based missiles against naval forces is found in Raymond A. Robinson, 'Incoming Ballistic Missiles at Sea', *US Naval Institute Proceedings*, June 1987, pp. 67–71.

20. See, for example, Hung P. Nguyen, *Submarine Detection from Space: A Study of Russian Capabilities* (Annapolis, Md.: Naval Institute Press, 1993). This is the most comprehensive unclassified analysis of this subject to be undertaken to date.

21. Such a system would be based on a combination of the current Tomahawk cruise missile and the near-term Fasthawk cruise missile.

11 The Land/Sea Dimension: the Role of the Army in Future Warfare
Colin McInnes

This chapter analyses the relationship between land and sea power. Specifically it focuses on the British Army's views on the future of warfare and the role of sea power within its vision of future operations. The chapter begins by discussing the relative importance of the Army and Navy to British defence policy and how this has changed over the course of the past hundred years. It then outlines the Army's traditional view of the relationship between land and sea power and the situation which had developed immediately prior to the end of the Cold War. The chapter then suggests why there was a prima facie case that this relationship might change with the end of the Cold War and details why the change has in fact been quite limited, to the extent that the current relationship – at least from the Army's perspective – appears to be a very traditional one.

THE ARMY, THE ROYAL NAVY AND BRITISH DEFENCE POLICY

Prior to this century the British Army and the Royal Navy had a very distinctive relationship. The Navy was the 'senior service'. It was the first and most important line of defence and secured the critical link with Empire. As the world's leading trading power, *pax Britannica* and with it Britain's trading strength rested on the broad shoulders of the Royal Navy. In contrast the Army was the junior partner. Its primary task was the defence of Empire, both from internal insurrection and also from external powers. The Army's second home was India, and although it had fought sometimes with great distinction on continental Europe, the 'continental commitment' was generally seen as something to be avoided.[1] Britain was a maritime power and its Navy the source of much of its military strength.

In the twentieth century, however, this relationship began to change. The First World War saw the British Army taking on and ultimately defeating the engine of the German military, its land army, while the Royal Navy's *Dreadnoughts* spectacularly failed in their declared mission of sinking the German High Seas Fleet. Further, the popular memory of the First World War is almost entirely focused on the land campaign – from the contemporary poetry of Wilfred Owen, Robert Graves and Siegfried Sassoon to more recent films and television. In a very real sense, it was the British Army and not the Royal Navy that had won the First World War for Britain. Although the Royal Navy fared rather better in the Second World War, it proved ineffective in defending the British mainland from attack – this time by strategic bombing – while once again it was the Army, albeit with substantial American assistance, which took on and defeated the main body of German military strength in Western Europe and North Africa. By the end of the Second World War the Royal Navy had clearly slipped from a position of pre-eminence in British defence policy, and indeed in the early years of the Cold War it was the Royal Air Force with its strategic nuclear mission which took priority in government planning.[2] In a general war, after the Army briefly held the line in Germany, the RAF's nuclear weapons would ultimately wreak destruction. In the Cold War against communist insurrection outside Europe, it was the Army's presence overseas which mattered with the other two services merely providing ancillary support.

Although in the 1960s the Royal Navy gained the strategic nuclear role from the RAF with the purchase of the Polaris system, and NATO's new strategy of flexible response rendered the sea lines of communication relatively more important, by the early 1980s the Navy had sunk to its nadir with John Nott's 1981 review cutting a swathe through the surface fleet and limiting the Royal Navy's role to primarily one of an anti-submarine warfare force.[3] The Falklands War provided some respite from the Nott cuts as well as a welcome boost in prestige for the Navy, but for the rest of the decade the other two services matched and, arguably, exceeded the Royal Navy in terms of defence priorities (the special case of Trident aside). For the Army, its two main commitments – the defence of NATO territory and internal security in Northern Ireland – were topped in the list of government defence priorities only by the strategic nuclear deterrent. Although the early post-Cold War years suggested a shift back to more traditional priorities – the 1990/91 *Options for Change* exercise (a defence review in all but name) emphasized air defence of the UK and the Royal Navy's out-of-area role, while cutting disproportionately British Army forces in Germany – by the mid-1990s the Army had established itself as critical to government security policy, performing a variety of roles in places as diverse as the Persian Gulf, Bosnia and Rwanda.

Consequently, the post-Cold War strategic environment has not led to a fundamental shift in the relative importance of the three services. Although there have been changes, no one service has emerged pre-eminent. The shift away from a focus on the Soviet threat to a more generalized policy dealing with security 'risks' has not yet been accompanied by an equally fundamental shift in the relationship between the three services. What the remainder of this chapter therefore focuses on is not the relative significance of the Army versus the Navy *per se*, but the Army's view of future operations and the role of sea power within that.

LAND POWER AND SEA POWER

The relationship between land power and sea power, and the relative merits of a continental versus maritime strategy, have been two of the key questions debated by naval theorists over the past hundred years or more – from historical classics such as Alfred Thayer Mahan's *The Influence of Sea Power upon History*[4] to more contemporary works such as Colin Gray's *The Navy in the Post-Cold War World*.[5] It has not, however, been a topic which has much engaged land power theorists nor indeed the British Army. The works of the key British interwar thinkers on land power, Captain Sir Basil Liddell Hart and Major-General J. F. C. Fuller, focused on different questions, as indeed do those of more recent writers such as Richard Simpkin and Chris Bellamy.[6] Liddell Hart's *The British Way in Warfare*[7] and, at the end of the nineteenth century, C. E. Callwell's *The Effect of Maritime Command on Land Campaigns* are rare exceptions to this general rule. In general, however, land power theorists have focused on a different set of questions: the relationship between offence and defence, the impact of new technology (the tank in the 1930s, nuclear weapons in the 1950s, precision guided munitions (PGMs) and the helicopter in the 1970s and the so-called 'Revolution in Military Affairs' in the 1990s), strategies of manoeuvre versus those of attrition, and the relationship with air power.[8] The relationship with sea power has, in contrast, rarely been debated by land power theorists.

Instead a consensus has developed that the Navy's task, crudely put, is to get the Army to where it needs to be and to keep it supplied there. Once in the theatre of operations, the Army will engage the enemy's main force in the decisive land-battle. Since it is this which will determine victory, the Army and land power theorists have focused on the question of how to win the land campaign, happily leaving the question of how to keep the sea lines of communication open to the Navy. Although this may appear to be little more than a caricature, simplifying a much more complex relationship, the Army and its theorists' understanding of the relationship has not traditionally developed much beyond this level because the question of the relationship between land and sea power is so rarely considered by them. Indeed, if anything, during the last two decades of the Cold War the Navy was even more in the background for the Army for two reasons. First, under the Healey reviews of the 1960s the Army had lost its out-of-area role, meaning that it was no longer reliant on the Navy to move and support it overseas. Second, despite the advent of flexible response and attempts to raise the nuclear threshold, the common assumption was that a war in Europe would be over before the Navy could establish sea control and exert a major influence on the land campaign.

In the post-Cold War era, however, there are a number of possible reasons why this relationship might be changing and suggestions that the Army is becoming more aware of, and sensitive to, the role and utility of sea power. A key indicator here is the growing emphasis upon the tri-service nature of future campaigns – what is termed 'jointness'. Indeed 'jointness' has become the shibboleth of the 1990s. New joint structures have appeared, most notably the new Permanent Joint Headquarters (PJHQ), the Joint Rapid Deployment Force (JRDF) and the Joint Services Command and Staff College (JSCSC) which replaces the three single-service staff colleges. Doctrine has also emphasized the joint nature of future operations. The Royal Navy's *The Fundamentals of British Maritime Doctrine*, for example, states that 'most major campaigns and operations will be *joint*; that is, they will involve forces of more than one Service and will frequently be combined.'[9] Similarly the 1996 version of *British Military Doctrine*, one of the Army's key doctrinal publications, states that 'at the operational level activity on land, at sea and in the air must be conceived, planned and conducted as a single entity, usually involving all three Services and is therefore "joint".'[10] It is not simply campaigns which are seen in joint terms, but operations including battle. The 1996 version of *British Military Doctrine* develops the joint theme with the statement that 'the joint battle is indivisible', and then devotes a number of pages to a detailed discussion of how air and sea power can be used to support the land battle.[11]

This move towards 'jointness' may be seen as part of an ongoing trend in modern war: that the combined arms battle of the Second World War became the land/air battle – or, in American doctrinal terminology, Air-Land Battle[12] – in the 1980s and from this moved to joint operations in the 1990s. This is driven at least in part by technology producing systems which transcend the simple air/land/sea divide, most obviously electromagnetic spectrum (EMS) operations, but also the development of long-range weapons such as the Tomahawk cruise missile. In the UK it is also driven by the diminishing capabilities of the single services on the assumption that the synergistic benefits of jointness may be used as a force multiplier to offset other weaknesses. Since 1989, defence budget reductions have already led to substantial cuts in the size of all three UK armed services to the extent that the British Army, for example, has been cut by roughly one quarter, while there is a growing recognition that the government may be unable and/or unwilling to fund the purchase of some new technologies. Moreover, the speed of technological change, particularly in the electronics and computing fields, continues to accelerate, almost certainly beyond the government's ability to pay for all or even most of their military applications. Although in the early 1990s the Conservative government planned to offset force reductions with an emphasis upon maintaining or even enhancing the armed services' technological competitiveness – what was termed a 'leaner but meaner' force structure – this was greeted with considerable scepticism at the time[13] and subsequently because of a series of cuts in the defence budget. As a result the armed services may find themselves deployed in a position where they are not only outnumbered but where they may also lack a dominant technological edge in some key areas. In this situation, 'jointness' may prove to be a force multiplier whereby the whole is greater than the sum of the parts. According to the current orthodoxy joint operations may offer greater efficiency, a means of maximizing what is available and of exploiting areas of relative advantage.

In addition to this emphasis on jointness, the likelihood that future operations will be expeditionary in nature also suggests a closer relationship between land and sea power. This represents a major change from the policy assumptions of the 1970s and 1980s, when the Army was based in or near where it would have to fight – primarily West Germany – and when the limited expeditionary capability rested almost wholly with the Royal Navy and the Royal Marines.[14] If the Army now has to be moved to where it is needed, and if it is to do so in strength and over any period of time, then sea power will be critical for power projection and in controlling the sea lines of communication. For although air transportation is increasingly capable and can reach a theatre of operations in hours or days (whereas sea transportation may take weeks or months), moving heavy equipment and large stockpiles can only be done by sea.

Finally the nature of post-Cold War crises suggests a possible change in the relationship between sea and land power. It has become a commonplace in the UK to talk of the unpredictability of future crises – the uncertainty over where and when they might occur and against whom British forces may have to fight. Nor might it be clear whether British *military* involvement is required or, even if it is required, whether the government is willing to respond. This has created the possibility that naval forces might be despatched to maintain a presence and demonstrate concern while limiting risk and involvement, but at the same time retaining the ability to escalate if and when required – what the Royal Navy terms 'poise'.[15] If land power does become involved, then it may do so at a later stage when the Navy is already established in theatre having developed some local knowledge and expertise, as happened in the crises in the former Yugoslavia and the Persian Gulf.

THE ARMY AND FUTURE WAR

The above suggests that there may be good reasons to think that the relationship between sea and land power may be changing in the 1990s, certainly when compared to that of the 1970s and 1980s. In particular the emphasis upon joint operations, the likelihood that future Army operations will be expeditionary in nature, and the unpredictable nature of future crises all suggest a closer relationship between the two. This is not, however, borne out by the Army's vision of the nature of future war, and in particular its view of campaigns and battle. In a series of documents, including new versions of its key doctrinal manuals *British Military Doctrine*[16] and ADP Volume 1, *Operations*, the Army has detailed its view of how future wars will be fought. What is remarkable is how, despite the rhetoric of 'jointness', the Army's view of the relationship between land and sea power is very traditional: that the Royal Navy's job is to get the Army to where it needs to be and to support it there, but that the Army will win the war through a decisive land/air engagement in which the Navy will play little part. This is demonstrated most clearly in the Army's view of how future campaigns will be structured and how battle will be fought.

Although the Army does not have a formal model for the shape of future campaigns, and indeed is intent upon avoiding an overly rigid perspective on how campaigns might develop, it does seem to have a generalized and informal view that future campaigns will consist of three overlapping phases: an initial phase involving the deployment to the theatre of operations and preparation for the campaign; a main engagement with enemy forces; and post-conflict activities.[17] The precise emphasis to be placed on each phase is not fixed, though should war come then clearly the second phase is seen as being decisive. Nor is it necessarily the case that a crisis will go through all three phases. In some instances the first phase will have a deterrent effect preventing escalation, while in others, namely defeat during the second phase, the final phase might not be required. Nevertheless Army doctrinal publications do, albeit largely implicitly, see future campaigns in terms of these three distinct, though possibly overlapping, phases.

The first phase is preparatory in nature and would involve establishing sea control for strategic mobility and power projection, securing command of the air, the battle for EMS supremacy and deep operations to 'shape the battlefield'. At this stage the Army's roles would be largely secondary – establishing a secure rear area from which to operate and contributing to deep operations through the use of special forces, intelligence and reconnaissance assets, long-range fire (including attack helicopters) and electronic warfare assets. In contrast the Navy would be much more heavily involved in securing the sea lines of communication. Deployment of forces in this phase may, of course, have a deterrent effect. If so, the crisis would not escalate and *by default* this would be the decisive phase.[18] However, if the crisis does escalate into a main force engagement, then the campaign would move into a second phase. At this point land forces would take centre-stage in conducting a short but intense land/air campaign designed to destroy enemy forces and capture territory.

> It will be fought day and night... and without respite for some days. It will be fought through out [sic] the area of operations, that is with simultaneous and synchronised deep, close and rear operations at each appropriate level and with little clear geographical delineation between the three. The nature of extreme violence, in an attempt to dislocate an enemy, will place high demands on the moral component of an army... *Conclusion of the campaign is likely to be sought in the land campaign.*[19]

Ordinarily this would be the decisive phase in the sense that this is where victory over enemy forces would be achieved. Even in operations other than war, this phase would be decisive in determining the outcome of a crisis. The third and final phase of a campaign would involve post-conflict activities. The end of combat operations may not mean the end of military involvement in theatre; instead a variety of possible tasks may emerge once the conflict is over. These range from rebuilding the infrastructure to humanitarian relief, to disarmament and decommissioning of weapons through to protection of civilians, as happened with the Kurds following the Gulf War. Again land forces would be heavily involved in this stage, though such operations might require very different skills from the previous stage and would probably take much longer.

Although the Army acknowledges the importance of the other services to the successful outcome of a campaign, particularly in the first phase, it is clear that should a crisis escalate into major conflict then the Army views the decisive phase as the land/air battle in which it would take the leading role. In other words, any future war would be won by the Army supported by the other services. Land, or more accurately, land/air, power would remain the dominant form of future warfare. Sea control is necessary but not sufficient for victory, while its contribution to the land/air battle, although growing, especially through air power and long-range missiles, is 'nice to have' rather than essential. In operations other than war a not dissimilar view is held – at the end of the day it is what happens on the ground that matters. States are territorial entities and the ability of sea power to affect directly what happens on the ground is limited. Sea power is relatively more important in the first phase where its 'poise' may have a deterrent effect as well as its role in aiding preparations for land operations. Finally, post-conflict activities which may be critical in ensuring long-term stability and security are also seen as primarily an Army task, with the Navy very much in a secondary role.

Even more revealing is the Army's view of how the decisive phase – the land battle – will be fought. During the 1980s the British Army moved away from the pattern of operations which it had developed from the days of Montgomery – a pattern which emphasized firepower, attrition, tactical-level set-piece engagements and, in the NATO context, an almost entirely defensive orientation – to a new manoeuvre-orientated approach which attempted to fight at the operational level, seizing the initiative by bold actions and targeting the enemy's weaknesses rather than meeting their strengths. Although this new approach was largely prompted by developments in the Warsaw Pact and was adopted primarily for operations on NATO's Central Front, it was a critical underpinning to Major-General Rupert Smith's concept of operations for the 1st British Armoured Division in the Gulf War. In other words, an approach developed for a defensive war in Europe was successfully used for offensive operations in the Persian Gulf area. Partly as a result of this, the Army's doctrine for conventional warfare has not been wholly rewritten in the light of the changes in the 1990s; rather there has been a remarkable degree of continuity. The changes which have occurred have been evolutionary rather that revolutionary, fine-tuning and improving upon what already existed rather than discarding and replacing. Critical to this approach are three concepts: the integrated battlefield, the operational level of war and manoeuvre warfare.

The British Army plans to fight not only a joint campaign, but also an integrated battle whereby all elements – close, deep and rear – are combined for synergistic effect. Deep operations would be used to shape the battlefield and would involve long-range weapons such as multiple launch rocket systems (MLRS) and the new Apache attack helicopters. Intelligence would be provided by modern, long-range sensors as well as human intelligence (HUMINT), particularly special forces. The importance of linking this directly to the close battle was one of the key doctrinal shifts for both the British and Americans in the 1980s. In the 1990s, however, it has received increased attention from the British Army due to digitization allowing a potentially much greater integration of systems. Command, control and communications (C3), battlefield sensors, weapons and combat support can now be knitted together into a single synergistic whole. Deep operations are now widely recognized as a critical element in the overall scheme of battle, and if anything their importance is increasing in British Army doctrine. Nevertheless this does not mean that the close or contact battle has disappeared. The deep battle assists the contact battle by disrupting and degrading the enemy's position; it is not intended wholly to replace it. The ability to take and hold ground, to confront the enemy at close quarters and prevail will remain an important element in overall battlefield success, although its importance may be declining relative to the deep battle as the ability to execute the latter improves. Finally, the modern battlefield requires effective C3 and the efficient resupply of forces. The complex, fast-moving and multi-dimensional nature of modern warfare has placed a premium upon the ability to maintain effective command and control of forces in battle. Indeed, C3 is not only a force multiplier but a potential battle winner. Similarly the ability of modern forces to consume huge quantities of fuel and ammunition, as well as the requirement to repair and refit forces, has led to the greater integration of logistics into battle planning. Rear operations are therefore very much part of the integrated battle. The overall aim of the integrated battlefield therefore is to maximize effectiveness by the synergistic use of forces.

Attacks throughout enemy forward and rear areas must be co-ordinated so that a cumulative effect can be created in the decisive place ... the synergistic effect of taking action simultaneously in several different places is far greater than the sum of the individual actions.[20]

The second key element in the British Army's doctrinal thinking on the modern battle is that both the joint campaign and the integrated battlefield is enabled by a focus on the operational level of war. From the 1980s, the British Army has moved decisively away from the view that battle consists of a series of tactical engagements within an overall framework of battle, to one whereby all actions are geared towards a single campaign objective and must be viewed in that context. A series of tactical successes is, on its own, insufficient, as the Germans found on the Eastern Front in the Second World War; what is important is the manner in which these are used as part of a wider *operational* level plan, a point the Soviets emphasized in that war to great effect. Therefore, current doctrine assumes that 'it is at the operational level that military resources are directed to achieve the campaign objectives.'[21] This operational level perspective has, if anything, been strengthened in the 1990s. The 1996 version of *British Military Doctrine* emphasizes the significance of the single joint commander in theatre who will command all forces and who will work at the operational level. The operational commander will decide on which tactical objectives are necessary, in which order and with what force level *in order to achieve the campaign objective.*[22]

British Army doctrine also continues to be manoeuvre-based, though the term 'manoeuvrist approach' is now used in an attempt to broaden the use of these doctrinal principles to operations other than war. This approach emphasizes attacks not upon the enemy's combat power, but upon his willingness to fight and upon his operational cohesion. The manoeuvrist approach is not simply 'the movement of mass' as opposed to 'masses of movement' – though the requirement to find, fix and strike the enemy remains. Rather, it is a distinctive view of warfare which focuses upon the human dimension rather than the material. Warfare is seen as a clash of wills as well as a clash of machines. The enemy's will is perhaps the key target in the Army's doctrine, while great emphasis is placed upon efforts to ensure that the British Army is better led, better trained and has the greater will to fight and win. High morale is necessary to overcome the shock of battle – forces must be psychologically as well as physically robust – while leadership and the ability to make rapid decisions on a fast-moving battlefield are critical in maintaining the initiative and keep the enemy off balance.

What is striking in this approach to battle is the marginal role played by sea power. The integrated battlefield is a land/air battlefield, not a land/*sea*/air battlefield, because the joint commander will command what is essentially a land/air battle with little or no contribution from sea power. Despite the rhetoric of jointness, and despite the emphasis on the integrated battlefield and the operational level of war, it is clear from both editions of *British Military Doctrine* as well as ADP *Operations* that the key relationship is between land and air power. This is most clearly seen in the sections on the manoeuvrist approach, the very heart of British Army doctrine, where discussion centres almost exclusively on land/air operations with little contribution from sea power. Sea power is strategically important in securing the sea lines of communication and in creating the conditions necessary for operational success; but at the operational level and in the decisive phase of war, its relationship with land power is limited, while at the tactical level it hardly exists at all.

CONCLUSION

This chapter began by discussing the relationship between the Army and Royal Navy in British defence policy. Although the Royal Navy has clearly slipped from the position of primacy it held at the turn of the century, reaching its nadir with John Nott's 1981 defence review, the post-Cold War defence review initially suggested something of a reappraisal in the relative importance of the two services. The removal of the Soviet threat to Europe implied that one of the Army's key roles, namely that of a contribution to the defence of NATO territory, could be dramatically reduced, while new security risks were likely to arise outside NATO's traditional geographic area of responsibility requiring an expeditionary, and hence heavily naval, capability. But the Army's importance in the post-Cold War world was quickly and amply demonstrated in a series of crises in the early and mid-1990s – particularly in the Persian Gulf, Bosnia and Rwanda. In all of these the Army played at least an equal role to the other services and arguably the most important. Similarly, although there is a prima facie case for a reappraisal of the relationship between land and sea power in future warfare – not least because of the increased emphasis on 'jointness' but also because of the likely expeditionary nature of future crises, new technologies leading to greater synergy between land, sea and air power, and the unpredictability of future crises – an examination of current Army doctrine reveals a very traditional view of the relationship: that the Navy's role is to get the Army to where it needs to be and keep it there, but that the decisive phase of a conflict will be the land/air battle in which naval forces will have little role. Even in post-conflict activities, increasingly important in maintaining security and stability in potentially volatile areas of the world, the Army sees the Navy as playing little role. From the Army's perspective sea control is a necessary but not sufficient condition for success in future operations; what is decisive however is the land/air campaign.

NOTES

1. See Sir Michael Howard, *The Continental Commitment: The Dilemma of British Defence Policy in the Era of Two World Wars* (London: Temple Smith, 1972); and, Capt. Sir Basil Liddell Hart, *The British Way in Warfare* (London: Penguin, 1942).
2. R. Ovendale, *British Defence Policy since 1945* (Manchester: Manchester University Press, 1994).
3. See Cmnd 8288, *The United Kingdom Defence Programme: The Way Forward* (London: HMSO, 1981); and, W. Jackson and E. Brammall, *The Chiefs: The Story of the United Kingdom Chiefs of Staff* (London: Brassey's, 1992).
4. A. T. Mahan, *The Influence of Sea Power upon History, 1660–1783* (London: Methuen, 1965; first published in 1890).
5. C. Gray, *The Navy in the Post-Cold War World: The Uses and Value of Strategic Sea Power* (University Park, Pa.: Pennsylvania University Press, 1994).
6. See: B. Bond, *Liddell Hart: A Study in Military Thought* (London: Cassell, 1977); B. Holden Reid, *J. F. C. Fuller: Military Thinker* (London: Macmillan, 1987); R. Simpkin, *Race to the Swift: Thoughts on Twenty-First Century Warfare* (London: Brassey's, 1985); and, C. Bellamy, *The Future of Land Warfare* (London: Croom Helm, 1987).
7. Liddell Hart, op. cit.
8. C. McInnes, *Hot War, Cold War: The British Army's Way in Warfare, 1945–95* (London: Brassey's, 1996).
9. BR 1806, *The Fundamentals of British Maritime Doctrine* (London: HMSO, 1995), p. 14.
10. *Design for Military Operations: The British Military Doctrine*, Army Code 71451, 2nd edn, 1996, 4–12.
11. Ibid., 4–28, 4–13.
12. See Boyd D. Sutton, John R. Landry, Malcolm B. Armstrong, Howell M. Estes III and Wesley K. Clark, 'Deep Attack Concepts', *Survival*, vol. 26, no. 2, March/April 1984, pp. 50–70.
13. See General Sir Martin Farndale, 'The British Army: Implications of Change', *RUSI and Brassey's Defence Yearbook 1992* (London: Brassey's, 1992); and Major-General K. Perkins, 'Smaller – but Better? Military Capabilities versus Resources', *RUSI Journal*, vol. CXXXVII, 1992, pp. 65–6.
14. The 1975 Defence Review saw the disbandment of the airportable division of three brigades together with the parachute brigade. In their place nominally remained a single airportable brigade which contained a parachute battalion. However, this was not equipped with an assault capability (see *Statement on the Defence Estimates 1975*, Cm 5976, pp. 11 and 18). This was

partially improved after the Falklands War with the redesignation and improvements to 5 Airborne Brigade (see John Stanley, House of Commons Parliamentary Debates, vol. 48, Sixth Series, Session 1983–84, 7–18 November 1983, *Debate on the Army*, 17 November 1983, Col. 104).

15.   Rear-Admiral J. J. Blackham, 'Maritime Peacekeeping', *RUSI Journal*, vol. CXXXVII, no. 4, 1993, p. 20.
16.   *Design for Military Operations*, op. cit.
17.   *Force Development Yellow: The Future Battlefield*, D/DGD + D/1/124/14/ LW3, 12 December 1996, pp. 2–3.
18.   But note it would not be the deployment itself which would deter, but the threat of escalation implied in that deployment.
19.   *Force Development Yellow*, p. 3, emphasis added.
20.   *Design for Military Operations*, 4–34.
21.   Ibid., 4–9.
22.   Ibid.

12 The Royal Air Force and the Future of Maritime Aviation
Christina J. M. Goulter

Like the other two Services, the Royal Air Force (RAF) has been compelled to reassess its roles since the end of the Cold War. As part of this there has also been a recent attempt to revise the RAF's doctrine, since it was felt that the last edition was too closely tied to a NATO–Warsaw Pact confrontation.[1] While revisions are necessary, they need to be done carefully. There is a temptation to reason that because particular roles were dominant during the Cold War, they are no longer required in the new post-Cold War world. The RAF's own history has shown the dangers of eliminating whole capabilities in periods of downsizing rather than effecting cuts across the board. History has also shown that some of the RAF's roles are easier targets than others during cost-cutting exercises, and one role to have been targeted repeatedly is shore-based maritime aviation. Maritime aviation played an important role during the Cold War, but recent RAF restructuring shows that it is again under threat. Yet, in the future, there is likely to be as much, if not more, of a need for shore-based maritime aviation. Not only have most traditional roles for maritime aviation persisted beyond the Cold War, but as the RAF heads into the next century as part of the new joint service structure, the emphasis will be on littoral warfare. In this environment, the need for the RAF to maintain a strong maritime force is obvious. The uncertainties as to what the future holds also point to an increased, rather than decreased, need for a balanced force structure, which includes a credible shore-based component.

Regardless of what period we are talking about, Britain has always relied upon freedom of the seas to conduct the bulk of her overseas trade.[2] With some £300 billion in global investments today, Britain still depends on the maintenance of her sea lines of communication (SLOCs). Defence of these SLOCs has always been a priority. In addition to trade, these SLOCs play a vital part in Britain's ability to protect her offshore resources, most notably her oil and fish stocks, and SLOCs also provide an essential link to her traditional allies upon whom she has depended for manpower and material support during wartime. It is widely acknowledged that Britain is unlikely to enter a major war in the future without allied support, so these links will continue to be important. For these reasons, SLOCs in the Atlantic, Mediterranean, Norwegian and North Seas are of particular importance. Higher defence policy also talks about protecting the UK, her allies and her dependent territories, even when there appear to be no threats to the UK directly. This involves, among other things, maintaining and protecting a credible nuclear deterrent. Historically, Britain has also been concerned about a 'balance of power' on the Continent and the stability of Western Europe, particularly those countries bordering on the North Sea, will continue to be a key element in UK defence policy.[3]

It is generally accepted that the size and character of any force structure should reflect perceived or actual threats. So, what are the future threats to these UK defence interests likely to be, particularly from a maritime perspective? The familiar bipolar world of the Cold War, which made long-range planning relatively easy, has been replaced by a world full of non-aligned and newly independent states, many asserting their national identities in ways that should be of concern to the Western community. Recent history shows that Britain does not even have to be at war with states such as these for her trade interests to be affected. The Iran–Iraq war between 1984 and 1988 showed just how expensive it can be to implement a free trade policy. Four hundred and thirty-two US Navy and international seamen died while attempting to keep oil flowing to the West. As 43 per cent of the world's oil supplies have to pass through the Straits of Hormuz, Operation *Earnest Will*, as it was known, was of critical importance. Wars between neighbouring states are not a thing of the past, and civil wars, which have tended to spill over into adjoining nations, are on the increase. Given the scope of British overseas interests, Britain is bound to be affected increasingly in the future. As a recent study noted, 'free trade is seldom a free good for very long.'[4]

The difficulty facing defence analysts in the West is to know when and where the next conflict is likely to arise. Actions by rogue states are, by definition, difficult to predict. For that reason, many within the wider defence establishment have concentrated on the more easily identifiable traditional threats. In the US, for example, the focus is on four countries: Russia, China, North Korea and Iran. While Britain does not necessarily place the same emphasis on these countries, as America's chief ally, such states are also of interest to Britain. The four nations head the list of a group of states which routinely exert influence within their own regions and often have a global influence. Relations between the US and these four, in particular, will be a primary factor in shaping the future global security environment.[5]

Turning first to Russia, the main argument put forward is that because the future of Russia's democratic and economic reforms remains uncertain, an eye should be kept on the country. Russia certainly possesses capabilities which places it above other regional powers in importance, and of the former Soviet states, it is the most credible threat to European security. Elements of a siege mentality have already been witnessed among Russia's senior defence establishment in response to NATO's expansion, and should an ultra-nationalist take the reins of power in Moscow, then we may see a return of the traditional 'Russia versus the West' scenario. Russia is not stagnant. In spite of severe economic constraints, the Russians have augmented elements of their defence structure and strategic nuclear forces have received top priority. Fleet Admiral Felix Gromov stated recently 'the Navy's main task is deterrence, nuclear deterrence. . . . ', and, consequently, the SSBN fleet has been the focus of recent developments.[6] The Russian Navy began construction of a new fourth generation ballistic missile submarine/nuclear fueled (SSBN), referred to as the *Borey* (or *Arctic Wind*), in November 1996, and a large proportion of current research and development funding is devoted to silent running technology. Meanwhile, current generation SSBNs (*Yankee*, *Delta* and *Typhoon* classes) have been monitored exercising regularly both off North Cape and in the Far East.[7]

Despite continuing budgetary difficulties, the Russian Navy still maintains a significant conventional capability. The average age of vessels has fallen over the last eight years, and several large cruisers and an aircraft carrier, the *Admiral Kuznetzov*, have been completed. Some may dismiss Russian carrier capability because the *Kuznetzov's* sister ship was never finished, and it can be argued, of course, that the Russians lack the ethos and know-how to operate a significant carrier fleet. However, what must be said is that the Russians possess the potential to build such vessels should they wish to do so in the future. All these developments have alarmed the Americans, and they were particularly perturbed in March 1996 when the Russian Northern Fleet conducted the largest naval exercise since the dissolution of the Soviet Union. The exercise included 13 submarines, 16 surface vessels and 40 aircraft. It confirmed that the basic Russian defence strategy (deploying multiple defensive layers) remains unchanged from the Soviet era. The consolation for the Americans, one would have thought, is that if operational analysis of the former Soviet Union continues to be at least partially applicable today, then there should be sufficient advanced warning of

Russian hostility and some knowledge of how to deal with a threat from that source.[8]

But perhaps of greatest concern to Britain and the US is the sale of former Soviet hardware to the rest of the world. Three *Kilo* class submarines have been sold to Iran, and this type has proved to be among the quietest and most difficult to detect. It is thought that the Iranians may have the ability to surge-deploy all three during a crisis, or, alternatively, maintain a near continuous at-sea-presence with at least one submarine. A recent US study suggests that Iran's weapons acquisitions go well beyond a defensive capability, and that the country may be in a position soon to control the Persian Gulf.[9]

Another part of the world to attract increasing interest from the US and Britain is in the Pacific. Of concern is the way in which the Chinese Navy is transforming itself from a coastal defence navy into a force capable of sustained open-ocean operations. From China's perspective, the air and naval threat from the east (the US or Japan) is seen as a greater danger to its security than any ground threat from Russia. The effectiveness of long-range cruise missiles, in particular, has convinced the Chinese leadership that the first line of China's maritime defence must be moved hundreds of miles out to sea. There has been a move to extend China's maritime influence to a second island chain (well beyond 130 degrees east, that is as far as New Guinea). A vital element in the nation's developing blue-water capability is its submarine force. The recognition that the current force, comprising ageing *Romeo* and *Ming* class vessels, was outdated has led to a modernization programme which includes production of the indigenous *Song* diesel-electric submarine, first seen in 1997.[10] However, more ominous is China's long-term goal of building a nuclear retaliatory force. Already in its possession is the *Xia* SSBN, and there is a new submarine design (Type 094) currently under development for introduction early next century. The new type is expected to have improved silent running capability, and may carry as many as 16 missiles. If these projects reach fruition, then China will possess the most challenging submarine force, next to Russia's, in the foreseeable future. The recent flexing of Chinese muscle in the Pacific, as demonstrated by its live firing tests off the coast of Taiwan in 1995, is certainly a destabilizing influence in the region, and it will be interesting to see how Russia, or Japan for that matter, react in the future. The Taiwan issue remains a potential flashpoint, and other territorial disputes may well flare into periodic crises.[11]

Another major source of instability in the Pacific region is North Korea. There is mounting pressure on the economy, society and military, and internal collapse, accompanied by a leadership change, is highly probable within the next few years. The change is likely to be violent, and will undoubtedly affect South Korea. Reunification of the peninsula has always been the primary goal of the communist leadership of North Korea, and in such a volatile environment, an attack on South Korea is widely predicted. In spite of economic ruin, the North Koreans have continued to acquire weapons of mass destruction, missiles and artillery. They also own the fourth largest submarine force in the world, and although most of the submarines date from the 1950s or early 1960s, these would, nevertheless, be capable of interfering with any reinforcement or resupply operations on the Korean peninsula. The ability of small diesel submarines to operate undetected in shallow coastal waters was demonstrated in September 1996, when a *Sango* coastal submarine embarked on a reconnaissance of South Korean waters.[12]

The countries discussed above have been highlighted by recent studies in the US, but the potential threats to Britain's interests are also pertinent. Over twenty countries in the third world now operate conventional submarines, many of them quiet diesel-electric types produced in the West, such as the *Oberon, Daphne* and Type 209 classes.[13] Because of the cost of nuclear submarines, small states are more likely to buy conventional submarines, and many of the enhancements to improve performance are relatively inexpensive. It may, of course, be said that these nations lack the ethos and know-how necessary to operate credible submarine forces, but Britain cannot afford to be complacent and consider these acquisitions as mere status symbols. It is difficult to be specific about the conventional submarine threat in the wider world in the future, but the northwest Indian Ocean and the Gulf can be considered high-risk areas.[14] Overall, the trend among non-aligned nations seems to be towards the procurement of diesel submarines and fast-attack craft. For example, Iran has received ten *Houdong* fast-attack vessels from China, and these are equipped either with the Chinese C801 or C802 anti-ship cruise missiles, thus posing a considerable threat to shipping in the Gulf.[15] The proliferation of advanced modern weapons which can be fired from a variety of platforms widens the spectrum of potential threats that the UK must face, and the amount of advanced warning that Britain will receive if some of these nations become hostile or indirectly affect British interests is unlikely to be substantial. She should not bank on the lead-time the Coalition enjoyed in the Gulf War, for example. Britain should also be mindful of the fact that the smaller her defence forces become, the greater the lead-time she will require.

Whatever the main source of threat is considered to be, almost all defence analysts have moved away from global and large-scale conventional scenarios to littoral warfare against small states or small coalitions. If this is the way of warfare in the future, then the conventional submarines and fast-attack craft just referred to could prove to be major obstacles to British operations. Littoral warfare has been presented by some as a new scenario, but history is replete with examples of littoral engagement which offer important lessons for the future, as illustrated in Malcolm Murfett's chapter. In preparing for D-Day in 1944, for example, the planning staffs were preoccupied by two principal threats to the cross-Channel invasion: seaborne, in the form of submarines, submersibles and torpedo boats, and aerial, particularly anti-shipping attacks and the type of dive-bombing and strafing which was experienced four years earlier at Dunkirk. Operation *Overlord* demonstrated clearly the need for air supremacy and control of the sea. Another important lesson from the Second World War was that a nation controlling the high seas does not automatically have control of the littoral environment, and this is a point that both the US and Britain need to consider carefully. As both nations have downsized their forces since 1990, the protection of the assets that remain becomes even more vital. However, Britain and the US should guard against abandoning 'blue-water' superiority in favour of littoral dominance because their forces will still need to operate over long distances. British forces will have to operate over a wide range of environments and conditions, but because of the cost of pre-positioning these forces around the world would be too great, UK forces must be available at short notice to deploy over long distances (hence the current emphasis on the Joint Rapid Deployment Force). But if this force is to have any chance of success, its SLOCs need to be secure. If Britain and her allies cannot have access to a country by sea, then that operation is unlikely to be approved. Intervention by Britain or the US in limited wars of the past has been made possible by control of the sea. This was certainly true in Korea, Vietnam, the Falklands and the Gulf. In the latter case, 94 per cent of the resupply and reinforcement operation was done using sealift.[16]

Sea control and security of SLOCs will be increasingly important as Britain and her traditional ally, the US, are denied forward bases. With the passing of the Cold War, fewer countries are prepared to contribute resources for operations, unless those operations are considered to be within a country's national interests. At the height of the Cold War in the late 1950s, the US could rely on 115 major overseas bases; by 1995, it had 27.[17] While most of these reductions were implemented by the US after 1989, bases were also lost at various times as a result of political differences between the US and host nations. The classic example here is the loss of bases in Libya after Qaddafi came to power in September 1969.[18] The implications of the trend to withdraw from overseas basing are obvious: Britain and the US will be more dependent upon forces which are afloat and forward deployed.

Operations in the littoral environment highlight the importance of shore-based aviation. The chief advantages offered by shore-based aircraft are their ability to deploy quickly, their range and payload capacity. Even if basing is problematic, air-to-air refuelling will ensure that maximum ranges can be sustained. For these reasons, maritime aviation should not be focused solely in the carrier. This is particularly important for Britain, which currently has a limited carrier force of three vessels. This is not to say that the carrier will not continue to be an important means of force projection, especially in those cases where there is advanced warning of hostilities and basing is problematic. If basing cannot be secured, then the carrier offers a means of sustaining localized air superiority.

Most of the roles required of aircraft in the littoral environment have remained constant. The protection of the amphibious force will require anti-submarine warfare (ASW) and anti-surface unit work, surveillance, reconnaissance and support of the Navy in its anti-surface operations. In ASW, attention is now focused on conventional submarine threats, although it must be said that, in contrast to the US Navy, the RAF has always trained intensively for operations against both nuclear and conventional submarines. Because it is unlikely that Britain will act unilaterally in the future in any major operation, there will be a need to coordinate with European allies in ASW work, and Britain will be expected to take the lead. Much of the European ASW capability is restricted to coastal and close-range self-defence, and many nations cannot afford maritime patrol aircraft of their own. So, there is a clear requirement for the type of long-range maritime aircraft the RAF possesses. Furthermore, there are no guarantees that all of Britain's European friends will contribute to coalitions to the desired extent. Some European allies have become noticeably less cooperative now that the Cold War has ended, especially after suffering their own defence cuts. This is something Britain should have anticipated, as history has shown that coalitions and alliances become fragile when the threat that prompted their formation dissipates. Britain also has to be mindful of the fact that the US Navy's P-3 force has been cut in half since 1989, from 24 to 12 regular squadrons.[19] So, the RAF should not depend upon the Americans to carry the burden of ASW operations, even in parts of the world traditionally considered to lie within US interests such as the Mediterranean and the Indian Ocean. During the Gulf War, for instance, the Americans were dependent upon the RAF's Nimrod force to patrol the northern half of the Persian Gulf, in spite of their desire to keep operations in that part of the Gulf an all-American affair.[20]

Beyond Europe, the RAF's patrol work will prove more difficult, not only because of the crews' relative unfamiliarity with non-European and non-Atlantic zones, but also because the sonar environment will be less ideal. One of the important lessons of the Gulf War was the need for a high standard of littoral ASW, especially against diesel submarines. In the Gulf, the ASW aircrews experienced a high rate of false alarms, as radar plots were crowded by oil rigs, wrecks and other debris in the coastal waters. This is likely to be a problem in any littoral environment, but especially beyond Europe, where environmental regulations are generally less stringent.[21]

One of the most interesting shifts in emphasis is the one that has occurred in anti-surface unit warfare (ASUW). The ASUW role, long considered of only secondary importance, now ranks alongside ASW after it was acknowledged that many potentially hostile nations will deploy sizeable small-craft forces. It is widely believed in maritime aviation circles that the air force will not be called upon to attack major war vessels of the scale once employed by the Soviets, although this eventuality should not be dismissed too quickly because, as we have said, of the 'blue-water' aspirations of non-aligned nations. However, the present focus on small craft brings attendant changes in operational doctrine, tactics and weaponry which the RAF needs to address. There is, for example, an urgent need for a short-range weapon which can be fired in close proximity to the target. This was demonstrated in the Gulf War during the first sanctions enforcement operations, when RAF aircraft needed to show intent with shots across the bow, but did not want to make multiple passes over vessels which might have been armed with anti-aircraft weapons. Once the war started, stand-off weapons were found wanting in an anti-shipping role against small, fast vessels. Anti-shipping attacks on smaller targets also raises a question about the suitability of an aircraft the size of a Nimrod in this role. Once again, the Gulf War reinforced what had been established during the Second World War: that attacks on small craft or selected vessels within convoys require fast, manoeuvrable aircraft. The size of the Nimrod also made the aircraft vulnerable to surface-to-air and air-to-air attack, and there were concerns over the safety of the platform, in spite of Coalition air cover. Hand-held SAMs, especially the SA-18, launched from vessels posed the greatest threat.[22]

This raises a subject which the RAF has doggedly avoided discussing in a meaningful way since its creation: air attack on merchant vessels. The RAF undertook such operations between 1940 and 1945, but this work was regarded as a wartime expedient and the subject has not been revisited. There are two reasons for this: it is a sensitive subject and no service wishes to risk the inevitable public vilification if planning against this type of target is done in peacetime. Second, the assumption has always been that the weapons, tactics and operational doctrine for use against naval units are transferable to attacks on merchant vessels. As has been described elsewhere, this does not necessarily follow. The subject requires much closer attention from the RAF, as the littoral warfare envisaged is sure to involve blockading operations, especially if a conflict escalates into an unlimited war.[23]

Another important lesson from the Second World War is that an effective aerial blockade force cannot be created overnight. A number of conditions must be met if aerial blockade is to be anything other than a blunt instrument, effective only in the mid to long term. Heading the list is the need for accurate intelligence. This is particularly important in a limited war scenario, where one of the main objectives is to prevent escalation of the conflict. Accurate intelligence allows one to target only the adversary's shipping, and focuses attention on those cargoes of greatest value to the enemy. This is vital if the aim is to undermine a specific feature of the enemy's war-waging capacity, whether this is industrial production or imports of weapons or food. Accurate intelligence on the enemy's supply mechanisms also helps to economize on effort, and this will be increasingly important in the future, if downsizing trends continue. Therefore, intelligence should be viewed as a force multiplier. However, Britain should be conscious of the fact that gathering intelligence on an adversary's sea trade cannot be done easily after a war breaks out, and so most of the intelligence mechanism needs to be in place before this point is reached. This is why it is false economy to cut military intelligence organizations in peacetime.[24]

There are a number of other roles for shore-based maritime aircraft which have endured beyond the Cold War. The first is the ongoing requirement for the protection of Britain's nuclear deterrent. The second is the counter-terrorism role. The ability of aircraft to locate and shadow vessels suspected of smuggling and gun-running has been well documented but not widely publicized for security reasons. Although the Irish Republican Army (IRA) threat to mainland Britain has decreased, Britain cannot rule out the possibility of terrorist action by splinter groups. These will continue to stockpile former Soviet Union weapons, which have flooded onto the international market at bargain basement prices. In 1996, Russia surpassed the US as the world leader in arms exports by securing over 30 per cent of the world market.[25] The arms trade is much more diverse and discreet compared with the Cold War era, and the monitoring of arms cargoes has become increasingly important in recent years. Over 90 per cent of arms transfers go via the sea, and among the items found more commonly today are components capable of facilitating weapons of mass destruction.[26] There is also the increasing threat of terrorism sponsored by certain countries in the Middle East, and although Britain has not been affected directly to the same extent as the United States or France, it may prove a problem for British interests in the Mediterranean and Middle East. Five US-named state sponsors of terrorism (Libya, Sudan, Iran, Iraq and Syria) are located in close proximity to major shipping routes through this area.[27] Piracy and hijacking have also impacted on British shipping interests, particularly in the Pacific region. Every year, five or six ships 'vanish', never to be recovered. The annual cost of piracy to the US alone is estimated conservatively at $450 million.[28]

Over the last decade, economic sanctions and embargoes have been used extensively by the United Nations (UN) as a means of punishing aggressors, and maritime patrol aircraft have worked in close concert with naval vessels in enforcing a number of UN Resolutions. For example, RAF Nimrods have been involved in the Multinational Interception Force (MIF) in the Gulf. Its prime responsibility is to enforce the sanctions imposed on Iraq since August 1990, and in the intervening time, 10 000 vessels have been boarded and 119 diverted for violations.[29]

Another function performed by the maritime aircraft is search and rescue, and, in the littoral context, this role will be very important. The success of maritime aircraft in this role was amply demonstrated during the Second World War, when nearly 6000 aircrew and some 5000 others were saved by Air Sea Rescue operations mounted by Coastal Command between 1941 and 1945.[30] In the Gulf War, it transpired that there was little need for search and rescue, but the expectation was that there would be high casualties. It is important to maintain this capability also for the inevitable maritime disasters, such as the 'Piper Alpha' North Sea oil rig fire in 1988. Finally, maritime aircraft can provide valuable support to ground commanders, as the Gulf War demonstrated. Nimrod radars were used to 'look inland', and this work was considered one of the great 'joint' success stories of the war.[31]

The latter function is being marketed heavily by the advocates of the US Navy's P-3 force since 1991 in an attempt to compensate for its lost

Cold War role. It is a function the RAF's maritime sector should emphasize with greater vigour, along with the other roles discussed above, because the maritime component of the RAF is far from immune from the types of cuts experienced by the US Navy. The successive cuts in the British defence budget which have occurred since the end of the Cold War are disturbing, particularly for anyone who has studied the 1920s when the RAF was reduced to below cadre levels. The maritime element of the RAF is the greatest cause for concern, because maritime aviation has traditionally been an easy target in periods of downsizing. It has usually suffered proportionately greater cuts than other sectors of the RAF. This was certainly the case after the First World War, when the shore-based maritime element was reduced to 5 per cent of its immediate pre-Armistice figure, compared with 26 per cent for the non-maritime portion, as the RAF focused on strategic bombing after 1919. A similar de-emphasis of the maritime component of the RAF occurred in 1945, even before the Second World War ended. This was particularly true of the offensive (strike) element in Coastal Command. The RAF returned to 'Trenchardism' – equating air power with strategic bombing – and, once again, this was largely in order to preserve the RAF's share of the defence budget after the war. However, the impact on the non-strategic bombing portion of the RAF became even more severe once the service assumed responsibility for the nuclear deterrent in 1947. It was also reasoned in the late 1940s that the Soviet fleet could be bottled up in the Baltic, so dispensing with the need for anti-shipping squadrons. As we examine the current defence picture, we see strong parallels with both of these periods, especially in the way the RAF is treating the maritime force. There are ominous signs in procurement, manning and organizational changes.[32]

The number of maritime patrol aircraft in the RAF has declined steadily, from 32 in 1990 down to 26 in 1997, and three of these are considered 'reserve' aircraft. Those who are not troubled by these developments may point to the RAF's programme to update the Nimrod force, which is planned to cost £1.8 billion. Some may argue that this is a significant sum, but it actually represents only 8.5 per cent of one year's defence budget for equipment, and the programme is being spread over nine years. Furthermore, at the end of the programme, there will be 21 Nimrods, 11 fewer than in 1990. Yet, there will be as much, if not more, of a demand for maritime patrol aircraft in the future. Some have associated the maritime patrol aircraft purely with the Cold War, and once this passed away, it was reasoned that there was no longer a requirement for investment in maritime aviation. This is reminiscent of the Admiralty's argument in the 1960s that it needed aircraft carriers for a peacekeeping role east of Suez. When there was a withdrawal from 'East of Suez', the navy was unable to justify retention of carriers on any other grounds. The RAF must not fall into the same trap. The fact that the Soviet Union collapsed does not mean that there is no longer a need for maritime patrol aircraft. Nor should we be seduced into thinking that developments in space technology will take over all the functions currently performed by maritime patrol aircraft. The reliability and security of satellites for military purposes are areas of concern, and this is why US Space Command has set about developing a space doctrine which, they hope, will give the US programme coherence and a lead over potential peer competitors.[33]

More troubling for the maritime air advocates is the fact that maritime patrol aircraft are now being referred to as maritime patrol and *attack* aircraft, and the separate strike function currently being undertaken by two Tornado GR1B squadrons is likely to disappear. Anti-shipping skills will be degraded and ultimately lost if this happens. Multi-functional aircraft are rarely a success, and, in an earlier age, Coastal Command's crews who were trained in bombing, torpedo dropping and reconnaissance were the proverbial Jacks with very little mastery. Success in either the ASW or anti-shipping roles during the Second World War was achieved only after the various roles were separated out and the crews were given specialized platforms and training. This was seen again in the Gulf War, when US A-6 crews engaged on combat air patrol were less than effective in an anti-shipping role, especially in poor weather. On many occasions, Royal Navy helicopters had to be used to fly under low cloud to locate vessels for the A-6s.[34]

Regardless of the platform, what the RAF must remember is that maritime aircrew skills are perishable, possibly to a greater extent than most air force roles. ASW and ASUW are complex functions, and training needs to be frequent. Yet this is becoming increasingly difficult because of the steady attrition of personnel and loss of aircraft. Corporate knowledge is important in any of the roles performed by the RAF, and it must guard against the type of downsizing of personnel suffered by the US Navy's P-3 force. There is widespread concern among the US Navy's ASW aviators that their downsizing since 1990 has caused irreparable damage to their future capability. In the UK, there is only a handful of senior officers with maritime expertise left, and there is a strong sense that maritime interests are not being represented at the higher levels. Whether it is conscious or not of this, the RAF continues to perpetuate a trend which started shortly after the service was created. Maritime representation has always been kept on the margins, and as a symptom of this, the typical Chief of Air Staff has come from either a bomber or fighter background. Of the 25 Chiefs of Air Staff since 1918, only two can claim true maritime backgrounds, and in neither case was their maritime experience recent.[35]

There have also been a number of organizational changes which are symptomatic of a marginalized maritime voice. In 1996, No. 18 (Maritime) Group and No. 11 (Air Defence) Group were amalgamated to form the awkwardly named 11/18 Group, and this has eroded the amount of influence the maritime lobby has in Whitehall. On paper, at least, this amalgamation might have appeared logical. If any of the RAF roles had to be combined as a cost-cutting exercise, it should probably have been air defence and maritime strike. As has been discussed earlier, the strike function calls for small, agile aircraft, and, as D-Day in Normandy in 1944 and the Falklands campaign in 1982 showed, operations in the littoral environment need effective air defence. However, the danger is that the maritime strike role will be accorded secondary status, especially if the Group's budget continues to decline at a steady rate. There was also a recent reorganization of the RAF's Directorate structure in the Ministry of Defence. The initial proposals for the reorganization failed to include any maritime interests, and the maritime sectors were finally tacked onto that Directorate which had space on the organizational chart.[36]

These criticisms of the RAF should not be taken as the author's advocacy of Navy ownership of shore-based maritime aviation. There have been no fewer than six serious attempts by the Navy and its supporters to claim control over the RAF's shore-based assets, and in each of these cases, the adjudicating bodies were correct to rule in favour of the RAF. The decisions were based on the following factors: first, the disruption caused by handing over resources and responsibility for shore-based aviation to the Navy would be too great, even in the mid to long term; that there would be a duplication of effort and resources if this were to happen; that the RAF could always provide a larger and more efficient support organization for shore-based aircraft; and, finally, that the Navy might be tempted to spend the budget allocated to shore-based aviation on carrier aircraft. While the Navy has a strong tradition of fleet support aviation, its experience in other realms of naval and maritime aviation is limited. This is particularly true in the areas of amphibious support, convoy protection and blockade operations. These arguments remain true today and will continue to be so in the future.

However, it is also true that the RAF has always wanted to have its proverbial cake and eat it. Maintaining control over shore-based assets has traditionally been used as a means of pegging the RAF's budget at a certain level. The best example of this occurred in the 1920s, when the three services were vying for an ever decreasing share of the defence budget. In 1919, before the full weight of budgetary constraint fell on the military, the Chief of Air Staff, Sir Hugh Trenchard, indicated that he would be content to see army and naval support aviation handed back to the other services in due course. However, after this point, Trenchard and the Air Staff strongly resisted all bids to fragment the RAF. The most bitter of the debates were those between the air force and the Navy concerning the ownership of the carrier and shore-based aviation. Similar debates resurfaced after the Second World War, prompted again by defence cuts and the RAF assuming responsibility for the nuclear deterrent in 1947, which meant that the maritime squadrons were being left out in the cold and were vulnerable to Navy predations. Should the RAF allow its maritime function to deteriorate any further then it may need to prepare to do battle with the Navy. Such debates over the ownership of maritime aviation have always drained vital energies in both camps and neither can afford to waste any time or resources.[37]

The success of maritime aviation to date has been in no small way the result of the close relationship between the Navy and the RAF's maritime units at the operational level. This is one of the few high points in an otherwise very chequered history. This close association has made the transition to the new 'joint' world relatively easy for the maritime squadrons. However, it will be interesting in the future to see how much emphasis the Air Staff place on maritime aviation within the joint structure. If the defence budget is pruned any further, we are likely to see increasing weight being given to the RAF's 'deep strike' capability against industrial, command, control and communication (C3), and similar objectives. This is the one unique role the RAF can point to, just as the air force had to preach strategic bombing doctrine in the 1920s and 1930s to preserve its independence. The air force will not need much prompting because of the perceived air power successes in the Gulf War.[38]

While he was Chief of Air Staff in the 1950s, Lord Tedder said that 'loose purse strings lead to loose thinking.'[39] The opposite can also lead to an overly narrow, inflexible doctrine, and what Britain cannot afford is a return to a 1920s scenario in which maritime and army support aviation withered on the vine. The new joint doctrine may prevent this from happening, but for all the reasons discussed above, the maritime sector cannot afford to be complacent.[40] What the RAF and the wider defence establishment need to appreciate is that in an age of uncertainty and limited budgets, a flexible doctrine and a balanced force structure are vitally important. Human nature, being what it is, means that most defence establishments feel more comfortable planning for scenarios which have some basis in history, such as a renewed Gulf War or a second Korean War. But the more serious scenario is the unexpected one, for which there are no guidelines. Britain must also guard against the view that when war breaks out in the future, the country will be able to reconstitute the services and all its supports easily and quickly. She was scarcely prepared for war in 1939, and this was after a rearmament programme lasting five years. As a microcosm of this, the RAF must appreciate that it cannot create an effective maritime force overnight, as it tried to do in 1939. The 1930s rearmament was also focused on an identified enemy, Germany. Today, there are multiple potential threats, large and small, and no concrete planning can be undertaken against specific states. This has allowed the budget drafters unusual latitude, and now Britain is trying to cut a coat according to the cloth available, and the coat is in danger of becoming a straitjacket.

NOTES

1. AP 3000, *Air Power Doctrine*, 2nd edn (London: HMSO, 1993).
2. *Statement on the Defence Estimates, 1995: Stable Forces in a Strong Britain*, Cm 2800 (London: HMSO, 1995), p. 10.
3. Air Historical Branch (RAF), AHB 1, Ref. 1; Office of Naval Intelligence, *Worldwide Maritime Challenges, 1997* (Washington, DC: US Government, March 1997).
4. Ibid., p. 26. See also pp. 24, 27–8.
5. Statement for the Senate Select Committee on Intelligence, 'Global Threats and Challenges: the Decades Ahead', dd. 28 January 1998, p. 8.
6. Office of Naval Intelligence, *World Submarine Challenges, 1997* (Washington, DC: US Government, 1997), p. 9. See also pp. 10–17; Statement for the Senate Select Committee on Intelligence, op. cit., p. 8.
7. See *Jane's Fighting Ships, 1997–98* (Coulsden: Jane's Information Group, 1997), p. 25.
8. Interviews with author, Ministry of Defence (MoD) Main Building (April 1997); AHB, Ref. 1; Office of Naval Intelligence, *Worldwide Submarine Challenges, 1997*, op. cit., p. 13; Office of Naval Intelligence, *Worldwide Challenges to Naval Strike Warfare, 1997* (Washington, DC: US Government, 1997), p. 22.
9. Office of Naval Intelligence, *Worldwide Submarine Challenges, 1997*, op. cit., p. 31; Statement for the Senate Select Committee, op. cit., pp. 15–16.
10. *Jane's Fighting Ships, 1997–98*, op. cit., p. 115.

11. Office of Naval Intelligence, *Worldwide Submarine Challenges, 1997,* op. cit., pp. 18–23; Statement for the Select Committee on Intelligence, op. cit., p. 12.

12. Office of Naval Intelligence, *Worldwide Submarine Challenges, 1997,* op. cit., pp. 24–8; Statement for the Senate Select Committee on Intelligence, op. cit., p. 11; *Jane's Fighting Ships, 1997–98,* op. cit., p. 393.

13. IISS, *The Military Balance 1997–98* (Oxford: OUP for IISS, 1997), pp. 299–302; D. Miller, *An Illustrated Guide to Modern Submarines* (New York: Arco, 1982), pp. 110–11, 120–1, 146–7.

14. Office of Naval Intelligence, *Worldwide Submarine Challenges, 1997,* op. cit.

15. *Jane's Fighting Ships, 1997–98,* op. cit., p. 320; Office of Naval Intelligence, *Worldwide Maritime Challenges, 1997,* op. cit., p. 21.

16. PRO AIR 41/74. AHB, 'The RAF in the Maritime War', vol.V, 'The Atlantic and Home Waters: the Victorious Phase, June 1944–May 1945', p. 29; C. J. M. Goulter, *A Forgotten Offensive: Royal Air Force Coastal Command's Anti-Shipping Campaign, 1940–1945* (London: Frank Cass, 1995), pp. 224–5; Office of Naval Intelligence, *Worldwide Submarine Challenges, 1997,* op. cit., p. 32.

17. Office of Naval Intelligence, *Challenges to Naval Expeditionary Warfare, 1997,* (Washington, DC: US Government, 1997), p. 7.

18. IISS, *Strategic Survey, 1970* (London: IISS, 1971), p. 90.

19. Compare figures in *The Military Balance, 1989–90,* p. 20, and *The Military Balance, 1997–98,* op. cit., p. 21. Discussions with Capt. J. O'Rourke, USN, US Naval War College, Newport, RI, April 1997.

20. AHB (RAF), AHB 1, Ref. 2; AHB 2, work in progress.

21. Interviews with the author, MoD Main Building (April 1997); AHB 2, work in progress (maritime).

22. Interviews with author, MoD Main Building (April 1997); discussion with Lt F. Ford, RN, Bracknell (February 1998); AHB 2 work in progress; Goulter (1995), op. cit., chs 4–8 esp.; Office of Naval Intelligence, *Worldwide Challenges to Naval Strike Warfare, 1997,* op. cit., p. 21.

23. Goulter (1995), op. cit., esp. Chaps. 4–9.

24. For a discussion of the importance of intelligence in blockading operations, see C. Goulter, 'The Role of Intelligence in Coastal Command's Anti-Shipping Campaign, 1940–45', *Intelligence and National Security,* vol. 5, no. 1, January 1990.

25. Office of Naval Intelligence, *Worldwide Maritime Challenges, 1997,* op. cit., p. 20.

26. Ibid., p. 20.

27. As defined by the US Office of Naval Intelligence in ibid., p. 33.

28. Ibid., pp. 32–3.

29. Ibid., pp. 18–19; AHB 2, work in progress.

30. AHB 'Coastal Command War Record', p. 8.

31. AHB 1, Ref. 2; AHB 2, work in progress.

32. Goulter (1995), op. cit., p. 38. See also pp. 317–21; AHB Narrative, *Defence Policy and the Royal Air Force, 1956–1963,* 1987, pp. xiii–xviii, 1–23, 173–8; interviews with the author, US Naval War College, 1997 (Captain J. O'Rourke).

33. Using the 1996/97 budget for comparison. *SDE UK Defence Statistics*, 1992–96. See also J. Bourn, *Securing Value for Money in Defence Procurement*, Whitehall Paper No. 25 (London: RUSI, 1994); *Air International*, September 1996, p. 130; A. Hezlet, *Aircraft and Sea Power* (London, 1970), ch. 14; discussions with Dr Brian Sullivan, team leader of the US Space Doctrine development (November 1997); Scott, W. 'Milspace Maturing into Warfighter Roles', *Aviation Week and Space Technology*, 1 September 1997, pp. 46–8.

34. Goulter (1995), op. cit., esp. chs 4–5; interviews with the author, MoD Main Building (April 1997).

35. Marshal of the Royal Air Force Sir William Dickson (1953–59), who served in the Royal Naval Air Service during the First World War, and MRAF Sir Denis Spotswood (1971–74), who served in Coastal Command between 1937 and 1943. Two postwar Chiefs of Air Staff, Slessor and Douglas, were AOCs-in-C of Coastal Command during the war (1943–44 and 1944–45 respectively), but neither had a maritime background prior to these appointments. Interviews with Captains J. O'Rourke, S. Lavender, US Navy, and Commander R. Schoonover, US Navy (Rtd), US Naval War College, 1997.

36. Interviews with the author, MoD Main Building (April 1997); *SDE UK Defence Statistics*, 1992–96.

37. For a full discussion of the interwar debates, see Goulter (1995), op. cit., chs 1–3, and G. Till, *Air Power and the Royal Navy, 1914–1945* (London: Jane's, 1979), pp. 29–55. See also PRO AIR 41/45, RAF Narrative, 'The RAF in the Maritime War: the Prelude'; AHB Narrative, 'Defence Policy and the Royal Air Force, 1956–1963' (1987), pp. 64–6, 173–8, Appendix L, 'Coastal Command: the 1958–59 Controversy'.

38. Goulter (1995), op. cit.; AHB Narrative, 'Defence Policy and the Royal Air Force, 1956–1963', Appendix L; AP 3000, op. cit., esp. p. 71.

39. AHB Narrative, 'Defence Policy and the Royal Air Force, 1956–1963', p. xiv.

40. *British Defence Doctrine*, Joint Warfare Publication (JWP) 0–01 (1996).

13 'Back to the Future': the Royal Navy in the Twenty-First Century
Andrew M. Dorman[1]

INTRODUCTION

As it enters the new millennium, the size, composition and outlook of the Royal Navy promises to be considerably different from the one which existed a mere decade ago. If the Navy is successful in getting its case accepted within the Ministry of Defence (MoD), we could, once again, see a Royal Navy containing relatively large aircraft carriers earmarked for the projection of British military power overseas,[2] supported by a brigade level amphibious assault capability and nuclear-powered attack submarines equipped with conventionally armed land-attack cruise missiles (TLAM).[3] What this would amount to is a return to a far more traditional defence policy than we have seen over the last fifty years with a maritime rather than continental emphasis.[4] Incorporated within this would be a defence policy that utilizes available technology to project power from the sea to a far greater distance and far more accurately than has previously been possible.

Such a scenario would have been hard to imagine a decade ago, let alone 17 years after the infamous Nott review of 1981 which seemed to sound the death knell of a balanced fleet.[5] The reasons for change are varied, but the most significant of them has been the willingness of successive post-Cold War British governments to re-examine the role of military power within the changed strategic environment. This has not, unsurprisingly, been without significant internal division, particularly from those who wish to maintain the land–air emphasis of the 1980s. But, what is already clear is that a new priority has been given by successive governments to the relative importance and ability to 'punch above our weight' and a renewed discussion about the concept of expeditionary warfare.[6] Within this thinking the latest strand to emerge has been the new Labour government's reference to 'defence diplomacy'. Although this concept has not been fully worked out yet the implications of this are, according to Christopher Bellamy, already clear:

The foreign policy objectives emerging from the Government's review, stressing the need to ensure security through diplomatic means, and to protect British and European interests world-wide, begin to suggest a maritime strategy. Maybe, for Britain and the US, a new maritime era is dawning...

Given our objectives and much of our history, it makes sense. If we want to make a real contribution to international security in the new world order, a maritime contribution would be most welcome.[7]

This chapter therefore sets out to consider the Royal Navy's role within the changing domestic and international environment brought about by the end of the Cold War. The chapter is subdivided into three parts. First, it will examine how government policy towards the use of military power has evolved since the end of the Cold War and consider how it is likely to develop into the twenty-first century. Second, it will look at the extent to which the Royal Navy has adapted to the changing strategic environment to date and then review how it plans to evolve in the early part of the twenty-first century. Third, the analysis concludes by examining the compatibility of the Royal Navy's response to government policy towards the use of the military, considers the likelihood of the Royal Navy's plans being implemented, and then explores the implications for the Royal Navy in the next millennium.

'PUNCHING ABOVE ITS WEIGHT:'[8] THE BRITISH GOVERNMENT AND THE ROLE OF MILITARY POWER

Defence writers frequently quote statistics to highlight the increasing tempo of military operations and other 'peacetime commitments' currently confronting the armed forces of the West. Britain is no exception to this role,[9] with the issue of the rotation of army units and the regular breaching of the 'harmony rules'[10] by the Royal Navy being a source of continuing concern to successive Service Chiefs.[11] What these statistics also reveal is an increasing willingness of successive British governments to use military power in the pursuit of Britain's interests.

For all the major Cold War belligerents the bipolar system imposed considerable restraints upon their use of force. Fear of crises escalating into a Third World War resplendent with nuclear weapons placed considerable restrictions upon the use of force by participating states. For Britain the principal objective of its defence policy throughout this period remained constant, to deter the Soviet Union and its allies from expanding into Western Europe.[12] The British armed forces, including the Royal Navy, were therefore useful only in a negative sense in their primary mission – the prevention of the Soviet Union using direct force against Britain's national interests (deterrence being an essentially negative concept).

The end of the Cold War transformed this situation. The diminution of the threat posed by the Soviet Union and its Russian successor has allowed successive British governments to view the use of force in a more positive fashion. Constraints on the use of force still exist within the international system but these constraints are fundamentally different from those imposed by the Cold War.[13] Thus the end of the Cold War has also allowed British security policy to focus on its wider interests and the use of force has again become one of the tools available to pursue its foreign policy.[14]

Five principal reasons why Britain might want to resort to the threat or use of force can be identified. First, Britain as an ex-colonial power retains the vestiges of empire in a number of parts of the world, despite the return of Hong Kong to China in 1997.[15] The Falklands War of 1982 and the continuing military commitment is an obvious example of this.

Second, Britain, like the rest of Western Europe, is dependent on the supply of essential raw materials including oil to maintain its economy. A number of academics have argued that the significant participation of a number of West European states in the Gulf War was directly attributable to this interest.[16] Dilip Hiro takes this argument a step further. In his own analysis of the Gulf War he links Western involvement directly to the inward investment by Kuwait in Europe. Developing this hypothesis in more detail it can be argued that as the world becomes increasingly interdependent states will use their military power more frequently to protect their exposed interests.[17]

Third, there will continue to be internal and external political pressure on the British government to use its military forces. Internally, domestic politics has had an increasing role to play since the end of the Cold War, a trend that has been significantly influenced by the media particularly on the humanitarian front.[18] Externally, the United States has, historically, relied significantly upon its allies for support when its own interests have been at stake. The 'special relationship' between the US and United Kingdom has varied in its closeness[19] but the interaction of the respective militaries remains strong. The US has consistently looked to the UK among its principal allies for support and this was nowhere more evident than in the British decision to despatch the aircraft carrier, HMS *Invincible*, to the Persian Gulf in January 1998 in support of the deployed US forces.[20]

Fourth, concern remains within government about the future of Britain's status as a permanent member of the United Nations Security Council. This has led to Britain's consistent involvement in the majority of UN operations since the end of the Cold War. This fear was neatly summed up by the House of Commons Select Committee on Defence:

> The United Kingdom's position in the world owes much to its defence expertise, and the level of national commitment to defence. *The main-tenance of that position is at risk if the United Kingdom does not respond to the international peacekeeping requirement on a scale commensurate with membership of the Security Council, let alone the legitimate demands of UK public opinion.*[21]

Finally, there remains Britain's historic interest in the balance of power in Europe. The reduction in the Soviet/Russian threat has led to concern about ethnic unrest in the states bordering Western Europe. These have the potential to escalate into a wider conflict and help to explain the ongoing involvement of British forces in Bosnia. The above arguments were encapsulated in a statement made by the then Foreign Secretary, Douglas Hurd, in 1992:

> Some problems – state sponsored terrorism, for example, or the pro-liferation of ballistic missiles – may prick our skin more than our consciences. But, if we really want a world that is more secure, more prosperous and more stable, then humanitarian problems can be just as threatening and must be seen not just as a moral issue, but as a potential security threat as well.[22]

This view has been continued with the new Labour government. George Robertson, the new Secretary of State for Defence, attempted to sum this up at the first Labour Party conference after the 1997 General Election:

> As we approach the end of the 20th century, we stand at a genuine cross-roads in our history – the Cold War over, Russia now moving towards democracy, but at the same time simmering tensions and rivalries coming to the surface in other parts of the world.
> The proliferation of weapons of mass destruction; the growth of ethnic brutalism; terrorism; organised crime; and the scourge of an international drugs trade – the evil billion dollar industry starting in poppy fields on the other side of the world and reaching into our streets and schools, touching our children – these are just some of the new security challenges which we must be prepared to meet.

Because what distinguishes us from the Tories is that we believe that Britain can, and should, be a force for good in the world. We are not isolationists. We are internationalists and proud of it.[23]

The result of this change in emphasis over the last eight years has been the commitment of British forces to a variety of operations worldwide in support of the varying strands of British foreign policy. This foreign policy emphasis partly explains the current government's emphasis on the latest defence review being foreign policy led[24] and resulted in the term 'Defence Diplomacy' emerging. This appears, in some respects, to be a 'politically correct' version of the more traditional naval term 'gunboat diplomacy'. But the concept also incorporates the wider roles that military forces can be used for, the majority of which fall short of actual war.[25]

ADAPTING TO CHANGE: THE ROYAL NAVY IN THE NEW STRATEGIC ENVIRONMENT

Since the end of the Cold War the Royal Navy has undergone a significant reduction in its size. In the seven years between the 1989 Defence Estimates and 1996 Defence Estimates the fleet has shrunk from 4 to 2 SSBNs[26] (with another 2 in the process of construction), 16 SSNs to 12, 12 to 0 SSKs, 13 to 12 guided missile destroyers and 36 frigates to 24.[27] The Royal Navy is therefore considerably smaller than originally envisaged by the 'Options for Change' process and the Strategic Defence Review may well lead to further reductions.[28] Like the majority of its Western counterparts the Royal Navy has, therefore, undergone considerable change both in its size and composition.[29] However, of perhaps greater importance has been its change in outlook.[30]

By the end of the Cold War the Royal Navy was principally concerned with the maintenance of Britain's independent nuclear deterrent, second its wartime roles in NATO and lastly, and very much the junior role, the maintenance of a naval presence in various parts of the world.[31] The first role was initially taken over from the Royal Air Force in 1969 by the *Resolution*-class SSBNs equipped with Polaris missiles. Their replacement was announced in 1980 with the decision to purchase a new class of SSBNs equipped ultimately with the Trident D-5 missile. Throughout the Cold War the role of the Polaris force remained essentially unchanged as the ultimate guarantor of Britain's defence. With the end of the Cold War the decision has been announced that they will not carry their full complement of warheads, but instead be limited to the same number of warheads that were held in the Polaris force. This represents a significant diminution in the throw-weight that Britain can now deliver since the Trident warheads are significantly smaller than the Polaris warheads. Furthermore, the Trident force has also been earmarked to replace the RAF's WE-177 bomb in the sub-strategic role.[32]

The relative importance of the other NATO tasks did not, however, alter over time. There were four main naval tasks for the Royal Navy during the Cold War, apart from the SSBN force. The first of these tasks was the containment of Soviet surface and subsurface forces in their northern bases which involved the forward deployment of NATO submarines. This task remained important throughout the Cold War, but it was the Nott Review of 1981 which increased its significance *vis-à-vis* the other NATO naval tasks.[33]

The second task was the reinforcement of Northern Norway using 3 Commando Brigade, together with its Dutch attachment, by the Navy's specialized amphibious warfare vessels. This task consistently remained the 'Cinderella' of the Royal Navy's tasks. Support for this role was first brought into question with the then Labour government's decision to delete the replacements for the two landing pad docks (LPDs) from the LTCs[34] in 1975.[35] This was reinforced by the subsequent Conservative government in 1981. After initially contemplating abolishing the Royal Marines altogether it decided to scrap prematurely the main amphibious units – the LPDs.[36] However, the domestic impact of the Falklands War, the upgrade of the Trident missile system to the D-5[37] and the political significance of abandoning this NATO commitment meant that these vessels were retained. However, from 1982 onwards the forces earmarked for the task were effectively being left to wither on the vine in the face of increasing defence stringency evidenced by the paying off and subsequent sale of HMS *Hermes* in 1984 without replacement in the landing platform helicopter (LPH) role.[38]

The third NATO task was the provision of anti-submarine warfare (ASW) support for NATO's strike fleet of US aircraft carriers. The Royal Navy's contribution centred upon the provision of an ASW-orientated aircraft carrier group together with supporting submarines and maritime patrol aircraft. This role received increased significance from the mid-1980s as the US Navy shifted its strategy to a more offensively orientated posture.[39] This involved the early deployment of a UK aircraft carrier group into the Norwegian Sea in order to provide ASW support for the US carrier battle force.[40]

The fourth task was the defence of reinforcement shipping bringing supplies from North America to the European mainland, together with the protection of reinforcements being deployed from the United Kingdom. This task centred upon the provision of destroyers, frigates and submarines to conduct barrier patrols and convoy protection for shipping carrying reinforcements from North America to Western Europe. However, the Nott Review and the subsequent financial constraints meant that this area suffered disproportionately larger reductions compared to the other roles.[41] The Navy therefore sought to stress the need for more destroyers and frigate numbers as their numbers consistently dwindled.

The last role, the maintenance of a naval presence around the world, was undertaken in two forms: first, by the permanent stationing of units in particular areas of the world, such as the Armilla Patrol in the Persian Gulf; and second by the periodic despatch of a naval task group to the Asia-Pacific region usually headed by an aircraft carrier. Both were viewed as secondary roles, although this did not stop the Naval Staff from attempting to use them as a means of preserving fleet numbers.[42] The permanent establishment of a presence in a region immediately ensured that a replacement cycle of ships was needed to cover the task, even if the ship's wartime role actually required them to be elsewhere.

The priority within the Navy was therefore principally on subsurface forces, the need to maintain destroyer and frigate numbers, and the Navy's support for Britain's NATO roles. This was most evident in the frequently political debates during the 1980s about the size of the destroyer/frigate force and their replacement timescale. Since then the order has, in many ways, been reversed. A renewed emphasis has been given to the role of the navy worldwide and the role of the deterrent has been downplayed. This change in emphasis was not, however, clear to those involved in the initial post-Cold War reductions and was as much a result of in-fighting between the three services as it was a clear vision ahead.

The 'Options for Change' process left the Royal Navy with essentially the same basic force composition as it had during the Cold War but on a smaller scale. Like the other two services, the Navy agreed to an across-the-board cut-back based on the premise that there would be no further cut-backs for five years in preference to the alternative of a more rigorous defence review. This acquiescence was understandable because throughout the late-1980s the increasing divergence between the procurement plans envisaged within the long-term costings and fiscal reality had particularly impacted on the Navy. The strategic nuclear deterrent, home defence including the air defence of the UK and the commitment of land and air forces to West Germany remained the government's priority.[43] As a result, the Navy had suffered continuing delays to its procurement programme. 'Options for Change' allowed the navy to retire many of its elderly and costly to maintain ships and retain the newer vessels in service while ensuring that the other two services also bore equally the cut-backs. Thus the remaining *Leander*-class frigates were rapidly retired from service and the *Amazon*-class frigates were sold to Pakistan. Their planned replacements, the Type 23s, continued to trickle into service and the combined destroyer and frigate number was reduced to 40. Orders for additional conventional submarines were cancelled and the older *Oberon*-class vessels were quickly phased out of service together with the older SSNs.

The first half of the 1990s witnessed a government ideologically committed, and a MoD reacting, to the need to quantify defence. The end of the Cold War had heralded considerable talk about a 'peace dividend' at a time of economic slump. The MoD therefore found itself the prime target of the Treasury which sought to reduce government expenditure where it could. The Army's and later the Air Force's doctrinal statements helped to elaborate and justify their force construction. The Navy, as Eric Grove rightly highlights in this volume, left itself open to a funding squeeze through its lack of an explicit statement of doctrine. The Royal Navy therefore remained largely on the defensive in its Whitehall battles with the other services and suffered disproportionate cut-backs in the Defence Cost Studies process.[44] Moreover, the timing of the Gulf War, just after the announcement of the 'Options for Change' conclusions, further undermined the Navy's position within the MoD. The Navy played a largely supporting role to the other two Services which were then able to make the most of this political capital once the government broke its promise for a five-year moratorium on defence cuts.

The Army, having lost 1 (Br.) Corps, succeeded in underpinning its forces through Britain's command of the newly formed Allied Command Europe Rapid Reaction Corps (ARRC). This prestigious NATO command required a significant troop commitment of two divisions and an air-mobile brigade which, when combined with the ongoing deployment to Northern Ireland, helped to undermine any ministerial consideration of further troop reductions.[45]

The Royal Air Force consolidated its position through its support for land operations, the need to retain an air defence capability and the requirement to introduce a far greater range of precision-guided munitions for the new strategic environment. Their principal concern remained the preservation of the Eurofighter programme and in this they were assisted by the collaborative nature of the project and the apparent lack of an adequate air superiority fighter within the Air Force's armoury.

The Navy's response was quite impressive and drew upon its own close links with the US Navy and Marine Corps. By late 1995 BR1806, *The Fundamentals of British Maritime Doctrine*, was released. As the last of the three Services doctrinal statements to be published it was able to project a joint philosophy with naval units being presented as joint rather than single-service assets. This joint outlook, as Eric Grove alludes to in his chapter, was in part a manifestation of the changed international environment in which Britain found itself. 'Jointery' also appealed to ministers on cost grounds – it appeared to offer them a means of maintaining Britain's defence capabilities on a shrinking budget.[46] In BR1806 the Navy tied its procurement plans neatly into the changed strategic thinking within the MoD of the mid-1990s. It was therefore hardly surprising that the authors of BR1806 emphasized maritime (i.e. joint) rather than naval doctrine.

BR1806 also highlighted the changed strategic environment by differentiating between the various levels of conflict and played down the risk of general war. This fitted into the changed strategic thinking within the MoD resulting from the experiences of the first few post-Cold War years. BR1806 therefore emphasized the far greater likelihood of Britain's involvement in lesser conflicts and the diplomatic role of military forces. In many respects this move to a Navy orientated towards limited war and peacekeeping was a replay of the Sandys review of 1957.[47]

Of fundamental significance was the decision to abandon the traditional policy of the Navy Board arguing about ship numbers within Whitehall. The new focus was instead on three interlinked core capabilities and the core units needed to fulfil them, namely: aircraft carriers, amphibious forces and the SSN force. The major tasking for the Royal Navy was thus centred on power projection and the need to conduct expeditionary warfare. Sustaining the three components also required the full plethora of supporting forces, such as air defence destroyers, frigates, mine-countermeasures vessels and the Royal Air Force's maritime forces in No. 18 Group. In this respect, therefore, the three core components requirement for a balanced fleet finally undermined the conclusions of the 1981 Nott Review. Yet, in emphasizing capability and reach rather than ship numbers it directly reflected the philosophy that John Nott attempted to espouse to the Navy. But, more importantly, within the corridors of the MoD, the emphasis on core capabilities was a far more substantial piece of ammunition to use than the pros and cons of retaining 30, 35 or 40 destroyers and frigates. The danger for the Navy of this changed approach lies in the three capabilities being interlinked. If one link is undermined or dispensed with then the other two will become vulnerable.

The re-emphasis upon aircraft carriers has increased to a level last seen in the early 1960s. The naval argument in favour of aircraft carriers neatly ties into the 'defence diplomacy' concept:

> Carriers can be moved quickly through international waters to signal Britain's intent to potential aggressors without having to fire a shot. If things turn nasty, a carrier can provide air cover for rapid deployment of troops without needing permission to use local bases.[48]

The contrast between the flexibility of carrier-based air power and the problems associated with the reliance on foreign bases has been evident in the crisis with Iraq since November 1997.[49] The apparent Saudi Arabian veto on the use of its bases for offensive strikes against Iraq forced the United States and subsequently the United Kingdom to rely on carrier-based aircraft. In November 1997 HMS *Invincible* was rapidly redeployed from the Caribbean to the Mediterranean to give the British government the option of deploying a carrier to the Gulf. By January 1998 further rising tension led to the decision to deploy HMS *Invincible* to the Gulf itself.[50]

The Navy's current force of three *Invincible*-class aircraft carriers remains unchanged from the Cold War and two remain operational at anyone time with the third in refit or reserve.[51] These 20 600 tonne carriers support an air group of Sea Harrier FA2s, Sea King AEW2 airborne early warning aircraft and Sea King HAS6 anti-submarine warfare helicopters. Their major weakness is the small size of their embarked air group. During the Falklands War HMS *Hermes* usually carried an air group 50 per cent larger than that in HMS *Invincible* and thus supplied the major part of the air effort.[52] To meet these deficiencies in the short-term the decision has therefore been taken that their Sea Dart surface-to-air weapon system should be removed in order to allow the embarkation of three more Sea Harrier/Harrier GR7s, together with the additional munitions carriage brought about by the inclusion of the RAF Harrier GR7s.[53] However, 'senior staff are keenly aware that the ships were not specifically designed for the operational role they are being called upon to fulfil...'[54]

In the longer term strong arguments exist that their replacements should be far more capable vessels able to carry a larger air group than the existing vessels. According to Rear-Admiral Richard Philips, Assistant

Chief of Defence Staff (Operational Requirements (Sea)), what is required is a vessel that

> will enable one to take a 'golf bag' approach to meet specific mission needs and vary the Air Group composition in scenarios where either a high quality or numerous threat exists. A carrier may then embark extra aircraft numbers, or other aircraft types. Examples may be the embarkation of powerful attack helicopters, support helicopters, or a normally land-based ground attack aircraft.[55]

The Navy argues that the aircraft carriers are the obvious platforms for the Joint Forces Headquarters and Joint Force Commander when operations are staged away from the existing base infrastructure, a scenario which is increasingly likely.[56]

Four 'solutions' have so far been put forward[57] with current preference being given to a STOVL-equipped[58] carrier capable of carrying approximately 30–40 aircraft on a displacement of roughly 35 000 tonnes. The Navy has therefore set out its stall on procuring a significantly larger vessel than it currently has, although a decision has yet to be taken. The key concession that the Navy appears willing to take in order to get these ships is to replace the existing three *Invincible*-class ships by only two new carriers.

The current plan is to equip these aircraft carriers with the Joint Strike Fighter (JSF), an Anglo-American collaborative venture which is currently in the concept demonstration phase. The specification includes the requirement to be able to operate from the existing *Invincible*-class carriers.[59] The current intention is to purchase 80 JSF aircraft for the Royal Navy.[60] The Navy has also pushed through the argument that the future replacement for the Royal Air Force's Harrier GR7 force should be compatible with the new aircraft carriers. This has led the Royal Air Force to separate the Harrier replacement from the Future Offensive Air System requirement.[61] However, the key driver behind which aircraft carrier configuration will be ordered lies in the choice of AEW platform. According to Rear-Admiral Philips:

> A number of options are being considered which encompass conventional helicopters, Advanced Compound Helicopters (ACH), tilt rotor technology and Unmanned Air Vehicles (UAVs). The current Merlin airframe is an attractive baseline option, reducing the carrier air group to one rotary type with the benefits of shared support.[62]

However, if a conventional AEW platform is chosen, such as the American Hawkeye, this will require a return to a conventional steam-catapult operated configuration. This, however, looks unlikely and the STOVL concept of the *Invincible*-class looks set to continue.

Of the three core capabilities the amphibious capability is currently the most developed. The Royal Navy is scheduled to receive a number of new and capable ships in service over the next ten years.[63] Moreover, 3 Commando Brigade has been given a central role within the newly formed Joint Rapid Deployment Force (JRDF) and is currently receiving new equipment. However, the current state of the amphibious fleet is the subject of some concern and a 'window of vulnerability' looks likely to remain until the first of the new LPDs enters service. The existing two LPDs, HMS *Fearless* and HMS *Intrepid*, are increasingly showing their age with high maintenance costs, reduced reliability and large crew requirements.[64] The replacement of the two ageing LPDs has now been agreed and contracts signed. HMS *Intrepid* should be replaced by HMS *Albion* in 2002 with HMS *Fearless* being replaced by HMS *Bulwark* in 2003.[65]

HMS *Ocean*, the new helicopter carrier, will be commissioned in 1998 and thus resurrect a capability that was lost with the paying off and subsequent sale *of* HMS *Hermes* in 1984.[66] Her standard air group will comprise 12 support helicopters and 6 light helicopters although Appache attack helicopters and Chinooks can be embarked. Limited C4I facilities have been accepted and *Ocean* will only be able to support a single commando group rather than a larger brigade size amphibious assault force, this being the role of the LPDs or aircraft carriers.[67] The other weakness lies in *Ocean* being a single unit. RFA *Argus* could act as a limited helicopter carrier but this would take her away from her hospital duties and provide a significantly reduced capability. If the Navy is looking to maintain a two task group capability, one deployed and the other in refit or being made ready to relieve, then a second *Ocean* is required.

The current generation of LSLs[68] are also getting old. While the *Sir Galahad* is relatively young and the *Sir Tristram* was upgraded after the Falklands War, the other three are showing their age. Consequently, *Sir Bedivere* has undergone a major upgrade as part of a ship life extension programme (SLEP) but this process has proven to be extremely costly.[69] It is likely therefore that the other two LSLs will instead be replaced by two new vessels. The MoD has already earmarked funds to build two alternative LSLs (ALSLs) to replace the *Sir Geraint* and the *Sir Percivale* in 2002 and 2003[70] but their future depends on the Strategic Defence Review.

The Navy also has funds set aside for the charter of two roll-on/roll-off ships for the RFA.[71] The role of these ships is primarily heavy lift in support of the Joint Rapid Deployment Force (JRDF), but there is a hope that they could be fitted with a stern ramp to allow the use of mexi-flotes and landing craft in sheltered anchorages.[72] They thus have the potential to contribute to amphibious operations and would be more suited to the role, if modified, than the SS *Canberra* was in the Falklands War. Consequently, if all these plans go ahead then by 2005 the special-ized amphibious force will comprise two groups each comprising a new LPD, *Ocean/Argus*, 2–3 LSLs and a roll-on/roll-off vessel.

The third core capability currently comprises 12 SSNs. This is made up of 7 *Trafalgar*-class and 5 older *Swiftsure*-class boats. Before the 'Options for Change' and 'Defence Cost Study' reviews the force had 16 SSNs and 11 SSKs.[73] The loss of the SSKs, in particular, has caused considerable disquiet in the Navy, especially given the move towards littoral rather than blue-water operations. Moreover, of the existing force of 12 boats 4 are likely to be in refit which leaves only 8 boats for operational and training requirements.[74] The credibility of this force remains of concern especially when it is remembered that the Falklands War utilized 5 SSNs and 1 SSK.[75] This implies that only one operation can be supported at any one time especially when one recalls that some of these boats would also be required to support the Trident force.

This deficiency in numbers could well be compounded by the fact that current policy assumes that each boat will be replaced on a one-for-one basis with a new class of SSNs. However, the previous Conservative gov-ernment announced an order for only 3 *Astute* class SSNs to replace the 5 *Swiftsure*-class boats with options being taken out on a further two vessels.[76] However, the future size of the SSN forces remains a matter of contention and this raises significant questions about sustainability.[77] Nevertheless, the capability of this force will be significantly increased as the existing and new boats are equipped with the Tomahawk Land Attack Missile (TLAM). This will give the Navy the capacity to strike deep in land, a capability lost with the demise of the conventional aircraft carriers equipped with the Buccaneer. However, there are only 65 missiles on order which raises questions about the sustainability of the TLAM force in any conflict.[78]

CONCLUSIONS

The decision to adopt a three-core capability has not been without prob-lems and all three core areas require significant improvements in equip-ment for them to be sustained. This situation has been compounded by the fact that, with the exception of the SSN fleet, each role was of low priority during the latter years of the Cold War. Until the Royal Navy achieves the requisite force capability the service remains in a period of risk where these capabilities could, at best, be described as basic, with old, and at times inappropriate, ships being used to cover these roles.

Nevertheless, the 1997 deployment, *Ocean Wave*, to the Far East is indicative of the potential capability that the Navy could have to project military power. It represented the largest demonstration of British naval presence 'East of Suez' in thirty years, comprising more than twenty ships including an aircraft carrier, an LPD and two SSNs.[79] What remains to be seen, therefore, is the degree of success the Navy will have in putting its vision into practice in the midst of the Strategic Defence Review. A failure to generate the requisite capability in each area has the potential to undermine completely the whole vision and raise fundamental questions about the future viability of the Royal Navy.

NOTES

1. The views expressed in this chapter represent the views of the author and should not be interpreted as representing the official policy of the Royal Navy or the Ministry of Defence.
2. See Martin Edmonds (ed.), 'British Naval Aviation in the 21st Century', *Bailrigg Memorandum 25* (Lancaster: Centre for Defence and International Security Studies, 1997).
3. *Statement on the Defence Estimates, 1996*, Cm. 3223 (London: HMSO, 1996), p. 58.
4. Christopher Bellamy, 'Gunboat Diplomacy for the 21st Century', *Independent*, 24 July 1997, p. 19.
5. *The United Kingdom Defence Programme: the Way Forward*, Cm. 8288, (London: HMSO, 1981).
6. It is interesting to note the inaugural conference at the new Joint Services Command and staff College in June 1997 was entitled 'Jointery in an Expeditionary Era'. See Andrew Dorman, 'Western Europe and Military Intervention', in *Military Intervention in the Post-Cold War World: From Gunboat Diplomacy to Humanitarian Intervention*, eds Andrew Dorman and Thomas Otte (Aldershot: Dartmouth Publishing, 1995), pp. 114–17.
7. Christopher Bellamy, op. cit., p. 19.
8. Douglas Hurd, 'Foreign Policy and International Security', *RUSI Journal*, vol. 138, no. 2, April 1993, pp. 1–6.
9. For an indication of current deployment levels see Tim Butcher, 'Duty Comes First for Forces at Christmas', *Daily Telegraph*, 26 December 1997, p. 6.

10.	These were supposed to govern the amount of time individual ships spent away from their home port and thus ensure personnel spent sufficient time at home.
11.	House of Commons Defence Committee, *Seventh Report – Statement on the Defence Estimates, 1996*, HC. 215, Session 1995–96 (London: HMSO, 1996), pp. xxi–xxii; Bruce George and Nick Ryan, 'Options for Change: A Political Critique', *Brassey's Defence Yearbook, 1993*, ed. Centre for Defence Studies (London: Brassey's, 1993), p. 44.
12.	Stuart Croft and Phil Williams, 'The United Kingdom', in Regina Cowen Karp (ed.), *Security with Nuclear Weapons? Different Perspectives on National Security* (Oxford: Oxford University Press for SIPRI, 1991), p. 147.
13.	See Thomas G. Otte, 'Military Intervention: Conclusions and Reflections', in *Military Intervention in the Post-Cold War World*, op. cit., pp. 193–209; Colin S. Gray, *The Navy in the Post-Cold War World* (University Park, Pa.: Pennsylvania State University, 1994); Eric Grove, *The Future of Sea Power* (London: Routledge, 1990).
14.	*Statement on the Defence Estimates, 1996,* op. cit., p. 3; Douglas Hurd, 'Foreign Policy and International Security', op. cit., pp. 1–6.
15.	*Statement on the Defence Estimates, 1996*, op. cit., p. 3.
16.	For a fuller explanation of this argument see John Roberts, 'Oil, the Military and the Gulf War of 1981', *RUSI Journal*, vol. 136, no. 1, Spring 1991, pp. 11–16.
17.	Dilip Hiro, *Desert Shield to Desert Storm: The Second Gulf War* (London: Harper Collins, 1992).
18.	A good example of this was Britain's involvement in the air evacuation of a number of seriously ill individuals from Bosnia during the Civil War after attention in the media was focused on the suffering of a particular child – Operation *IRMA*.
19.	'Two Views of Britain's Place in the World', *The Times*, 7 April 1997, p. 8.
20.	Michael Evans and Michael Theodoulou, 'British Carrier to Aid US Against Saddam', *The Times*, 17 January 1998, p. 17.
21.	In bold in original. House of Commons Defence Committee, *Fourth Report – United Kingdom Peacekeeping and Intervention Forces: Report together with the Proceedings of the Committee Relating to the Report, Minutes of Evidence and Memoranda*, HC. 188, Session 1992–93 (London, HMSO, 1993), p. xxvi.
22.	Douglas Hurd, op. cit., pp. 1–6.
23.	George Robertson, *Speech to the Labour Party Conference*, 1997.
24.	*Ministry of Defence Press Release 055/97*, 28 May 1997.
25.	See the seven mission types and various military tasks set out in *Statement on the Defence Estimates, 1996*, op. cit., pp. 18, 105–16.
26.	SSBN – nuclear-powered ballistic missile carrying submarine; SSN – nuclear-powered attack submarine; SSK – conventionally powered attack submarine.
27.	*Statement on the Defence Estimates, 1989*, Cm. 675 (London: HMSO, 1989); *Statement on the Defence Estimates, 1996*, op. cit. Note: there was no Statement on the Defence Estimates 1997, this was deferred whilst the Strategic Defence Review was undertaken.

28. Joris Janssen Lok, 'New Challenges Force Change on Royal Navy', *Jane's Defence Weekly*, 3 September 1997, p. 41.
29. Scott C. Truver, 'Budget Squeeze Blurs the Long-Range Vision', *Jane's Navy International*, vol. 101, no. 5, June 1996, pp. 28–39; 'The Future of Seapower', *Jane's Navy International*, January/February 1996, pp. 22–32; Richard Scott, 'Which Course will Russia's Navy Steer', *Jane's Navy International*, October 1996, pp. 18–21.
30. Sam Bateman, 'Sea Change in Asia-Pacific', *Jane's Navy International*, October 1996, pp. 24–35; Richard Scott and Kathleen Bunten, 'Stretching to Keep a Global Reach', *Jane's Navy International*, March 1997, pp. 34–49; Richard Scott and Mike Wells, 'Flexing Joint Muscle: Mixed Air Groups Aboard Carriers', *Jane's Navy International*, December 1997, pp. 14–22.
31. Colin McInnes, *Trident: The Only Option?* (London: Brassey's, 1986); Robert H. Paterson, *Britain's Strategic Nuclear Deterrent From before the V-Bomber to Beyond Trident* (London: Frank Cass, 1997), chapter 4.
32. *Statement on the Defence Estimates, 1996*, op. cit., p. 24.
33. *The United Kingdom Defence Programme: the Way Forward*, op. cit.
34. LTC – long-term costings.
35. *Statement on the Defence Estimates, 1975*, Cm. 5976 (London: HMSO, 1975), p. 11.
36. *The United Kingdom Defence Programme: the Way Forward*, op. cit.
37. In the negotiations with the Americans to move from the Trident C-4 to D-5 system the British accepted US concerns about the implications for British conventional forces by agreeing to retain the LPDs in operation together with some other measures. The decision to retain these had already been taken but was kept secret so that it could be offered to the Americans as a concession. Private communication with author.
38. 'Amphibious Advancement', *Jane's Navy International*, September 1998, p. 28.
39. See introductory chapter to this text by Mike Smith and Matthew Uttley.
40. See Norman Friedman, *The US Maritime Strategy* (London: Jane's, 1988).
41. *The United Kingdom Defence Programme: the Way Forward*, op. cit.
42. Interview with Admiral Sir William Staveley by author.
43. On one occasion the Navy agreed to forego the purchase of three Type 23 frigates to help the Army fund its purchase of Challenger 2 main battle tanks. Interview with Admiral of the Fleet Sir William Staveley.
44. David White, 'Strategy Outlined for Blitz on Defence Costs', *Financial Times*, 6 July 1993; Christopher Bellamy and Colin Brown, 'Rifkind Squeezes Budget as Peace Dividend Falls Short', *Independent*, 8 July 1994, p. 2.
45. Bruce George and Nick Ryan, 'Options for Change: a Political Critique', *Brassey's Defence Yearbook, 1993*, ed. Centre for Defence Studies (London: Brassey's, 1993), p. 44.
46. For an elaboration of this argument see Keith Hartley, 'Jointery: Just Another Panacea? An Economist's View', in A. Dorman, M. Smith and M. Uttley (eds), *Defense Analysis Special Edition*, vol. 14, no. 1, April 1998.
47. Eric Grove, *Vanguard to Trident: British Naval Policy since World War II* (London: The Bodley Head, 1987), p. 212.

48. Bernhard Gray, 'Forces Dig in to Debate their Role in the World', *Financial Times*, 10 March 1997, p. 7.
49. Michael Evans and Michael Theodoulou, 'British Carrier to Aid US Against Saddam', *Times*, 17 January 1998, p. 17.
50. Bernhard Gray, 'Forces Dig in to Debate their Role in the World', op. cit., p. 7.
51. Joris Janssen Lok, 'New Challenges Force Change on Royal Navy, *Jane's Defence Weekly*, 3 September 1997, p. 42.
52. David Brown, *The Royal Navy and the Falklands War: The Epic, True Story* (London: Arrow, 1989), p. 358.
53. Anton Hanney, 'Sizing-up the Next Carriers', *Navy News*, October 1997, p. 2; 'UK Navy SAMs to Make Way for More Aircraft', *Jane's Defence Weekly*, 17 September 1997, p. 5.
54. Anton Hanney, 'Sizing-up the Next Carriers', op. cit., p. 1.
55. Rear-Admiral Richard T. R. Philips, 'Naval Aviation in a Changed Strategic Environment' in 'British Naval Aviation in the 21st Century', op. cit., p. 17.
56. BR1806, *The Fundamentals of British Maritime Doctrine* (London: HMSO, 1995), p. 173.
57. Martin Edmonds, 'Navy Procurement, Industrial Strategy and the Future Carrier', in 'British Naval Aviation in the 21st Century', op. cit., p. 51.
58. STOVL – short take-off and vertical landing.
59. Rear-Admiral Richard T. R. Philips, 'Naval Aviation in a Changed Strategic Environment', op. cit., p. 19.
60. Martin Edmonds, 'Navy Procurement, Industrial Strategy and the Future Carrier', op. cit., p. 29.
61. Richard Scott and Nick Cook, 'UK Air, Naval Forces Sign on Joint Future Aircraft', *Jane's Defence Weekly*, 7 January 1998, p. 3.
62. Rear-Admiral Richard T. R. Philips, 'Naval Aviation in a Changed Strategic Environment', op. cit., p. 17.
63. Vincent Grimes, Richard Scott and Mike Wells, 'Amphibious Advancement', *Jane's Navy International*, September 1998, p. 28.
64. Andrew Pierce, 'Worn-out Warships Must Limp On to 2002', *Times*, 15 August 1997, p. 4.
65. 'Amphibious Ships', *Globe and Laurel*, July/August 1997, p. 208.
66. 'Amphibious Advancement', *Jane's Navy International*, September 1998, p. 28.
67. 'Amphibious Ships', op. cit., p. 208.
68. LSL – landing ship logistics.
69. 'Amphibious Advancement', op. cit., p. 28.
70. Richard Scott, 'Alternative LSLs Put Paid to SLEP', *Jane's Navy International*, December 1997, p. 4.
71. RFA – Royal Fleet Auxiliary.
72. 'Amphibious Ships', op. cit., p. 208.
73. IISS, *The Military Balance, 1989–90* (London, IISS, 1989), p. 79.
74. Joris Janssen Lok, 'New Challenges Force Change on Royal Navy', op. cit.
75. David Brown, *The Royal Navy and the Falklands War*, op. cit., p. 360.
76. *Ministry of Defence Press Release 035/97*, 17 March 1997; Christopher Bellamy 'Britain to Spend £2bn on Three New Nuclear Submarines', *Independent*, 18 March 1997, p. 9.

77. Joris Janssen Lok, 'New Challenges Force Change on Royal Navy', op. cit., p. 42.
78. *Statement on the Defence Estimates, 1996*, op. cit., p. 58.
79. Tim Butcher, 'Royal Navy Proves It Is Still a World Force', *Daily Telegraph*, 20 March 1997, p. 13.

14 The Changing Face of Maritime Power
Mike Lawrence Smith and Matthew R. H. Uttley[1]

The broad context of this volume is the extent to which the shift from Cold War to post-Cold War has impacted on the nature of maritime power. It is clear that the end of the Cold War has changed the basis for strategic planning among the major powers. The underlying theme addressed in this volume is whether the changes in the international scene have propelled strategic thinking into innovative, ground-breaking territory, or represent merely an alteration in emphasis back towards traditional ways of looking at military power, both maritime and otherwise, the only innovation being in more elaborate and fanciful names to cover really quite traditional notions of military activity. While any definitive conclusions will, naturally, be disputable, the scope and coverage of this volume permits a tentative assessment of the extent of the changes since the end of the Cold War and in which areas they are taking place.

INNOVATION AND TRADITION IN MARITIME THEORY AND DOCTRINE

At the level of maritime strategy in terms of theory, George Baer's and Geoffrey Till's contributions indicate that little has changed fundamentally. The end of the Cold War has not ushered in new strategic or geopolitical theorizing that has displaced established thinking about the utility of naval force. Instead, the crucial precepts of naval strategy as elaborated by Alfred Thayer Mahan and Julian Corbett fit effortlessly into the post-Cold War strategic environment.

Mahan is best known as a 'blue-water navalist' because most commentary has focused on the aspects of his work that emphasize achievement of security through control of the sea and blue-water battle fleet operations. Debates over the utility of these 'blue-water' and 'naval' aspects of Mahan's work in the post-Cold War strategic milieu continue: Jan Breemer, for example, comments that Mahanian codification of the proper roles of blue-water fleets provide 'very few historical lessons' for 'the [contemporary] naval officer who must be indoctrinated to fight for land control';[2] in contrast, Colin Gray argues that 'naval strategy is not "dead", rather it is resting pending the next call to action when bad times return to world politics, as surely they will.'[3] However, other recent commentaries have focused on Mahan's consideration of, and relevance for, littoral operations in his writings.[4] In this context, George Baer's chapter demonstrates the relevance of Mahan's thinking for today's US Navy.

One commentator has argued that the post-Cold War shift away from defending a fleet's battle-space in open water towards dominating an enemy's battle-space in littoral waters means that 'manoeuvre warfare at sea is joining with manoeuvre warfare on land and Sir Julian Corbett must be standing up and applauding from his grave.'[5] Geoffrey Till's contribution clearly establishes why much of what Corbett wrote at the beginning of this century remains apposite as we approach its end. Similarly, in outlining the long- and short-term factors and processes leading to the formulation of the Royal Navy's BR1806 *The Fundamentals of Maritime Doctrine*, Andrew Lambert and Eric Grove outline in a very practical way the application of Corbett's ideas to the formulation of contemporary doctrine.

It can be argued on this basis that Mahan and Corbett did articulate the lasting essence of naval power. While it is true that the belief that national power lay through command of the sea and the search for a conclusive decision in warfare through sea battle dominated much naval thinking right up to the Second World War, few analysts and practitioners now deviate from the notion that sea power is relevant only so far as it affects events on land.[6] In this sense the truly timeless values of maritime strategy have been enunciated, and what has followed has simply been a reaction to, and a refinement of, pre-existing ideas. Commentators on maritime affairs accept that even recent experience of intensive naval engagements in the Falklands War of 1982 and the Persian Gulf War of 1991 did not point to 'much that was very new from the doctrinal point of view'. More often these conflicts served only to confirm 'old truths at the operational/strategic level'.[7] One therefore does not have to go too far out on a limb to proclaim that these existing ideas about maritime theory and practice themselves will remain extant unless there is a radical transformation of the international system. What analysts are left with at the strategic level, then, as George Baer's and Geoffrey Till's analyses indicate, is to debate shifts of emphasis and nuance within pre-established parameters of maritime power.

CHANGING ROLES FOR NAVIES?

At the operational level, in terms of the known roles that navies perform, this volume suggests that the post-Cold War démarche has not resulted in any breakthrough in thinking but, rather, in a recrudescence of 'gunboat diplomacy'. The concept of gunboat diplomacy encompasses the application of 'limited naval force' in areas such as power projection from the sea, 'illegal immigration, national encroachment on the freedom of the seas, piracy, terrorism, pollution and the smuggling of drugs and other unwelcome cargoes' in addition to 'humanitarian relief to the innocent victims of violence'.[8] The contributions by Michael Clarke, Malcolm Murfett, Michael Pugh and Tim Benbow indicate that all of these tasks have been accentuated in the post-Cold War world at the expense of Cold War operational plans which emphasized large-scale 'blue-water' naval confrontation, but no major innovations in the range of tasks *per se*.

What these studies do illustrate, however, is the paradox that surrounds contemporary gunboat diplomacy in terms of new constraints and new opportunities that affect individual states. On the one hand, the post-Cold War employment of naval forces in gunboat diplomacy activities that include power projection and peace-support operations are occurring in an environment of constraints. As the chapters demonstrate, the combination of financial considerations, the need to operate in alliance or coalitions, increased economic interdependence and, for smaller powers, the opportunity for US exceptionalism, all serve to constrain the ability of individual states to engage in unilateral gunboat diplomacy. On the other hand, the increased range, accuracy and destructive power of weapons systems that contemporary Western navies can deploy from the sea offer a historically unprecedented opportunity to project military power. In essence, therefore, what the contributions by Michael Clarke, Malcolm Murfett, Michael Pugh and Tim Benbow show is that while the end of the Cold War may not have ushered in a new range of 'gunboat diplomacy' tasks, the post-Cold War political, economic and strategic environments in which gunboat diplomacy is exercised provide the novelty.

TECHNOLOGY AND THE FUTURE DIRECTION OF THE UNITED STATES THINKING

Norman Polmar's thesis is that the combination of the end of the Cold War and the emergence of the so-called 'information era' necessitate the development of new methods for measuring naval strength. Norman

Polmar's contention is that 'space', C4I and 'people' will become the keys to measuring the effectiveness of major navies. This approach marks a shift away from Cold War thinking whereby 'firepower' – measured in terms of the number of guns, missiles, aircraft or even warships in a fleet – was adopted as the primary measuring device. A notable aspect of this approach is its link with a developing US school of thought which advocates that 'force multiplier' opportunities may be achieved in the future by the fusion of systems that collect, process and communicate information with those that apply military force: the so-called 'revolution in military affairs' (RMA). Though debates continue over the extent to which the RMA concept is likely to be implemented in practice,[9] Norman Polmar's analysis indicates that technological innovations can necessitate a radical questioning of traditional approaches to the quantification of naval capability.

It is important to note that the end of the Cold War has stimulated major shifts in US thinking about power projection at the tactical-operational as well as the technological levels. Indeed, the novel approach and methodology advocated in Norman Polmar's analysis is also indicative of a series of dynamic US innovations taking place in the tactical-operational domain. Illustrative is the United States Marine Corps' (USMC) development of its core concept, 'Operational Maneuver From the Sea' (OMFTS), which has been an explicit reaction to the transformation of the strategic environment.[10] The rationale behind OMFTS 'lay in the need to replace the 20th century "industrial/attritional" mind-set with one that blends high-technology and manoeuvre warfare with the advantage of seabasing.'[11] Investigations by the USMC of the potentialities offered by the fusion of manoeuvre concepts of warfare with advanced data processing and intelligence technologies embodied in the vogue notion of the 'revolution in military affairs'[12] was given practical form in the setting up of the Commandant's Warfighting Laboratory at Quantico, Virginia in 1995. The 'Sea Dragon' enterprise that has emerged has generated interest and adherents further afield[13] and has already yielded important developments in amphibious power projection at the tactical level.

INNOVATION AND CONTINUITY IN UK MARITIME PLANNING AND OPERATIONS: 'JOINTERY' AND THE OTHER SERVICES

A major post-Cold War shift in the debate over maritime operations relates to the concept of jointery: the assumption that the shift to expeditionary warfare and projection of power from littoral sea areas necessitates synergy between the armed services in planning, operational and doctrinal terms. An important observation that emerges is that jointery in the United Kingdom has some way to go for the '*fusion* of effort in place of *ad hoc* arrangements'[14] to be achieved as far as the relationship between the Royal Navy and the other services is concerned. As Colin McInnes's chapter contends, there has been a prima facie case for a closer relationship between land and sea power in post-Cold War operations, not least because of the increased emphasis on jointery, but also because of the likely expeditionary nature of future crises. However, his analysis suggests that this is not borne out by the British Army's vision of the nature of future war, and in particular its view of campaigns and battles. In this regard, McInnes suggests that despite the rhetoric of jointery, the Army's view of the relationship between land and sea power reflects a high degree of continuity with Cold War thinking: that the Royal Navy's job is to get the Army where it needs to be and support it there, but that the Army will win the war through a decisive land/air engagement in which the Navy will play little part.

Similarly, Christina Goulter's chapter highlights some of the key constraints affecting the Royal Air Force (RAF) in formulating appropriate policies towards shore-based maritime aviation. The chapter contends that in the post-Cold War era of declining budgets and inter-service debates over responsibility for roles and missions there is a danger that, despite new joint doctrine, more weight will be given to the RAF's core 'deep-strike' capability at the expense of a flexible maritime aviation capability.

On a related theme, Andrew Dorman's chapter highlights some of the key issues confronting the Royal Navy, starting with an exploration of how successive British governments have changed their views on the use of force since the end of the Cold War. The analysis highlights how the Royal Navy was slow to adapt to the changed environment *vis-à-vis* the other services and its response in terms of the political rationale behind the 'core capabilities', and illustrates how this strategy has led to a 'window of vulnerability' being created within existing Ministry of Defence thinking. Extending this argument, Andrew Dorman concludes that if one of the core capabilities is undermined within the 1998 Strategic Defence Review then the future of the Royal Navy is in doubt.

Taken collectively, the final three chapters point to more general ambiguities that need to be addressed about what the concept of jointery actually means for naval planning and operations. Unlike other aspects of post-Cold War strategy, jointery has hitherto attracted little academic attention.[15] However, the observations in this volume all confirm that the concept of jointery and its application requires further elucidation before its viability as a force multiplier and synergizing factor can be evaluated.[16]

This volume set out to investigate areas of tradition and innovation in maritime thinking since the end of the Cold War. The various contributions show that while much has changed at the superficial level, post-Cold War maritime planning is characterized in many areas by a high degree of continuity. In part, this reflects the generic nature of maritime strategy and doctrine as well as the roles for which naval forces can be employed. Consequently, a conclusion of the book is that the changes in the international scene have not propelled maritime thinking into innovative ground-breaking territory, but rather have led to a shift in the balance within quite traditional notions of maritime activity. For the analyst, therefore, the challenge lies in monitoring and investigating this trend.

NOTES

1. The views expressed in this chapter are those of the author and do not necessarily reflect official opinion in any way.
2. Jan S. Breemer, 'The End of Naval Strategy: Revolutionary Change and the Future of American Naval Power', *Strategic Review*, Spring 1994, p. 49.
3. Colin S. Gray, 'The Limits of Seapower: Joint Warfare and the Unity of Conflict', *Joint Forces Quarterly*, Winter 1994–5, p. 60.
4. See J. T. Sumida, *Inventing Grand Strategy and Teaching Command: The Classical Works of Alfred Thayer Mahan Reconsidered* (Baltimore, Md. and London: Johns Hopkins University Press, 1997).
5. S. Bateman, 'Strategic Change and Naval Roles', in S. Bateman and D. Sherwood (eds), *Strategic Change and Naval Roles and Issues for a Medium Naval Power* (Canberra: Australian National University, 1993), p. 39.
6. Colin S. Gray, *The Leverage of Sea Power: The Strategic Advantage of Navies in War* (New York: Free Press, 1992), p. 26.
7. Geoffrey Till, 'Maritime Power in the 21st Century', in Geoffrey Till (ed.), *Seapower: Theory and Practice* (London: Frank Cass, 1994), p. 90.
8. James Cable, *Gunboat Diplomacy, 1919–1991: Political Application of Limited Naval Force*, 3rd edn (London: Macmillan/IISS, 1994), pp. 147–8.
9. See, for example, Lawrence Freedman, 'Britain and the Revolution in Military Affairs', *Defense Analysis*, vol. 14, no. 1, April 1998.
10. For a broader discussion, see Lieutenant-Colonel H. T. Hayden, *Warfighting: Manoeuvre Warfare in the US Marine Corps* (London: Greenhill Books, 1995).

11. General Charles Krulak, 'Innovation, the Warfighting Laboratory, Sea Dragon and the Fleet Marine', *Marine Corps Gazette*, December 1996, p. 14.
12. For an informative discussion of this concept see Colin S. Gray, 'The American Revolution in Military Affairs: An Interim Assessment', *The Occasional*, Strategic and Combat Studies Institute, no. 28, 1997.
13. See, for example, 'The Commandant's Warfighting Laboratory: Sea Dragon', *Beach Head – The Amphibious Forces Journal* (Headquarters Royal Marines), no. 5, July 1996.
14. J. S. Breemer, 'The End of Naval Strategy', op. cit., p. 46.
15. An exception as far as the UK academic community is concerned is Martin Edmonds, 'Maritime Manoeuvre: Expeditionary Warfare, Jointery and the Role of the Carrier', *Bailrigg Memorandum 28* (Lancaster: CDISS, 1997).
16. See A. Dorman, M. L. Smith and M. R. H. Uttley, 'Jointery and Combined Operations in an Expeditionary Era: Defining the Issues', *Defense Analysis*, vol. 14, no. 1, April 1998; and, M. T. Owens, 'The Use and Abuse of "Jointness"', *Marine Corps Gazette*, November 1997, pp. 50–9.

Index

193